ÉTUDES ÉCOSSAISES

Numéro 13

Exil et Retour

———

Exile and Return

Université Stendhal - Grenoble 3
2010

Numéros disponibles

ÉTUDES ÉCOSSAISES

RESPONSABLE : David Leishman

RESPONSABLE ADJOINT : Pierre Morère

ÉQUIPE DE RÉDACTION ET COMITÉ DE LECTURE : Ch. Civardi, K. Dixon, S. Kleiman-Lafon, D. Leishman, P. Menneteau, P. Morère, M. O. Pittin-Hédon, B. Sellin, R. Watson.

COMMANDES :

Ellug / Revues
Tél. 04 76 82 43 75 / Fax : 04 76 82 41 12
Courriel : Brigitte.Pautasso@u-grenoble3.fr
Adresse postale :   Université Stendhal
                         BP 25 – 38040 Grenoble cedex 9
                         Chèques postal ou bancaire à libeller à l'ordre de :
                         Mᵐᵉ l'Agent comptable de l'université Stendhal

Prix : 19 Euros   (+ 2,50 Euros de frais de port et 1 Euro pour les suivants)
ISBN 978-2-84310-173-1   —   ISSN 1240-1439

Sommaire

THE OOTLIN[1]

I'm back to Starnyfinnan efter fifety years awa,
An' hardly meet a livin' sowl wi' whom I essed to
jaw;
I fin' mysel' an ootlin I' the pairis' that wis hame;
I coontit upo' cheenges here, but naething noo's
the same.

The hoosies o' the clachan, 'at I left in claes o'
thack,
They're spick an' span wi' cans an' sclaits upo'
their heid an' back;
Nae doot, it's richt an' up to date; but, man, I
miss the breem,
An' this is nae the clachan o' my homesick, nichtly
dream.

The kirks are nae the same to me; the ministers
are new;
I dinna see sae mony fowk on Sawbath i' the pew;
The dominie is nae like fat I haed fin at the
skweel;
The doctor's unco wise-like, but I dinna ken the
chiel.

Ye bed me stop my chirmin, for ye say that it's
ill-faured;
But, min' ye, I'm an ootlin here excep' i' the kirk-
yard,
An' cronies there, they winna speak as i' the days
o' aul'—
My cert! they're seelent billies that are lyin' i'
that faul'.

I thocht to pack my pyockies, an' gae back across
the sea,
But Nance, my faithfu' pairtner, has refeesed to
gyang wi' me;
Ah weel, I'll hae a freen an' chum fin she's abeen
the sod,
An' I'll get back the ither anes when comes the ca'
o' God.

---

1. Selected verses (1, 2, 3, 8, 9) from George Abel, "The Ootlin" from the collection *Wylins fae my Wallet* (Paisley, 1917), pp. 37–41.

David Leishman
Stendhal University, Grenoble 3
Steve Murdoch
University of St Andrews
Siobhan Talbott
University of St Andrews
John Young [2]
University of Strathclyde

Exile and Return: Contexts and Comparisons / *Exil et retour : contextes et comparaisons*

An important recent trend in Scottish academia has been the emergence of a confident, vibrant, outward-looking and cutting-edge internationalist approach to Scottish history. Scholars have become increasingly involved in developing Scottish historical and cultural studies both within and outwith Scotland, particularly where specialised societies and academic bodies are established to pursue similar aims—societies such as the *Société française d'études écossaises* (SFEEc). Since October 2000 this important group has brought together scholars in a venture to pursue Scottish studies across a number of disciplines within France and further afield. In Scotland, the intellectual and institutional links between the universities of St Andrews and Strathclyde reflect and, to a certain extent, lead this movement among the younger academics with similar objectives. In both Scotland and France, these "new-internationalists" can be defined by their commitment to archive-based research excellence, the importance of non-Scottish archives for the study of Scottish history, and an open willingness to analyse Scotland and Scottish themes within the larger

2. The editors would like to express their gratitude to a number of people and groups who have helped bring this collection to fruition. We would like to extend our sincere thanks to Dr Alexia Grosjean of the Strathmartine Centre for giving the non-native contributions a language edit. We would also like to thank the numerous bodies who sponsored the conference from which these papers are drawn including the University of St Andrews, the University of Strathclyde, the Institute of Scottish Historical research at St Andrews and the Centre for French Studies at St Andrews. Last, and certainly not least, we thank the *Société française d'études écossaises* for allowing us to host the conference and for providing financial support to do so.

European and international academic community. More importantly, they show a desire to explore new approaches to scholarship through an active engagement and understanding with other disciplines, not least with those engaged in the study of literature, cultural studies, archaeology and sociology.[3]

In recent years, this thirst for an interdisciplinary approach has manifested itself in a burgeoning scholarship on the theme of migration, emigration and the formation of Scottish expatriate communities and networks of all descriptions.[4] Since 2006 the St Andrews-based "Scotland and the Wider World Project" has hosted a number of events on the themes of overseas migration, community development and network building. But there have been other events even more focussed on the theme of exile and/or return. A particularly "exiled" focused event was held at the University of Aberdeen in 2007, organised by David Worthington under the auspices of the Research Institute of Irish and Scottish Studies. More recently, the "Back to Caledonia" symposium organised by Mario Varricchio at the University of Edinburgh Centre for Diaspora Studies in May 2010 focused more particularly on the theme of "return". The University of Strathclyde is the Scottish partner in the International Research Network of the Institute of Ulster Scots Studies at the University of Ulster and it focuses specifically on the relationship between Scotland and Ulster in the early modern period. In September 2010 it held a conference on the theme of Scotland and the 400th anniversary of the Plantation of Ulster: Plantations in Context.[5] Yet while the pertinence of the topic remains constant for historians, scholars of literature and sociologists it is also of significance for those who have found themselves in exile, both historically and in the present day. However, we should not

---

3. For more on this recent interdisciplinary approach see also David Worthington's introduction to his edited collection, *British and Irish Emigrants and Exiles in Europe, 1603–1688* (Leiden, 2010), p. 27 and the authors within that collection, *passim*.

4. For the development of various types of Scottish communities abroad see Alexia Grosjean and Steve Murdoch (eds), *Scottish Communities Abroad in the Early Modern Period* (Leiden, 2005); For an interdisciplinary approach to Scottish networks, combining historical, sociological and social anthropological approaches see Steve Murdoch, *Network North: Scottish Kin, Commercial and Covert Associations in Northern Europe, 1603–1746* (Leiden, 2006).

5. Recent relevant publications from this institutional link include W. P. Kelly and J. R. Young (eds), *Ulster and Scotland, 1600–2000. History, Language and Identity* (Dublin, 2004) and W. P. Kelly and J. R. Young (eds), *Scotland and the Ulster Plantations: Explorations of the British Settlements of Stuart Ireland* (Dublin, 2009). Young has examined the role of return migration of Scottish refugees and descendants of Scottish migrants from Ulster to Scotland in the 1640s and at the Revolution of 1688–90. See, for example, John R. Young, "Escaping massacre: refugees in Scotland in the aftermath of the 1641 Ulster Rebellion", in D. Edwards, P. Lenihan and C. Tait (eds), *Age of Atrocity. Violence and Political Conflict in Early Modern Ireland* (Dublin, 2007), pp. 219–41, and John R. Young, "The Scottish Response to the Siege of Londonderry, 1689–90", in W. P. Kelly (ed.), *The Sieges of Derry* (Dublin, 2001).

think that the topic of exile is a particularly or peculiarly Scottish topic for consideration, although space here prevents a full run down of everyone else's "exile dilemma", or indeed every Scottish case-study.[6]

This present collection of essays has been drawn from a conference entitled *Exile and Return: Contexts and Comparisons / Exil et retour : contextes et comparaisons*, which built on continued interest in such themes, for both those who study it and those who experience it. The conference itself had several functions. First and foremost it was the annual conference of the SFEEc and as such it had several subtexts. This was the first time that the SFEEc had met outside France and this carried some considerable symbolic importance given that it coincided with the Scottish Government's "Year of Homecoming 2009". Although not directly connected to this event, the SFEEc decision to meet in Scotland not only acknowledged the historic relationship between Scotland and France but more importantly the ongoing Franco-Scottish relations in historical, political and cultural terms. The physical location of the conference in St Andrews was also significant and emblematic, not least due to the role of St Andrews in the Scottish Reformation. That event (which celebrates its 450th anniversary in 2010) redefined the Franco-Scottish, although the realignment was not as fatal as some pessimistic scholars might have us believe.[7] Moreover,

---

6. For a discussion of "exile" and the use of the word in its Irish historical context see Maria B. V. Garcia, "Irish Migration and Exiles in Spain: Refugees, Soldiers, Statesmen and Traders", in Th. O'Connor and M. A. Lyons (eds), *Irish Communities in Early Modern Europe* (Dublin, 2006), pp. 172–5; Raymond Gillespie, "Contrasting Communities: A Comparative Approach to Irish Communities in Baroque Europe", in Th. O'Connor and M. A. Lyons (eds), *The Ulster Earls and Baroque Europe* (Dublin, 2010), pp. 167–8. Some specific examples of the migrant experience might include Jason Harris, "Exiles and Saints in Baroque Europe: George Conn and the Scotic debate", in Th. O'Connor and M. A. Lyons, *The Ulster Earls*, pp. 306–26. For an English case-study see Caroline Bowden, "The English Convents in Exile, and Questions of National Identity, c. 1600–1688", in Worthington, *British and Irish Emigrants and Exiles in Europe*, pp. 297–314 and for a pan-British Isles case-study, see in the same volume Peter Davidson, "Perceptions of the British Isles and Ireland among the Catholic Exiles: The Case of Robert Cottington SJ", pp. 315–22. These three Catholic exile case studies can be contrasted with the Protestants discussed by Siobhan Talbot, "'My Heart is a Scotch Heart'; Scottish Calvinist Exiles in France in their Continental Context, 1605–1638", same volume, pp. 197–214.

7. There has been a long tradition of scholarship that has believed that "a significant element [of the Reformation of 1560] was rejection of the long-established association with France" (I. Whyte, *Scotland before the Industrial Revolution: An Economic and Social History* [London, 1995], p. 92), a view which has been propagated by assertions that "the onset of the Protestant Reformation [in Scotland] shattered Scotland's close relationship with France (enshrined in the 'Auld Alliance')" (J. Ohlmeyer, "Seventeenth Century Ireland and Scotland and their wider worlds", in O'Connor and Lyons, *Irish Communities in Early Modern Europe* [Dublin, 2006], p. 459). In recent years however, the continuation of a Franco-Scottish relationship in several spheres after 1560 has been recognised. Matthew Glozier has re-examined the continuing military links and Marie-Claude Tucker has emphasised the continuing presence of Scots in French universities during the seventeenth century. Most recently, ongoing research by Siobhan Talbott has reassessed the continuing commercial relationship between Scotland and France. M. Glozier, *Scottish Soldiers in France in the Reign of the Sun King* (Leiden, 2004);

and more interestingly in the present context, the Scottish Reformation was itself fomented largely by returning exiles, not least the one-time involuntary exile and French galley slave John Knox. Upon release he chose further exile in England and Geneva before his spectacular return home, which came to have far reaching religious and political consequences for Scotland.[8] This conference, however, was not concerned solely with exile and return between or within Scotland and France, but encompassed a far broader focus, encouraging not only focus on specific locations or relationships, but contrasts and comparisons between experiences of exile and return across geographic locations, ideological spheres and academic disciplines.

The importance of exiles in history should not be overlooked. Knox was not the only returned exile to serve as a catalyst for developments in Scottish society; others like Field Marshal Alexander Leslie assembled and formed the Army of the Covenant that humbled Charles I (1639–1640) and paved the way for the wider British Civil Wars.[9] It was returning exiles that formed the new Scottish government at the Restoration of 1660 (not least John Maitland, Duke of Lauderdale) and still more who engineered and helped overthrow that same restored Stuart regime in Scotland (1689) upon their return.[10] Further waves of exile sought to inform British politics throughout the ensuing Jacobite period, though with less success. However, the impact on home also came through economic enrichment. Alexia Grosjean has previously demonstrated the ways in which returning migrants could transform a particular parish through building projects, agricultural improvements and the development of a civic infrastructure in Scotland based on wealth earned abroad.[11] Nor should we forget the impact of exiles in actually writing

M. Glozier, "Scots in the French and Dutch Armies during the Thirty Years' War", in S. Murdoch (ed.), *Scotland and the Thirty Years' War* (Leiden, 2001); M. Tucker, *Maîtres et étudiants écossais à la Faculté de Droit de l'Université de Bourges 1480–1703* (Paris, 2001); M. Tucker, "Scottish Students and Masters at the Faculty of Law of the University of Bourges in the sixteenth and seventeenth centuries", in T. van Heijnsbergen and N. Royan (eds), *Literature, Letters and the Canonical in Early Modern Scotland* (East Linton, 2002).

8. Jane E. A. Dawson, "Knox, John (c. 1514–1572)", *Oxford Dictionary of National Biography*, Oxford University Press, Sept 2004; online ed., Jan 2008, <http://www.oxforddnb.com/view/article/15781> [accessed 9 June 2010]; R. A. Mason (ed.), *John Knox and the British Reformations* (Aldershot, 1998).

9. Alexia Grosjean, *An Unofficial Alliance: Scotland and Sweden, 1569–1654* (Leiden, 2003), pp. 165–90.

10. Ginny Gardner, *The Scottish Exile Community in the Netherlands, 1660–1690* (East Linton, 2004), pp. 178–206.

11. Alexia Grosjean, "Returning to Belhelvie 1593–1875: The Impact of Return Migration on an Aberdeenshire Parish", in Marjory Harper (ed.), *Emigrant Homecomings: The Return Movement of Emigrants, 1600–2000* (Manchester, 2005), pp. 216–32.

history or informing the public imagination through literature. Among these are many members of the SFEEc.

Though not exclusively so, the membership profile of SFEEc is also composed of exiles and/or the children of the diaspora. These include French academics, often with Scottish parents or partners with interests in Scottish studies, but also Scots now living and working in France. For many of these the 2009 *Exil et retour* conference represented a "return" to the homeland as "voluntary exiles" to speak on Scottish topics. They were joined by academics and postgraduates based in Scottish universities, many also voluntary exiles from further afield, some of whom have been particularly active in the SFEEc since the 2005 conference in Toulon. This increased participation from Scotland has unapologetically sought to bring the excellent research produced by the SFEEc to the attention of scholars in the non-Francophone world and facilitate a positive reception in a truly international and interdisciplinary environment. Although the vehicle for this project is a French journal, it is telling that ten of the eleven papers have been submitted in English, demonstrating that many French scholars wish to expose their work to the widest possible audience for international consideration, criticism and review.

The organisers of the SFEEc conference intended to build upon the previously mentioned corpus of work on exile communities by exploring the theme further, not least by looking at the subject through the lens of history, literature, culture and politics, but also by specifically homing in on the theme of "return" within the exile genre. Ginny Gardner's work on *The Scottish Exile Community in the Netherlands* (2004) had certainly already revived interest in studying the mechanisms for supporting a specifically exiled, rather than migrant, community abroad. However the section on the return of this community to Scotland after the Williamite Revolution forms only a part of one chapter out of seven. For historians, the "return" element of exile was a theme meaningfully explored in the excellent *Emigrant Homecomings*, edited by Marjory Harper (2005) which had a significant Scottish content.[12] More importantly, scholars who contributed to that collection, including Mark Wyman and Paul Basu, set what is probably the best conceptual framework for the historian of the topic.[13] But the theme has a much older pedigree among literary authors and the scholars who study them. Gaelic literature in particular

---

12. Marjory Harper (ed.), *Emigrant Homecomings: The Return Movement of Emigrants, 1600–2000* (Manchester, 2005).

13. Mark Wyman, "Emigrants Returning: The Evolution of a Tradition", pp. 16–31 and Paul Basu, "Roots Tourism as Return Movement: Semantics and the Scottish Diaspora", pp. 131–49—both articles in Harper, *Emigrant Homecomings*.

is famous for its voluminous corpus on the theme of enforced emigration, permanent exile and certainly the longing to return home. These themes have received sustained scholarly attention over the years, not least in the Gaelic/Highland context.[14] At its best, there can be no doubt that readers of this corpus, or audiences to the songs of migration are left moved and contemplative. This is a topic further explored by several of the contributors to this collection.

Several contributors also refer to the seminal work of Edward Said. Said's *Reflections on Exile and Other Literary and Cultural Essays* (London, 2001), provide a wider conceptual and interdisciplinary context in which the conference theme of "exile and return" should be placed. Two articles in Said's book stand out here. "Reflections on Exile", examines the experience of exile from a personal, international, interdisciplinary and modern perspective.[15] The strengths of an interdisciplinary approach are also advocated by Said in "History, Literature and Geography".[16] An internationalist approach to "Scottish Studies" as an interdisciplinary entity must therefore embrace such a conceptual approach. Said also reminds us that "although it is true that anyone prevented from returning home is an exile, some distinctions can be made among exiles, refugees, expatriates, and émigrés". According to Said, whereas exile was traditionally and historically associated with banishment, refugees were a creation of the state in the twentieth century. For Said, expatriates, on the other hand, "voluntarily live in an alien country for social and personal reasons". Indeed, France is the example given by Said here. Neither Ernest Hemingway nor F. Scott Fitzgerald was forced to live in France. It was their choice. Whilst expatriates may also experience the solitude and sense of detachment in exile, they do not suffer "under its rigid proscriptions". An émigré, for Said, is technically anyone who emigrates to a new country and there may be choice involved (indeed voluntary emigration from both the Highlands and Lowlands of Scotland is a key feature of Scottish emigration trends). Examples of émigrés given by Said include colonial officials, missionaries, technical experts, mercenaries and military advisers. Again, these examples represent key groups of people who formed the basis of many Scots abroad over the centuries. There is, however, a distinction between an émigré and an exile for Said, because

---

14. See for example John Macinnes's article "Gaelic Poetry in the Nineteenth Century", in Cairns Craig (ed.), *The History of Scottish Literature* (4 vols, Aberdeen, 1988), III [edited by Douglas Clifford], pp. 377–93. See also D. Thomson, *An Introduction to Gaelic Poetry* (Edinburgh, 1990 edition), especially chapter 6 where the cultural response to the exile and dispersal of the Gaels is discussed.

15. "Reflections on Exile", in *Reflections on Exile and Other Literary and Cultural Essays*, pp. 173–86.

16. "History, Literature, and Geography", in *ibid.*, pp. 453–73.

although émigrés may experience a sense of exile, they have not been banished.[17]

Yet, as Raymond Gillespie, among others, has articulated, it is quite possible to concede that "exile is a state of mind not linked solely to migration".[18] It is in literature, not history that this point can be most easily made. The return of "The Horses" to an appreciative human population after generations of exile in Edwin Muir's post-apocalyptic world is just one striking example of how "exile and return" can ignite our imaginations.[19] The impact remains evident in contemporary Scottish literature, where a novel like Irvine Welsh's *Trainspotting* (1993) culminates in a narrative of brutal, self-imposed exile that brings to light the vital tensions underlying the question of geographical displacement.

Thus the SFEEc conference sought to explore the theme of "exile and return" in its broadest context, encompassing themes of geographic displacement, intellectual, religious and cultural exile, and therefore exploring the theme of "return" not only in terms of the physical, but also in terms of the transfer of ideas and aspects of "return" through cultural osmosis or literature. The results were truly rewarding with stimulating contributions delivered across a number of fields. A selection of these is reproduced in the following pages and the rewards of an interdisciplinary approach are apparent.

Christian Auer and Gordon Pentland closely examine the theme of political exile, Auer in particular questioning whether political exile was of a specific nature or part of a wider trend in emigration. He argues that those in political exile, more than others, were able to retain a fundamental part of their identity, thus reinforcing the conclusions of scholars of earlier Scottish exile communities.[20] In her contribution, Kathrin Zickermann also explores the nature of an exiled community. Striking in her analysis was the fact that although the Scots she focused on were in exile due to politic-religious tensions within Scotland, once in exile they formed a community drawn from several different nations, showcasing in this German example both Anglo-Scottish and Franco-British co-operation abroad in response to a climate of religious uncertainty at home.

---

17. "Reflections on Exile", p. 181. The Scottish context to these remarks have been provided by the editors.

18. Raymond Gillespie, "Contrasting Communities", p. 168.

19. Edwin Muir, "The Horses", in *The Norton Anthology of Poetry* (3rd edition, London, 1983), pp. 992–3.

20. See for example Gardner, *The Scottish Exile Community in the Netherlands*; Rimantas Zirgulis, "The Scottish Community in Kedainiai, 1630–1750", in Grosjean and Murdoch, *Scottish Communities Abroad*, pp. 225–45; Rebecca Wills, *The Jacobites and Russia, 1715–1750* (East Linton, 2002).

The importance of these essays lies not only in the specific case studies they examine, but in the themes they shed light upon. There is, perhaps, a tendency to view "exile" as something inherently both forced and negative, and in some cases this was demonstrable. Thomas Brochard explores the experience of the exiled northern Highlanders, pressed into service by the British Crown in an attempt to both remove perceived troublesome elements from the Highlands and in a cynical bid to acquire cheap troops for foreign campaigns.[21] Yet, as several of the contributors to this volume have successfully argued, "exile" from the Highlands need not always have been enforced and was, in fact, often voluntary. Camille Manfredi explores the self-imposed exile of Sorley in Peter Urpeth's novel *Far Inland* (2006), who leaves his homeland on Lewis to travel to Glasgow in an attempt to improve his life. Although the journey is not forced as such, nonetheless he eventually becomes exiled from both his birthplace and his new community. This is a theme well known to scholars and readers of Iain Crichton Smith, who have commented previously on the dilemma of Gaels, for whom return to their unchanging native island is prevented by the changes that exile has wrought within themselves. For example, Roderick Watson observed that "As Lewismen, exiled in effect from the society in which they were raised, Iain Crichton Smith and Derrick Thomson have felt the pains of such separation with literal force".[22] Jean Berton here revisits the theme of exile and return in Crichton Smith's writing, skilfully adding to the existing corpus[23] through thoughtful reflections on subject. Berton in particular raises the question of how temporality intersects with language to shape the sense of loss experienced both by those who are exiled and by those who attempt the impossible return home.

Exile neither had to come as a result of some brutal oppression, nor even be something to be endured by those who left more willingly. The Scottish painters examined by Marion Amblard chose to travel abroad to train for their profession. The debate as to whether sojourning or even long-term occupational migration actually represents "exile" is one which frequently concerns scholars of the theme and is one which is

---

21. The relationship between the Highlander and service in the British Empire is explored briefly in Macinnes, "Gaelic Poetry in the Nineteenth Century", pp. 379–83. On the wider context of this, see A. Mackillop, *More Fruitful than the Soil. Army, Empire and the Scottish Highlands, 1715–1815* (East Linton, 2000) and R. Clyde, *From Rebel to Hero: Images of the Highlander 1745–1830* (East Linton, 1995).

22. Roderick Watson, "Internationalising Scottish Poetry", in Cairns Craig (ed.), *The History of Scottish Literature* (4 vols, Aberdeen, 1988), IV, p. 320.

23. See for example Moray Watson, "Iain Crichton Smith: Exile, Sparseness and the Clearances", in *Studies in Scottish Literature*, vol. 33 (2004).

tackled throughout the collection.[24] In the case of the artists it was certainly necessitated by a lack of opportunity to train in Scotland. These individuals voluntarily travelled abroad in order to further their careers, but they often found themselves thoroughly enjoying the experience. For some there may have been no opportunity to return to Scotland and thus many remained abroad to continue with their learning or on internal exile within Britain, usually in London, in order to make a living. Is there sufficient evidence to reveal to us whether they actually felt in exile or even longed for return? Amblard here attempts to answer these difficult questions. Indeed her paper reminds us of the very non-uniformity of the experiences of the exiles examined in this selection, including those who returned to Scotland. Christian Auer describes a "synecdoche form" of exile, one which was both geographical-spatial and ideological; thus a multi-dimensional form of exile. Aside from physical exile, more tangential elements of exile have been afforded attention—that of the imaginary exile suggested by Manfredi, or the distinction between physical and psychological estrangement as suggested by Celine Sabiron. Manfredi, for instance, analyses a form of exile which, while initially grounded in simple geographic terms, slips into the realm of the fantastic by appearing as an atemporal non-space accessible through Shamanic trances. The question of liminality is even more specifically addressed by Sabiron who chooses to focus on the moment of homecoming, when exile is at an end but the return home not yet fully accomplished. In this way, Sabiron furthers this important exploration of the liminal spaces, whether geographical or social, contained within the apparent binarity of "exile and return". Sellin too disrupts this duality in his study of Robin Jenkins, which focuses on the writer's "foreign" novels. Here the exiled characters' confrontation with a symbolic Other in Afghanistan or Malaysia often leads to a disintegration of established borders, value-systems and identities.

Throughout this collection a distinction emerges between those exiles who operated within distinct national communities, or those who operated within ideological arenas, and those who operated on several levels. Amblard's painters chose to operate within distinct national communities, despite becoming integrated into Italian artistic life. Auer raises the question of contrasting exile experiences, considering that while his exiled Scottish martyrs were often relatively comfortable, this was in stark contrast to the exiled Highland peasants, whom he describes as often "destitute". Zickermann's community of Reformed Protestant exiles were bound together by religion, yet fundamentally continued to remain

---

24. Raymond Gillespie, "Contrasting Communities", p. 168.

separate from their continental allies: the British Reformed exiles worshipped in different institutions to their European counterparts. She also raises the question of a figurehead for exiles, acting to draw the community of exiles together, in this example through the person of the Englishman William Waller. This in itself raises questions of nationality, identity and exile allegiance of those Scots under discussion.

What we learn from these papers is that exile could be both permanent and temporary, and both short- and long-lived. Amblard highlights the temporary nature of the settlement of her artists; recognising that a rise in the availability of training in Scotland, coupled with the development of the Romantic School, turned the attention of Scottish painters to the Middle East. This ended the need and the desire of this group to continue to exile themselves to Italian destinations, but it did not stop them travelling abroad. Zickermann's exiles were also fundamentally affected by political events in the locations they settled, be it the Netherlands, Bremen or Lüneburg. Moreover they were also affected by personal desire which allowed them to change location and/or return home whenever it suited them to do so—for example, Robert Hog opted to stay abroad some 20 years after the Williamite Revolution, the consequences of which could have seen him return home. Brochard, while also considering the temporary nature of the stay of the exiles he discusses, recognizes that the impact of such exile continued long after the time of return. It seems that people were (and are) fundamentally affected by protracted periods away from their homes, either within their own nation or during stays further afield.

If the impact of exile on the individual was traumatic, then it also had wider implications for the societies they left, settled and sometimes to which they tried to return. The consequence of the exile experience on both homeland and adopted land is a fundamental theme within this collection. The notion of cultural exchange is often key—as evidenced both by Amblard and Graham. Brochard sees the impact of the return of the Highland exiles as fundamental to that region's "civilization" and the development of bi-culturalism within Britain. Exchange of knowledge and experience is also fundamental—such as that highlighted by Graham when considering exchanges between Scotland and North-West France. Pentland distinguishes the political use of the notion of "exile"— particularly in shaping radical culture in Scotland. Most notably, perhaps, Sabiron suggests that the physical return home did not necessarily provide a meaningful "homecoming"—discerning a homecoming that was actual but not complete. This is again a notion frequently conjured up by those exiles moved to versify the subject. As George Abel described in his poem *The Ootlin* reproduced at the start of this journal, the theme of return migration and the associated feelings generated by the return, or the dream of the return home, are far from new, particularly in the field of literature.[25] We need only compare the feelings of loss for the exile in Charles Murray's *Hame* with the disappointment of the returnee in Myles Campbell's *Bogsa nan Litrichean / The Letterbox* for evidence of a continued pre-occupation with the theme of "exile and return" among the literati.[26] Iain Crichton Smith even ventured that there could be "No Return" at all due to the distance of the mind from home, let alone geographical considerations.[27] Again this literary evocation mirrors the findings of scholars who scrutinise exile groups, some of whom have articulated when and why a point of "no return" might be reached.[28]

Such thoughts of distance and the permanence of exile elicit a number of questions regarding the place of the migrant. Indeed one theme that pervades this collection perhaps more than any other is, unsurprisingly, the question of identity.[29] The particular importance for exiles of where they came from, or where they "belong", appears to be central to many of the exiles discussed in this volume. Both Graham and Sabiron note that "home" is fundamentally linked to a house or family, or, as Graham puts it, in "the place where one invests one's sense of self". Sabiron, interestingly, considers *two* homes—one original, one exile—suggesting that in some cases, at least, the destination to which individuals were exiled became a second home, which they often identified with no less than the original.[30] Jane Gray also sees identity as linked to knowing where one's "home" is, but as well as this, considers the issue of "divided" identity—of "hybridity"—of belonging to multiple identities but therefore of

25. George Abel, "The Ootlin" from the collection *Wylins fae my Wallet* (Paisley, 1917), pp. 37–41.

26. Charles Murray, "Hame", in Leslie W. Wheeler (ed.), *Ten Northeast Poets: An Anthology* (Aberdeen, 1985), p. 119; Myles Campbell, "Bogsa nan Litrichean", in Christopher Whyte (ed.), *An Aghaidh na Sìorraidheachd: In the Face of Eternity* (Edinburgh, 1990), pp. 44–5.

27. Iain Crichton Smith, "No Return", in *Selected Poems* (Manchester, 1985), pp. 110–2. In this evocative poem the author opens with the lines "No, really you can't go back / that island anymore. The people / are growing more and more unlike you".

28. See for example Éamon Ó Ciosáin, "The Irish in France, 1660–1690: The Point of No Return", in O'Connor and Lyons, *Irish Communities*, pp. 85–102.

29. In all scholarship of return migration, identity features strongly. See the arguments in Harper, *Emigrant Homecomings*, pp. 7–8 and contributors, *passim*. See also Siobhan Talbott who has also questioned the assumption that all Scots present in France adhered to a particular political ideology or Jacobite identity in Talbott, "Jacobites, Anti-Jacobites and the Ambivalent: Scottish Identities in France, 1680–1720", in B. Sellin, P. Carboni and A. Thiec (eds), *Écosse: l'identité nationale en question* (CRINI, 2009), pp. 73–88.

30. In so doing she reinforces the findings of a scholar of Canadian return migrants. See Marilyn J. Barber, "Two Homes Now: The Return Migration of the Fellowship of the Maple Leaf", in Harper, *Emigrant Homecomings*, pp. 197–214. Barber quotes a few lines from the diary of one Monica Storrs who wrote in 1938/1939 "And so I came Home. / But I've got two Homes now / Which is very puzzling".

identifying truly with none. In an exciting conclusion she demonstrates that the experience of exile can in its own way enhance the "experience of belonging". Gray and others conclusively demonstrate the validity of researching the "exile and return" theme, particularly in a climate where contemporary Scotland is forced to re-evaluate issues of gender, race, ethnicity and all that these imply for the contemporary understanding of Scottishness. Many exiles currently living in Scotland may contemplate these issues while living in their new adopted homeland—a country to which Scottish exiles living abroad may or may not one day return.

Thomas Brochard
University of Aberdeen

Exile and Return from the Far North of Scotland from the Reformation to the Revolution

The exile and return of individuals from the far north of Scotland from 1560 to 1640 can be viewed within the perspective of a "civilizing process" and its dual core of social discipline from above and social regulation from below. This framework sets the movement of exiles within the larger context of the relationships between the Scottish/British Crown and the clan communities of Caithness, Sutherland, Ross, and the Outer Isles. Indeed, the Government promoted "exile" as a way to canalize clan militarism. It intended to relocate the potential offered by private armies into the public sphere—i.e., as an official, governmental institution— and regulate it. The rationale behind this exile policy points towards its own "civilizing" agenda, namely the reform of these boreal communities and the removal of the most rebellious minorities. Another parallel phenomenon was at work in the exile and return of primarily, but not solely, members of the clan elite not only to other Scottish towns outside their native environment but also to Europe for educational motives. In this respect, the process of fosterage conveyed a significant cultural and educational function that complemented institutional formation. Moreover, the clan elite participated in the broader cultural experience of the British nobility with continental travels. The return after this intellectual and behavioural enrichment or trauma had an impact both at the personal and community level, as these individuals wielded substantial powers locally in judicial and administrative terms. The transformation and "civilizing" of the Scottish outlying shires over the period resulted to some degree from the manifold experiences of their people. Exile and return was an integral part of the process of integration. The mechanics behind it need to be studied so as to expose teachings for a civilizational model entailed by such a process. Like Penelope, let us unravel the rich web of the far-northern culture.

Exile and return: canalizing militarism

The concept of exile is ambiguous in the sense that its Latin root covers a broad spectrum of meanings. Unlike the "exulum trias" of Roman Cicero, Ovid, and Seneca, this paper has adopted one of the traditional etymological definitions of the Latin term *exilium*, essentially a change of place, a geographical movement "outside the land" *(extra solum)*. In essence, this encapsulated a move away from one's community, a separation from one's *patria*, the land of the *pater* indeed.[1] Traditional historiography has perceived the early-modern far north of Scotland—and the Highlands in general—and its people as a region that lacked dynamism to a degree and appeared sclerotic. The capacity for the exile of its people would thus seemingly be either low or high depending on whether one regarded inherent and exogenous factors as an obstacle or as an incentive to migration. In the conception of the Scottish far northern *homo peregrinator* over the period 1560 to 1640, two rich veins can be exploited to gauge such activity within these communities. The canalization of these people's militarism and their educational experiences in exile will be studied from the perspective of their integration within the greater Scottish/British polity and the so-called "civilizing" process of their perceived "barbarity".[2]

The military involvement of the clans at the local level in the Scottish far north provided the Crown with plentiful resources to be exploited in its "civilizing" process by its transposition to a structured national and

---

1. J. F. Gaertner, "The Discourse of Displacement in Greco-Roman Antiquity", in J. F. Gaertner (ed.), *Writing Exile: The Discourse of Displacement in Greco-Roman Antiquity and Beyond* (Leiden, 2007), pp. 1–20; G. H. Tucker, Homo Viator: *Itineraries of Exile, Displacement and Writing in Renaissance Europe* (Genève, 2003), pp. 37–51, underlines the inner, psychological elements that distinguish exile from travel.

2. This apparent absence of relative dynamism is found in I. F. Grant and H. Cheape, *Periods in Highland History* (1987, rptd. London, 1997), pp. 105–36; J. Goodare, *State and Society in Early Modern Scotland* (Oxford, 1999). Indeed, the two major works on the Highlands and Islands for the period are essentially political narratives of clan conflicts and the Crown's efforts to pacify these lands: D. Gregory, *The History of the Western Highlands and Isles of Scotland, from AD 1493 to AD 1625* (2nd ed., London, 1881); W. C. Mackenzie, *History of the Outer Hebrides* (Paisley, 1903). On the broader issue of "civilizing" and the State, one can turn to A. MacCoinnich, "'His Spirit Was Given Only to Warre': Conflict and Identity in the Scottish *Gàidhealtachd* c. 1580–c. 1630", in S. Murdoch and A. Mackillop (eds), *Fighting for Identity: Scottish Military Experience, c. 1550–1900* (Leiden, 2002), pp. 133–61; A. Cathcart, "Crisis of Identity? Clan Chattan's Response to Government Policy in the Scottish Highlands, c. 1580–1609", in *ibid.*, pp. 163–84; M. Greengrass, "Introduction: Conquest and Coalescence", in M. Greengrass (ed.), *Conquest and Coalescence: The Shaping of the State in Early Modern Europe* (London, 1991), pp. 1–24; J. H. Elliot, "A Europe of Composite Monarchies", *Past and Present*, vol. CXXXVII (1992), pp. 48–71; B. Dmytryshyn, "The Administrative Apparatus of the Russian Colony in Siberia and Northern Asia, 1581–1700", in A. Wood (ed.), *The History of Siberia: From Russian Conquest to Revolution* (London, 1991), pp. 17–36.

international setting. The central Government used and recycled the evident martial streak found in these local communities of the far north for service at home and abroad, whether it be on the restless Borders in 1581 or to support the Elizabethan campaign in the Nine Years' War (1594–1603) with the Iberian menace still potent. The Habsburg authorities replicated that move with the employment of the Senj uskoks in the Venetian and Austrian services.[3] With this ad hoc policy, the executive strove to contain and regulate the clans' "barbarity" and warlike behaviour to serve its own ends at a national and especially international level.

The Thirty Years' War constituted the main vector for this military exile on an international scale.[4] Military service in France offered comparable outlets throughout the period.[5] Highlanders thus fully participated in a military capacity in the expansion of British imperial operations under King Charles I. Additionally, selective operations equally drew recruits from the area. In 1612, George Sinclair, illegitimate nephew of the earl of Caithness, conducted an expedition to Norway during the Kalmar War with 100 to 150 men from Caithness.[6] The 1627–28

---

3. *The Register of the Privy Council of Scotland* [*RPC*], J. H. Burton *et al.* (eds), 38 vols (Edinburgh, 1877–1970), 1st ser., vol. I, pp. 136–7; vol. III, pp. 355–6; *Accounts of the Lord High Treasurer of Scotland* [*TA*], ed. T. Dickson *et al.*, 13 vols (Edinburgh, 1877–1978), vol. X, p. 147; *Collectanea de Rebus Albanicis: Consisting of Original Papers and Documents Relating to the History of the Highlands and Islands of Scotland*, ed. W. F. Skene (Iona Club, 1847), pp. 45–6. A fascinating insight can be found with the Senj uskoks: C. W. Bracewell, *The Uskoks of Senj: Piracy, Banditry, and Holy War in the Sixteenth-Century Adriatic* (Ithaca, 1992).

4. R. G. Asch, *The Thirty Years War: The Holy Roman Empire and Europe, 1618–1648* (Basingstoke, 1997). For Scotland, the collection of essays edited by Steve Murdoch presents a broad and wide-ranging view of the war: S. Murdoch (ed.), *Scotland and the Thirty Years' War, 1618–1648* (Leiden, 2001); A. Grosjean, *An Unofficial Alliance: Scotland and Sweden, 1569–1654* (Leiden, 2003), chs 2–3. The British imperial context is summarized in A. I. Macinnes, *The British Revolution, 1629–1660* (Basingstoke, 2005), pp. 47–54.

5. For far northerners in connection with the French army and the Scots Guard in France and its wider context, see Edinburgh University Library [EUL], Laing Collection, La. III. 666, p. 59; National Archives of Scotland [NAS], Edinburgh, Gordon Castle Muniments, GD44/14/4/5; F. Michel, *Les Écossais en France, Les Français en Écosse*, 2 vols (London, 1862), vol. I, pp. 9, 487–8; vol. II, pp. 50, 233–6, 283–5, 526; M. Glozier, *Scottish Soldiers in France in the Reign of the Sun King: Nursery for Men of Honour* (Leiden, 2004), chs 1–2; M. Glozier, "Scots in the French and Dutch Armies during the Thirty Years' War", in Murdoch, *Scotland and the Thirty Years' War*, pp. 117–41; W. Gordon, *The History of the Ancient, Noble, and Illustrious Family of Gordon, from Their First Arrival in Scotland, in Malcolm III's Time, to the Year 1690*, 2 vols (Edinburgh, 1726-27), vol. II, pp. 611–3, 624–30; R. Monro, *Monro His Expedition with the Worthy Scots Regiment (Called Mac-Keyes Regiment)* (London, 1637), vol. I, p. 45.

6. The military campaign in Norway features in National Library of Scotland [NLS], Edinburgh, P. Henderson, "Notes of the History of Caithness", Acc. 9798, under the year 1613; R. Gordon, *A Genealogical History of the Earldom of Sutherland* (Edinburgh, 1813), pp. 288-9; J. Calder, *Sketch of the Civil and Traditional History of Caithness, From the Tenth Century* (2nd ed., Wick, 1887), pp. 142–8, 301–2, 327; T. Michell, *History of the Scottish Expedition to Norway in 1612* (London, 1886); T. A. Fischer, *The Scots in Sweden: Being a Contribution towards the History of the Scot Abroad* (Edinburgh, 1907), pp. 75–84, 224. Far northerners also served in Holland: *Papers Illustrating the History of the Scots Brigade in the*

mission to the île de Ré and La Rochelle set sail with Sutherland and possibly Seaforth men, but no Clanranald men despite Clanranald's bond to
the earl of Morton for 150 men as a captain in his regiment.[7] The martial
training of clansmen had to be adjusted in order to integrate them into a
stricter military discipline and to reduce commotions and brawls within
this military milieu.[8]

The Crown actively sought the concurrence of the local elite with its
political and military decisions. Indeed, this move was doubly beneficial.
It was essentially a way of eradicating the most troublesome elements
of the region while securing cheap recruits for its foreign campaigns, as
practiced in the respective contexts of Ireland and the Ottoman Empire.
Towards that end, it repeatedly passed legislation to enlist social outcasts,
certain categories of criminals, and prisoners to join military service, particularly as recruitment already proved to be difficult by April 1627. But,
by means of the statute-book, the Crown regulated military recruitment
to prevent procedural abuses, notably impressment.[9]

Service of the United Netherlands, 1572–1782, vol. I, ed. J. Ferguson (Scottish History Society, 1899),
pp. 58–60, 62–3, 66, 69, 72, 74, 214–5, 226, 229 n. 5, 232, 291–2; A. Mackenzie, *History of the Mac-
kenzies with Genealogies of the Principal Families of the Name* (2nd ed., 1894, Markham, Ont., 1998, rpt.
2002), p. 61.

7. The expedition to the île de Ré is treated in *The Chronicle of Perth; A Register of Remarkable
Occurrences, Chiefly Connected with That City, from the Year 1210 to 1668*, ed. J. Maidment (Maitland
Club, 1831), p. 31; J. Balfour, *The Historical Works of Sir James Balfour*, ed. J. Haig, 4 vols (Edinburgh, 1824–25), vol. II, pp. 158–9; *Calendar of State Papers, Domestic Series, of the Reign of Charles I,
1625–49* [CSP, Dom.], J. Bruce *et al.* (eds), 23 vols (London, 1858–97), *1627–28*, pp. 285, 453, 515;
D. Gregory, "Notices Regarding Scotish Archery, Particularly That of the Highlanders; Together
with Some Original Documents Relating to a Levy of Highland Bowmen to Serve in the War
against France, in the Year 1627", *Archaeologia Scotica*, vol. III (1831), pp. 252–4; NLS, Morton
Papers, MS 82, nos. 32, 55; MS 84, no. 5; Gordons of Gordonstoun and Cummings of Altyre
Papers, Dep. 175/65, nos. 162, 177; Dep. 175/88/1; Gordon, *Earldom*, 408; *RPC*, 2nd ser., vol. II,
pp. 37–8, 55–6, 90, 118, 136, 285, 308, 577. In Aug. 1627, King Charles required Colin, 1st Earl of
Seaforth, to contribute men to serve in France: *The Earl of Stirling's Register of Royal Letters, Relative to
the Affairs of Scotland and Nova Scotia from 1615 to 1635*, ed. C. Rogers, 2 vols (Edinburgh, 1885), vol. I,
pp. 195–6.

8. *Extracts from the Council Register of the Burgh of Aberdeen, 1625–1642*, ed. J. Stuart (Scottish Burgh
Records Society, 1871), pp. 8–9; J. Mackay, *An Old Scots Brigade: Being the History of Mackay's Regiment
Now Incorporated with the Royal Scots* (Edinburgh, 1885), pp. 219–22.

9. NAS, Justiciary Records, Books of Adjournal, JC2/6, fo. 191v; *Earl of Stirling's Register*, ed.
Rogers, vol. I, p. 146; *RPC*, 1st ser., vol. XII, pp. 255, 431, 453; 2nd ser., vol. I, pp. 542–3, 546–7,
565–7, 580–1, 585, 589, 603–5, 608, 611–3, 635–6; vol. II, pp. 7–8, 32–7, 229, 332–3; vol. III,
p. 197; vol. VI, pp. 28–9; Fischer, *Scots in Sweden*, p. 91; G. Henry, *The Irish Military Community in
Spanish Flanders, 1586–1621* (Blackrock, Co. Dublin, 1992), pp. 22–37; K. Barkey, *Bandits and Bureau-
crats: The Ottoman Route to State Centralization* (Ithaca, 1994, rptd. 1997), ch. 6. In an echo to this policy
of levying unsubjected Highlanders, in the second half of the 18th century, the Hanoverian Government would enrol the defeated Jacobite clansmen for service in the British army in the colonies:
A. Mackillop, *"More Fruitful Than the Soil": Army, Empire, and the Scottish Highlands, 1715–1815* (East
Linton, 2000), ch. 2.

On the other hand, motivations for choosing military service and exile from one's community were complex and varied according to the situation of each individual. Besides, even more so within a clan society, collective causes complemented personal ones. Sets of push-pull factors, both personal and independent of one's will, moulded an individual's decision whether to enlist or not, whenever press-ganging was not involved. Financial rewards in the form of pensions, wages, and bounties were not altogether irrelevant.[10] Clanship and clan ties reinforced military participation, as did kinship overall for Scottish migration. People capitalized on these as networks to gain promotion or acquire position *inter alia* in the military sphere. Interestingly, William Gunn, the nephew of one of the arsonists at Sandside in 1615, served in the same company as John Innes, son of William whose corn was burnt in the process.[11] Additionally, direct and indirect correspondence between the continent and these boreal townships influenced military engagement through its encouraging or dissuading words.[12]

---

10. NLS, Culloden Papers, MS 2961, fos 27r-8v; NAS, Hamilton Muniments, GD406/1/9320; Scottish Catholic Archives [SCA], Edinburgh, Colleges Abroad, CA4/9/6; S. Murdoch, "Introduction", in Murdoch, *Scotland and the Thirty Years' War*, pp. 15–8; Henry, *Irish Military Community*, pp. 48–52. Religious allegiance was a variable factor as opposed to being clearly polarized along denominational divides: *Gordon under Arms: A Biographical Muster Roll of Officers Named Gordon in the Navies and Armies of Britain, Europe, America and in the Jacobite Risings*, C. O. Skelton and J. M. Bulloch (eds) (New Spalding Club, 1912), nos. 122, 1656, 1754; D. Worthington, *Scots in Habsburg Service, 1618–1648* (Leiden, 2004), pp. 88–9, 108–9, 146–50, 177–8, 239, 249, 278, 294–5; J. M. Bulloch, *The Gay Adventures of Sir Alexander Gordon Knight of Navidale* (Dingwall, 1925), pp. 13, 15, 19, 21–3; Fischer, *Scots in Sweden*, p. 266; M. R. Gunn, *History of the Clan Gunn* (Glasgow, 1969), pp. 126–9; S. Murdoch, "More Than Just 'Mackay's' and Mercenaries; Gaelic Influences in Scandinavia, 1580–1707", *Transactions of the Gaelic Society of Inverness* [*TGSI*], vol. LX (1997–98), pp. 167-8.

11. S. Murdoch, *Network North: Scottish Kin, Commercial and Covert Associations in Northern Europe, 1603–1746* (Leiden, 2006), chs 1–3; Grosjean, *Unofficial Alliance*, chs 3, 5; D. Armitage, "Scottish Diaspora", in J. Wormald (ed.), *Scotland: A History* (Oxford, 2005), pp. 280–1; Gunn, *Clan Gunn*, pp. 126–9; *The Munro Tree: A Genealogy and Chronology of the Munros of Foulis and Other Families of the Clan, A Manuscript Compiled in 1734*, ed. R. W. Munro (Edinburgh, 1978), L/10, L/17, L/29, L/30, M/5, M/35, M/37, Q/14, Q/39-Q/40, R/4, R/5, R/21, T, U. *Calendar of Documents Presented to H. M. General Register House, Edinburgh, by the Rt. Hon. the Baron Reay* [*Inventory of Reay Papers*], ed. C. T. Innes (1929), 8/1; J. A. Fallon, "Scottish Mercenaries in the Service of Denmark and Sweden, 1626-32" (Ph.D. Thesis, University of Glasgow, 1972), pp. 288, 292–3. If Munro is not mistaken, then Captain Innes was indeed John and not Robert as confused by Mackay and Riis: *Monro, His Expedition with the Worthy Scots Regiment Called Mac-Keys*, ed. W. S. Brockington (Westport, Ct., 1999), p. 116; J. Mackay, *An Old Scots Brigade: Being the History of Mackay's Regiment Now Incorporated with the Royal Scots* (Edinburgh, 1885), p. 205; T. Riis, *Should Auld Acquaintance Be Forgot...: Scottish-Danish Relations c. 1450–1707*, 2 vols (Odense, 1988), vol. II, p. 130. On networks see NLS, Dep. 175/65, nos. 146–7, 162–3; Sutherland Papers, Dep. 313/489, no. 9; NAS, Reay Papers, GD84/2/170; GD406/1/458; *The Sutherland Book*, ed. W. Fraser, 3 vols (Edinburgh, 1892), vol. II, pp. 152, 161–2; Fallon, "Scottish Mercenaries", pp. 46–54.

12. NLS, Dep. 175/65, nos. 143ff, *passim*; Dep. 313/491, no. 1778; *Social Life in Former Days: Second Series, Illustrated by Letters and Family Papers*, ed. E. D. Dunbar (Edinburgh, 1866), pp. 28–30, 32–3, 57–64; *Sutherland Book*, ed. Fraser, II, pp. 38, 152–65. For the positive influence of war correspondence

In order to assess the return of these soldiers and the effects of this homecoming on them and their society at large, it is necessary to understand the impact of the war on society at large. Death took an important toll on soldier numbers. Before even reaching the battlefields, the journey to and across the continent was itself a risky enterprise.[13] Diseases similarly ravaged the ranks and reduced the regimental rolls usually by 10% at least.[14] The war left a devastating trauma on individuals and to a lesser measure on the regional demographics in Scotland. It frustrated the potential for demographic growth through the depletion of the young male population. Conversely, demographic growth must also be related to the availability of land and of manufacturing processes. In the absence of either or both, a loss of population actually facilitated stability. Casualties among both the elite and ordinary clansmen distorted the social fabric of northern clanship, just as conscription did in the economically deprived area of Swedish Norrland.[15]

War inflicted psychological scars both on the exiles themselves and their home communities. For women and their expectation of returning soldiers, the poetry of war experience voiced the traumatic consequences they endured.[16] Undoubtedly, for those who survived and returned to Scotland, the ordeal occasioned them deep emotional and psychological strains as well as physical injuries. An inkling of this appeared in an undated petition by Donald, Lord Reay, to King Christian IV of Denmark.[17] Only this shared harrowing experience and heartfelt compassion towards his wounded fellow soldiers can explain Robert Munro's

---

in Scotland, see D. Horsbroch, "Wish You Were Here? Scottish Reactions to 'Postcards' Home from the 'Germane Warres'", in Murdoch, *Scotland and the Thirty Years' War*, pp. 245–69.

13. NLS, Dep. 175/65, no. 146; Gordon, *Earldom*, p. 473; Monro, *Expedition*, I, p. 64; II, pp. 3–4, 13; *The Celtic Magazine*, vol. X (1885), p. 235.

14. Monro, *Expedition*, vol. I, pp. 27, 65, 86; vol. II, pp. 8, 10, 12, 18, 23, 40, 47–9, 53, 59; Fallon, "Scottish Mercenaries", pp. 339–42; Fischer, *Scots in Sweden*, pp. 90, 100–2.

15. NAS, John MacGregor Collection, GD50/224/6; Munro of Foulis Writs, GD93/201; Cuninghame of Caprington Muniments, GD149/265/2, fo. 90r; NLS, Brydges MS, Adv. MS 6.1.17, fos. 92r-4r; Historical Manuscripts Commission [HMC], *Eleventh Report, Appendix, Part VI: The Manuscripts of the Duke of Hamilton*, ed. W. Fraser (London, 1887), p. 74; T. A. Fischer, *The Scots in Germany: Being a Contribution towards the History of the Scot Abroad* (Edinburgh, 1902), pp. 77–8, 90–1, 283–5; D. Kirby, *Northern Europe in the Early Modern Period: The Baltic World, 1492–1772* (London, 1992), pp. 138–9, 146–7. It is argued that in 18th century Scotland, net migration, which included temporary emigrants like soldiers and merchant mariners, had a much lesser impact on the population than that of fertility and mortality: R. E. Tyson, "Demographic Change", in T. M. Devine and J. R. Young (eds), *Eighteenth Century Scotland: New Perspectives* (East Linton, 1999), pp. 197-8.

16. One of these songs ran "Oh, woe unto these cruell wars That ever they began! For they have reft my native isle Of many a pretty man. First they took my brothers twain Then wiled my love frae me: Oh, woe unto these cruell wars In low Germanie!" (Fischer, *Scots in Germany*, pp. 73–4.)

17. I. Grimble, "The Royal Payment of Mackay's Regiment", *Scottish Gaelic Studies* [*SGS*], vol. IX (1961), pp. 28–30.

resolution to erect a hospital in Scotland for injured ex-servicemen in the spring and summer of 1634. However, a lack of funding and the later development of the Civil Wars meant that his project ultimately collapsed.[18]

Nevertheless, some of these military men needed little persuasion to continue their armed service either on the continent or in the British Isles in this belligerent context.[19] Others exploited their influential networks and military achievements to move into the diplomatic/political sphere, such as John Gunn of Golspie, for example, who rose to the rank of colonel and in 1638 assumed the governorship of Ohlau (Oława) in Silesia.[20] Scottish auxiliaries received and acquired estates and lands on the continent and advanced to the nobility. Though not a first generation Scot, Lieutenant-Colonel John Urquhart received three leaseholds from Queen Christina of Sweden in May 1645 for his military duties and was ennobled in 1648. Urquhart's case was part of the wider civilianization of the Scottish military in Swedish-held territories.[21] The official employment of far northerners in the army did not preclude their continued interest in their personal or clan interests. *Au contraire*, it somewhat supplemented and amplified them. Likewise, despite Muscovy's military

---

18. *Documents Relating to the Province of Moray*, ed. E. D. Dunbar (Edinburgh, 1895), pp. 113–4; Mackay, *Old Scots Brigade*, pp. 204–8; Clan Munro Association, *Clan Munro Magazine*, vol. V (1955), pp. 25–8; Monro, *Expedition*, vol. II, pp. 13, 20–1, 31–2, 54–5, 65–6, 70–2; *RPC*, 2nd ser., vol. V, pp. 333–6, 349, 352–6; SCA, CA4/9/6. It is worth pointing out that Munro initiated this project prior to the battle of Nördlingen. The colonel nonetheless lost most of his regiment. Munro certainly returned to Sweden and fought on until 1639 while the Swedish armies regrouped and strengthened: Grosjean, *Unofficial Alliance*, pp. 97–103, 172; W. S. Brockington, "Robert Monro: Professional Soldier, Military Historian and Scotsman", in Murdoch, *Scotland and the Thirty Years' War*, pp. 219–220; "Scotland, Scandinavia and Northern Europe, 1580–1707" [SSNE], S. Murdoch and A. Grosjean (eds), available online at <http://www.st-andrews.ac.uk/history/ssne/index.php>, accessed 19–20 February 2005, ID no. 94.

19. *Gordon under Arms*, Skelton and Bulloch (eds), nos. 122, 832, 1656, 1734; *Munro Tree*, ed. Munro, M/44, R/6, R/21; Mackay, *Old Scots Brigade*, p. 252.

20. Fischer, *Scots in Germany*, p. 316; W. Macfarlane (ed.), *Genealogical Collections concerning Families in Scotland*, ed. J. T. Clark, 2 vols (Scottish Historical Society [SHS], 1900), vol. I, p. 101. The ubiquitous William Gunn developed an ever wider network moving first into a limited local circle of influence to enjoy finally British and continental connections. Gunn, the son of an accessory to arson, ended his career as a major-general and baron of the Holy Roman Empire: Fischer, *Scots in Germany*, p. 112; Fischer, *Scots in Sweden*, pp. 118, 266; NLS, Gordons of Gordonstoun and Cummings of Altyre Papers, Acc. 10824/3, bundle no. 94, Dec. 1623; Dep. 175/65, nos. 107, 120, 146, 163, 300; Dep. 313/489, no. 28a; Dep. 313/491, no. 1770; NAS, GD406/1/857; HMC, *Eleventh Report*, App., pp. 101, 104; Monro, *Expedition*, vol. II, pp. 23–4; Fallon, "Scottish Mercenaries", pp. 63, 117, 120, 288, 290, 292–3, 344, 377, 382, 384; Worthington, *Scots in Habsburg Service*, pp. 239, 249, 278; D. G. Thompson, "In the Footsteps of Sir William Gunn", *Gunn Herald* (Mar. 1999), available online at <http://www.geocities.com/cgherald/Archive/SirWilliamGunn.html>, accessed 27 August 2009.

21. H. Tayler, *History of the Family of Urquhart* (Aberdeen, 1946), pp. 7, 21, 61, 92; Fischer, *Scots in Sweden*, pp. 117–8, 237–8, 260, 263–4; *Munro Tree*, ed. Munro, L/17, Q/15. This civilianization is researched in Grosjean, *Unofficial Alliance*, ch. 5; and see Murdoch, *Network North*, pp. 359, 361–4.

employment of Siberian Cossacks on the frontier, they still maintained their raids and combined their peripheral benefits with their national official position.[22] Indeed, the war was not all doom and gloom for soldiers. Happier moments punctuated its course in the form of marriage, for example.[23]

On the other hand, after his service, Hector Munro of Culcraggie sold the estate to his remote cousin, John Munro, burgess of Edinburgh. With the royal payments for his expensive military investments often failing to materialize fully, on time, or at all, Donald, Lord Reay, was still insolvent by 1637. He finally disposed of the lands of Strathnaver to John, Earl of Sutherland, in 1642.[24] Yet, military promotions and positions alternatively conveyed social and symbolic prestige. Indeed, beyond these material provisions, returning soldiers won appraisals and recognition from within the community, as experienced by brothers from Barra probably in around 1630-31:

> Gum bu sin na fir allail, 'S gum bu sin na fir fhurail, Fhuair an urram 's a b'fhiach e; 'S math ur gnothach 'sa Ghearmailt, Gur neo-chearbach ur gnìomh ann.

"Those were the famous men, Those were the watchful men, Who got honour and deserved it; You were well fitted to be in Germany, Your deed there was efficient."[25]

Through its manifold military arrangements, the Crown aspired to channel the potential offered by private armies into the public sphere for its own *mission civilisatrice*, namely the reform of the far northerners and the removal of the most troublesome minorities. It coerced them into partial submission by integrating them into the Scottish/British State rather than annihilating them outright. The experiences of returning soldiers were as multifarious as their reasons for joining the army had been.

---

22. C. Witzenrath, *Cossacks and the Russian Empire, 1598–1725: Manipulation, Rebellion and Expansion into Siberia* (London, 2007), pp. 24–6, 36–8, 61, 76, 127, 140–1, 148, 152.

23. *Munro Tree*, ed. Munro, M/24, Q/15; *The Scots Overseas: Emigrants and Adventurers from Argyll and the Northern Highlands (Part One)*, ed. D. Dobson (St Andrews, 1993), pp. 22, 27; D. [S.] Thomson, *An Introduction to Gaelic Poetry* (2nd ed., Edinburgh, 1990), pp. 60–1.

24. *CSP, Dom., 1628-29*, p. 555; A. Mackenzie, *History of the Munros of Fowlis* (Inverness, 1898), p. 360; NAS, GD84/2/173, pp. 178, 192; GD84/2/246, p. 33b; GD406/1/9656–7; *Inventory of Reay Papers*, ed. Innes, 3/1B, 2B, 3B, 4B; 8/2, 6, 12; 9/1–3, 7, 12; 12/1B–8B; 28/1–10, 1B–2B, 3B/1–4; 125/4–7; Gordon, *Earldom*, p. 509; Grimble, "Royal Payment", pp. 23–38; I. Grimble, *Chief of Mackay* (London, 1965), ch. 6; *Letters of Two Centuries Chiefly Connected with Inverness and the Highlands, from 1616 to 1815*, ed. C. Fraser-Mackintosh (Inverness, 1890), pp. 24–5, 34–6.

25. *Gaelic Folksongs from the Isle of Barra*, J. L. Campbell *et al.* (eds), (London, 1950), pp. 28–9. Sir Donald Mackay was made Lord Baron Reay in June 1628 in token of his military actions: NAS, GD84/2/169, 171; Mackay of Bighouse Muniments, GD87/2/2; *Registrum Magni Sigilli Regum Scotorum; The Register of the Great Seal of Scotland*, AD *1306–1668* [*RMS*], J. M. Thomson *et al.* (eds), 11 vols (Edinburgh, 1882–1914), vol. VIII, no. 1211.

The trauma of war left important psychological marks on society owing to its extensive influence especially in tightly-knit kinship communities of the early-modern Scottish far north. The readjustment to civilian life meant that, due to financial pressure, a large number of landholding military men had to part with all or a portion of their estates. Others were forced to carry on their martial career. However, others even managed to climb the social ladder through the social, political, and diplomatic preferment that their military service had earned them either in exile or in the *patria* after their return.

Exile and return: a cultural (re)vision

More peaceful opportunities also presented themselves notably, though not restrictively, to the clan elite. There was a recognition amongst the upper ranks that social promotion could be achieved in various ways away from unlicensed sword power. Education thus became a key aspect in the formation of the clan elite youth, as it was in other rural parts of Europe.[26] The education of children encompassed a broad segment of society through the active participation of the clan at large to meet these instructional needs, even if informally. As a consequence, exile from the communities occasionally took place at a relatively young age. For the well-to-do and aspiring gentry, peregrination in Europe opened up the means to cultivate oneself not merely academically but also culturally, and this had significant repercussions in the locality after their return given the powerful position of this social stratum.

Traditional historiography discredits any society mired in ignorance both of the knowledge of God and educationally. This biased picture is found in the contemporary Scottish Borders, the Mezzogiorno, and in late-medieval Tuscany, and is derived from secular and religious perceptions of its backwardness.[27] A revised approach to these societies reveals

---

26. G. Astoul, *Les Chemins du Savoir en Quercy et Rouergue à l'Époque Moderne : Alphabétisation et Apprentissages Culturels* (Toulouse, 1999), pp. 93–5; D. Allan, "'What's in a Name?': Pedigree and Propaganda in Seventeenth-Century Scotland", in E. J. Cowan and R. J. Finlay (eds), *Scottish History: The Power of the Past* (Edinburgh, 2002), pp. 161–2. This line of reasoning actually combined the two trends in the mainstream English humanist thought of the time whose ideal was to shape a belligerent aristocracy into gentlemanly scholar-soldiers rather than farmers or merchants: D. Shuger, "Irishmen, Aristocrats, and Other White Barbarians", *Renaissance Quarterly*, vol. 1 (1997), p. 520.

27. D. Withrington, "Education in the 17th Century Highlands", in L. Maclean (ed.), *The Seventeenth Century in the Highlands* (Inverness, 1986), pp. 60–9; M. M. Meikle, *A British Frontier?: Lairds and Gentlemen in the Eastern Borders, 1540–1603* (East Linton, 2004), ch. 5; S. K. Cohn, "Highlands and Lowlands in Late Medieval Tuscany", in D. Broun and M. MacGregor (eds), *Miorun Mòr nan Gall, "The Great Ill-Will of the Lowlander"?: Lowland Perceptions of the Highlands, Medieval and Modern* (Glasgow, 2009), pp. 111–2, 122; J. D. Selwyn, *A Paradise Inhabited by Devils: The Jesuits' Civilizing*

new elements and findings. Some of these mountain peoples were in fact educated locally after having received their initial education within the family home, as was common among the Scottish nobility and in families of the French Hautes Alpes.[28]

In addition to an institutional instruction, and as observed elsewhere across early-modern Europe, people in these lands sought alternatives and invested in the upbringing of their children, recognizing their potential as human capital.[29] The practice of fosterage was widely used throughout Scotland, Ireland, and western Eurasia and was important in the creation of networks of dynastic/clan or inter-familial allegiances and loyalties. Yet, its educational value is perhaps still somewhat under-valued.[30] Fosterage consolidated the system of patronage for superiors while presenting a prudent investment towards social advancement for depend-

Mission in Early Modern Naples (Aldershot, 2004), introduction and ch. 1. The denigration of people constitutive of the kingdom applied in the Swedish case against the Lapps: P. Burke, *Popular Culture in Early Modern Europe* (1978, 3rd ed., Farnham, 2009), p. 152. MacGregor claims this irreligious strain to be apparently a post-1560 construct as this did not feature in the late-medieval literati canon, except for William Dunbar: M. MacGregor, "Gaelic Barbarity and Scottish Identity in the Later Middle Ages", in Broun and MacGregor, *Lowland Perceptions*, p. 36.

28. A.-M. Granet-Abisset, "Entre Autodidaxie et Scolarisation : Les Alpes Briançonnaises", *Histoire de l'Éducation*, vol. LXXI (1996), p. 129. Gifts of chaplainries depicted a broad picture of local education: NAS, Register of Privy Seal, PS1/61, fo. 10v; PS1/63, fo. 98v; Church of Scotland Records, Miscellaneous Ecclesiastical Records, Register of Presentations to Benefices, CH4/1/1, fos. 101v, 104v, 107v; CH4/1/2, fos. 21v, 41r-v, 43v, 154r; *Origines Parochiales Scotiae: The Antiquities Ecclesiastical and Territorial of the Parishes of Scotland* [*OPS*], C. Innes and J. B. Brichan (eds), 2 vols (Bannatyne Club, 1851–55), vol. II, pp. 2, 422–5, 460, 586; Mackenzie, *Munros*, p. 302; *Old Ross-shire and Scotland As Seen in the Tain and Balnagown Documents*, ed. W. Macgill, 2 vols (Inverness, 1909–11), vol. I, no. 138; M. Dilworth, "Benedictine Monks of Ratisbon and Wurzburg in the 17th and 18th Centuries: émigrés from the Highlands of Scotland", *TGSI*, vol. XLIV (1964–66), pp. 96–7. The initial education of the nobility is discussed in K. M. Brown, *Noble Society in Scotland: Wealth, Family and Culture, from Reformation to Revolution* (Edinburgh, 2004), pp. 181–2.

29. R. A. Houston, *Literacy in Early Modern Europe: Culture and Education, 1500–1800* (2nd ed., Harlow, 2002), pp. 99–106, and pp. 106–23 for the motives and limitations in the search for the command of literacy; I. G. Tóth, *Literacy and Written Culture in Early Modern Central Europe* (Budapest, 2000), pp. 27–9; P. Bourdieu, "The Forms of Capital", in J. G. Richardson (ed.), *Handbook of Theory and Research for the Sociology of Education* (New York, 1986), pp. 243–6, 253; G. S. Becker, *Human Capital: A Theoretical and Empirical Analysis, with Special Reference to Education* (1964, 3rd ed., Chicago, 1993), pp. 15–26, 255–6.

30. This social geopolitical dimension of fosterage, namely the creation of alliances between and within kindreds, is discussed in A. Cathcart, *Kinship and Clientage: Highland Clanship, 1451–1609* (Leiden, 2006), pp. 80–5; F. Fitzsimons, "Fosterage and Gossiprid in Late Medieval Ireland: Some New Evidence", in P. J. Duffy *et al.* (eds), *Gaelic Ireland, c. 1250–c. 1650: Land, Lordship and Settlement* (Dublin, 2001), pp. 138–49. The utilitarian capitalization of fosterage in relation to kinship as exercised by Scots abroad is most aptly analysed in Murdoch, *Network North*, ch. 1. On comparative adoptive kinship within a socio-political angle, one should consult P. Parkes, "Celtic Fosterage: Adoptive Kinship and Clientage in Northwest Europe", *Comparative Studies in Society and History*, vol. XLVIII (2006), pp. 359–95.

ents.[31] Oral culture must have to some extent infused the youth with means to gain cultural and educational development which are difficult to quantify given the nature of that process. Within that Platonic framework, fosterage should not be disregarded as a mere lever for the reinforcement and utilitarian promotion of kinship bonds and loyalties. As a system, it filled the social and cultural interstices of biological descent and marital alliances.[32]

Furthermore, albeit extensive as a custom, fosterage was not the universal apanage of mountainous communities which were also dedicated to the formation of youth within the home.[33] It conveyed some educational and training values, if only minimally.[34] The phenomenon was wide-spread not only geographically and socially but also in terms of gender.[35] For example, prior to April 1602, Donald Thornton in the Chanonry of Ross entrusted his daughter Janet to Mr George Munro, Chancellor of Ross, for her education.[36] Sometimes progeny was placed within a separate environment away from the community, as happened with Torquil Macleod, son of the laird (or possibly the breive) of Lewis, brought up by his mother's relatives in Strathconon.[37]

As in the Eastern Borders, testamentary evidence attested to these educational concerns on the part of the parents.[38] The boarding of one's offspring with relatives, local/regional magnates, or even apparent strangers, by means of guardianship or otherwise, most certainly carried an

31. Parkes, "Celtic Fosterage", pp. 361–6; A. O. Curle, "Notice of Four Contracts or Bonds of Fosterage; with Notes on the Former Prevalence of the Custom of Fosterage in the Scottish Highlands", *Proceedings of the Society of Antiquaries of Scotland* [*PSAS*], vol. XXX (1895–96), pp. 12–4, 17, 19–21.

32. Murdoch, *Network North*, ch. 1; Cathcart, *Kinship*, pp. 80–5; Fitzsimons, "Fosterage and Gossiprid". For Plato, the art of reading and writing carried but the appearance of wisdom and only instruction led to true wisdom: Plato, *Phaedrus*, trans. H. N. Fowler (London, 1913), pp. 563, 565.

33. Granet-Abisset, "Entre Autodidaxie et Scolarisation", pp. 127–9 and 136–7, who contended that Alpine villages resorted to a mixture of home and school education, but also noted the possibility of a placement of the youth with a curate kin to learn Latin.

34. See the early Irish and Welsh practices and likewise that of the Ossetes in the North Caucasus in Parkes, "Celtic Fosterage", pp. 361–2, 362–3 n. 8, 374–5.

35. NAS, Commissariot of Edinburgh, Register of Testaments, CC8/8/31, p. 781; also CC8/8/29, p. 285; CC8/8/37, pp. 87, 329; NLS, Dep. 313/1597, year 1616, fo. 8v.

36. *RPC*, 1st ser., vol. VI, pp. 411–2; NAS, CC8/8/45, p. 183; Exchequer Records, Taxation Papers, E68/14/6, 5 May 1627; see also CC8/8/29, pp. 291–2. John Mackenzie of Gairloch had entrusted a daughter of his to Mr Robert Munro, most likely the treasurer of Ross, by 1607. Gairloch replicated the move with at least one of his sons cared for by Robert Leslie in the Chanonry. The location once again on the far north-eastern coast is significant: NAS, CC8/8/45, p. 669.

37. I. F. Grant, *The Macleods: The History of a Clan* (1959), p. 127; *The Book of Dunvegan*, ed. R. C. MacLeod, vol. I (Third Spalding Club, 1938), pp. 120–1. Some Mackenzie instances of fostering can be found in *Celtic Magazine*, vol. II (1877), p. 110. On the strengthening of kinship bonds through fosterage, see M. Rackwitz, *Travels to Terra Incognita: The Scottish Highlands and Hebrides in Early Modern Travellers' Accounts, c. 1600 to 1800* (Münster, 2007), pp. 242–7.

38. Meikle, *British Frontier*, pp. 165, 167.

educational function whether formally at a local school or informally by way of nurture in the family. By September 1607, a young Hector Munro, the son of the Munro chief, Mr Hector, was entrusted to Mr George Munro, Chancellor of Ross.[39] But, testamentary provisions towards the education of surviving children could only go as far as the goodwill of their tutors.[40] Throughout these provisions for the cultivation of children in a foreign environment, real and fictive kinship played a pivotal role.[41]

In terms of higher education and with the absence of local universities, exile from their native soil was compulsory for far northerners, just as it was for Borderers.[42] As had been the case from the Middle Ages, this required a knowledge in Latin, if not a conversance with it, to enable them to connect with the thinking and literature of the classical past and be in contact with the developing contemporary culture of Europe.[43] Overall, there were probably well over a hundred students from the far north of Scotland who attended Scottish and European universities

---

39. NAS, CC8/8/45, p. 183; and also CC8/8/20, p. 407; CC8/8/24, p. 179; CC8/8/25, p. 273; CC8/8/35, pp. 61, 782; NLS, Acc. 10824/3, charge crop 1621 and sett 1622. Other instances of boarding in towns of the area's eastern seaboard and the Lowlands suggest at least the possibility of school education and perhaps apprenticeship for boys, including for Wester Ross families. Even a minor landlord like Angus Macculloch in/of Craighouse (Tarbat parish) was able to place his son Walter with Alexander Morrison, indweller in Leith, by 1599: NAS, CC8/8/35, p. 781; CC8/8/45, p. 669. Island families opted for Glasgow for instruction facilities and/or positions of apprenticeship: NAS, Glasgow Commissary Court Records, Register of Deeds, 1585–88, 1604–1700, CC9/14/4, fo. 164r.

40. Thomas, the son of Sir John Sinclair of Greenland, was left in 1622 to "ye governement of ye laird of murkill [James Sinclair, Thomas' uncle] To be brocht up and trainit vp at scooles" (NAS, Caithness Commissary Court, Register of Deeds, CC4/8/1, fo. 4r). A generation before, in 1582, James Sinclair himself had been left with his cousin, Francis, Earl of Bothwell, to be governed, entertained, and sustained "at ye schuillis": SCA, Blairs Charters, BC14/4; also of interest is NAS, CC8/8/39, p. 321; Robertson of Kindeace Papers, GD146/10, testaments 1653–1793, Gilbert Robertson's testament.

41. In a number of instances, marital patterns are difficult to trace.

42. Meikle, *British Frontier*, pp. 168–72.

43. D. E. R. Watt, "Education in the Highlands in the Middle Ages", in L. Maclean (ed.), *The Middle Ages in the Highlands* (Inverness, 1981), pp. 80–9. On this Latinate culture in the far north, one should consult *Report of the Committee of the Highland Society of Scotland, Appointed to Inquire into the Nature and Authenticity of the Poems of Ossian*, ed. H. Mackenzie (Edinburgh, 1805), p. 50; J. Bannerman, "Literacy in the Highlands", in I. B. Cowan and D. Shaw (eds), *The Renaissance and Reformation in Scotland* (Edinburgh, 1983), pp. 214–35; R. Sharpe, "Roderick MacLean's *Life* of St Columba in Latin Verse (1549)", *Innes Review* [*IR*], vol. XLII (1991), pp. 111–32; *Highland Papers*, ed. J. R. N. Macphail, 4 vols (SHS, 1914–34), vol. I, pp. 8, 10–11; A. Cameron, *Reliquiae Celticae*, A. MacBain and J. Kennedy (eds), 2 vols (Inverness, 1892–94), vol. II, pp. 170–1; J. B. Craven, *Descriptive Catalogue of the Bibliotheck of Kirkwall (1683), with a Notice of the Founder, William Baikie, M. A. of Holland* (Kirkwall, 1897), pp. 20, 32; M. Anderson-Smith, "The Bibliotheck of Kirkwall", *Northern Scotland*, vol. XV (1995), pp. 128–30; Aberdeen University Library [AUL], Special Collections, volume shelf-marked "BK Rud [1–6]"; *Book of Dunvegan*, ed. MacLeod, vol. I, p. 184; NAS, GD146/10, inventory of old papers 1782.

over the period compared to the perhaps fifty to sixty students at European universities documented for the preceding two centuries, between c. 1200–1410. As one might expect, the vast majority of these students came from the nobility and landholding families, perhaps as much as 75%.[44] Moreover, the sons of clergymen attended universities, possibly to the amount of 15–20%, such as William Lauder at Aberdeen in the early 1630s, who was the son of James, minister at Avoch, or John Macrae, at both Aberdeen and St Andrews in the 1630s, whose father, Farquhar, officiated at the kirk of Kintail.[45] In a marginal but revealing capacity, higher education opened up the possibility of social mobility for a number of families, be they tenants, town inhabitants, or clan officials.[46] The relative absence of sons of burgesses in university records, as far as can be gathered, can be explained by their greater propensity to enter into indentured service with burgesses rather than going to university. It

---

44. Estimates of attendance are only tentative due to the partial survival of records, the proportion of attendants who never matriculated, the European-wide *peregrinatio academica*, and a high drop-out rate (Houston, *Literacy*, pp. 91-3). This number is the result of the perusal of a variety of sources too numerous to be listed, but primarily the *Fasti Ecclesiae Scoticanae*, ed. H. Scott, 8 vols (new ed., Edinburgh, 1915–50), vols VII–VIII, and the printed and manuscript registers of alumni and matriculations of the Universities of Aberdeen, Edinburgh, Glasgow, and St Andrews. There were about 64 students for whom their paternity was known and 48 of those were of noble or landholding stock. All the major families and clans of the far north had sons in higher education: Gordon, Gray, Macdonald, Mackenzie, Macleod, Macrae, Munro, Ross, and Sinclair, the last two perhaps underrepresented were it not for the fact that the name being found in these registers was a common one in Scotland. This is a major point as these registers mostly recorded first names and surnames with no other details, hence the difficulty in identifying Davidsons, Dunbars, Grays, Rosses, Sinclairs, Urquharts, and others. The medieval figures for the then dioceses of Caithness, Ross, Moray, and Argyll are taken from Watt, "Education in the Highlands", p. 87.

45. *Fasti*, ed. Scott, vol. VII, pp. 1, 33; *Officers and Graduates of the University and King's College, Aberdeen, MVD–MDCCCLX*, ed. P. J. Anderson (New Spalding Club, 1893), p. 185; A. Macrae, *History of the Clan Macrae: With Genealogies* (Dingwall, 1899), pp. 142–3; also *Selected Justiciary Cases, 1624–1650*, S. A. Gillon and J. I. Smith (eds), 3 vols (Stair Soc., 1953–74), vol. III, pp. 564–71. The ecclesiastics who sent their sons to the university at times combined a landholding position, hence the high percentage when the two figures for the landlords and clergy are added together.

46. For example, Archibald Davidson, son of Adam Davidson, burgess of Inverness and indweller in Thurso, went to the University of St Andrews: *Fasti*, ed. Scott, vol. VII, p. 106; vol. VIII, p. 674; *Accounts of the Collectors of Thirds of Benefices, 1561–1572*, ed. G. Donaldson (SHS, 1949), p. 208; *Early Records of the University of St Andrews: The Graduation Roll, 1413–1579, and the Matriculation Roll, 1473–1579*, ed. J. M. Anderson (SHS, 1926), pp. 297, 300, 304, 307; Royal Commission on the Ancient and Historical Monuments and Constructions of Scotland [RCAHMS], *Third Report and Inventory of Monuments and Constructions in the County of Caithness* (London, 1911), pp. 113–4. Mr Martin Macpherson, a graduate of Glasgow University, was the son of John Bain Macpherson, "warrior": *Fasti*, ed. Scott, vol. VII, pp. 194–5; vol. VIII, p. 690; Scottish Genealogy Society, *The Scottish Genealogist*, vol. I, nos. 2–3 (Apr.–Jul. 1954), p. 27; *Munimenta Alme Universitatis Glasguensis: Records of the University of Glasgow from Its Foundation till 1727*, ed. C. Innes, 4 vols (Maitland Club, 1854), vol. III, pp. 19, 82.

corroborates the view that work placement suited the economies of the pre-industrial West.[47]

The Lowland or English perspective of mono-centric civility, as solely radiating from the centre to the periphery, needs to be challenged. Cultural education was available in a Highland milieu among the peers of the realm. This meant that the "civilizing" process was partly an indirect one or even, one might say, a peripheral one. In the closing years of the sixteenth century, possibly in April 1596, Denis Campbell, Dean of Limerick, produced an account of the Western Isles for Queen Elizabeth of England. In it, he described a young Donald Macdonald of Sleat as having been "trained up in learning and civility" at the residence of Archibald, Seventh Earl of Argyll.[48] Under the influence of the House of Sutherland, the erstwhile rough Donald Mackay presented a different, softened aspect to his English audience at court for his knighthood in 1616 as "comely, firm and very portlike".[49] Less than two decades later, in 1631, the English comments on his appearance at his trial at Westminster for high treason had hardly evolved. Sir Donald still looked "comely [...] very port-like and of staid countenance".[50] Notably, the Strathnaver leader adopted an element of Latinate culture and changed the Gaelic slogan of the clan from *bi treun*, or "be valiant", to its Latin equivalent *manu forti*, "with a strong hand".[51] In essence, a component of

---

47. NAS, CC4/2/1, bundle 1633, legacy of the late William Strachan, 15 Jun. 1633. Albeit of a later date (1658), a good insight into indentured service can be found in NAS, Cromartie Muniments, GD305/1/147/2. On this point, one should consult Becker, *Human Capital*, p. 20. The search across the printed and manuscript registers of students enrolled at Scottish and English universities is not facilitated by the anonymity of the records which tended to list only the Christian names and surnames of the students. Undoubtedly, these would have incorporated sons of burgesses. However, the gift of chaplainries to fund schooling for children with a view for the recipients subsequently to enter the ministry was granted to a number of burgesses but these were not residents in the northern shires: NAS, CH4/1/1-4; PS1/53-67. Lastly, the fact that burgesses did not tend to use the title "Mr" suggests that they did not graduate but might have nonetheless attended university.

48. *Calendar of State Papers Relating to Scotland and Mary, Queen of Scots, 1547–1603* [*CSP, Sco.*], J. Bain *et al.* (eds), 13 vols (Edinburgh, 1898–1969), vol. XII, p. 205 n.; *Highland Papers*, ed. Macphail, vol. II, p. 267.

49. Grimble, *Chief of Mackay*, pp. 59–65. On some bellicose and lawless traits of character of Donald Mackay, one can consult Grimble, *Chief of Mackay*, p. 59; A. Mackay, *The Book of Mackay* (Edinburgh, 1906), p. 126; NAS, Particular Register of Hornings and Inhibitions, Inverness, 1st ser., DI62/4, fos. 134r-5v.

50. *Cobbett's Complete Collection of State Trials and Proceedings for High Treason and Other Crimes and Misdemeanors from the Earliest Period to the Present Time*, T. B. Howell and T. J. Howell (eds), 34 vols (London, 1809–28), vol. III, col. 486. The trial itself can be consulted in *ibid.*, Howell and Howell (eds), vol. III, cols 483–520.

51. A. Mackay, "An Account of the Aberach-Mackay Banner, Now Exhibited in the National Museum", *PSAS*, vol. XXXVIII (1903–4), pp. 527–9; A. Mackay, "The Aberach-Mackay Banner", *Celtic Monthly*, vol. VI (1898), pp. 171–5; J. Sinclair (ed.), *The Statistical Account of Scotland, 1791–1799* [*OSA*], D. J. Withrington and I. R. Grant (eds), 20 vols (Wakefield, 1973–83), vol. XVIII, p. 477. Much was probably lost in terms of banners and ensigns among the Scottish clans. A mere quote

social regulation from below complemented the pressure for behavioural reform contained within the top-down social discipline.

Finally, although difficult to decipher, cultural influences must have prevailed upon far northern leaders away from their residences when in the Lowlands, at court, or abroad altogether.[52] Just as Siberian Cossacks used literacy to exploit administrative and commercial opportunities and so pragmatically upheld their interests, Sir Robert Gordon, Tutor of Sutherland, likewise put to good use his interest in civil law while in France with access to leading institutions in that field at Poitiers, Orleans, and Bourges. Apologists of the emergent neo-Stoic thought endorsed the Tacitean aspiration for a reconfiguration of political morality along pragmatic lines, however disturbing these were. The defence of kinship thus became paramount over the immorality of the actual act(s) and justified it/them This philosophy peppered Sir Robert's genealogical work in the defence of the House of Sutherland and was carried out in actions and legal deeds in the defence of the comital House sometimes at the expense of morality.[53]

At a more practical level, contemporary fashion imposed itself on the clan elite who acquired stylish pieces of furniture and other goods, like the refined carved oak sideboard thought to have been imported from London alongside a silver communion cup by Sir Rory Macleod of Dunvegan during his stay at court in 1613. Yet, Sir Rory carved his coat-of-arms on the cup which featured two symbolic charges characteristic of Highland heraldry, namely the lion rampant, also a royal charge, and the galley.[54] Clan chiefs projected a pictorial personal pride of their

---

from a mid- to late-16th century piece of bardic praise-poetry of the Campbells revealed Clan Ranald as *ealta sluaigh na meirgeach maoth*, "those fighting bands of the ensigns of silk", and the Macleods as *Fine Leóid na mbratach mbodhbha*, "Tribe of Leod of the belligerent banners": *Duanaire na Sracaire Songbook of the Pillagers: Anthology of Scotland's Gaelic Verse to 1600*, W. McLeod and M. Bateman (eds) (Edinburgh, 2007), pp. 146–7, also 412–3; J. Macdonald, "An Elegy for Ruaidhrí Mór", *SGS*, vol. VIII (1958), pp. 40-1; A. Matheson, "Poems from a Manuscript of Cathal Mac Muireadhaigh", *Éigse*, vol. XI (1964–66), p. 1; *Gàir nan Clàrsach: The Harps' Cry*, C. Ó Baoill and M. Bateman (eds) (Edinburgh, 1994), pp. 86-7.

52. That is beside the other means responsible for the penetration of cultural influences in any given area either through books or trade for instance.

53. C. Witzenrath, "Literacy and Orality in the Eurasian Frontier: Imperial Culture and Space in Seventeenth-Century Siberia and Russia", *Slavonic and East European Review* [*SEER*], vol. LXXXVII (2009), pp. 63–77; D. Allan, "'Ane Ornament to Yow and Your Famelie': Sir Robert Gordon of Gordonstoun and the *Genealogical History of the Earldom of Sutherland*", *Scottish Historical Review* [*SHR*], vol. LXXX (2001), pp. 24–44, especially 40–44; Allan, "Pedigree and Propaganda", pp. 151, 159; NLS, Dep. 175/65, nos. 58, 84, 103. Beside networking, corruption lubricated legal businesses for prosperous far northerners.

54. F. T. MacLeod, "Notes on the Relics Preserved in Dunvegan Castle, Skye, and the Heraldry of the Family of Macleod of Macleod", *PSAS*, vol. XLVII (1912–13), pp. 118–9, 123–4 dated the sideboard to 1603 and of an Edinburgh origin; *Book of Dunvegan*, ed. MacLeod, vol. I, p. XLVI;

own sense of accomplishments in exile. Sir Donald Mackay, Lord Reay, reflected his martial feats in the Thirty Years' War by bearing a pikeman and a musketeer as dexter and sinister heraldic supporters respectively.[55]

Despite the partly intangible character of educational and cultural influences on exiled far northerners, it seems that they had an impact on at least a number of them once they returned to their home environment. This was an ongoing process of integration into wider Scottish and British society and of greater biculturalism with numerous variables that affected individuals and communities alike. At least the clan elite tended to retain elements of Gaelic culture, including those on the far northern-eastern seaboard, and associated these with non-native ones. The phenomenon amplified the pre-existing dual and hybrid culture and integration. However, the process needs to be studied over the *longue durée*. It was by no means a phenomenon that universally affected the far north but rather one that gradually unfolded with geographical and societal variations.

Conclusion

Just as Muscovy employed Tatars in its army and did not bestow high official positions on them while its Siberian Cossacks maximized their access to literacy, the Scottish far northerners, in similar circumstances abroad and back at home, exploited their situation through the use of

---

Grant, *MacLeods*, pp. 219, 243; A. Campbell, "A Closer Look at West Highland Heraldry", *Double Tressure*, vol. XIX (1997), pp. 46–7, 49–50, 59. The official guide to the castle comments that the sideboard bears the date 1603 and was brought by Sir Rory after his sojourn in London in 1613: John MacLeod, *Official Guide, Dunvegan Castle, Isle of Skye, Scotland* (2003, Dunvegan Castle, current [2009?] ed.), p. 19.

55. NAS, GD84/2/246, frontispiece; Lyon Office, Edinburgh, Kings and Nobilities Arms II, MS21, pl. 109. Sir James Balfour's and Pont's Manuscripts recorded the alternative heraldic charge of two hands holding two drawn swords rather than daggers: NLS, Scottish Heraldry, Blazons of Scottish Arms by Sir James Balfour of Denmilne, 1630, Adv. MS 15.1.11, fo. 34v; Lyon Office, Pont's Manuscript, MS1, p. 36 n. 46. On his 1623 targe, the hand does not grasp the sword: The Hunterian Museum, University of Glasgow, GLAHM C.72, available online at <http://www.huntsearch.gla.ac.uk/cgi-bin/foxweb/huntsearch/DetailedResults.fwx?collection=all&SearchTerm=C.72&mdaCode=GLAHM&reqMethod=Link>, accessed 30 April 2010. Aonghas MacCoinnich deserves our gratitude for this reference. It is significant that prior to Reay's time, the Mackay hand was displayed appaumé rather than associated with these bladed weapons (Mackay, "Account of the Aberach-Mackay Banner", pp. 527–32). Colonel George Matheson had his heraldic arms registered with the Lord Lyon on 5 October 1639 with an armed hand holding a naked sword for his crest, underlining his military exploits. Matheson traditions and genealogies have that he was George of Shinness in Sutherland: NLS, Adv. MS 15.1.11, fo. 35r; A. Mackenzie and A. MacBain, *History of the Mathesons with Genealogies of the Various Families* (2nd ed., Stirling, 1900), pp. 140–1; EUL, Sir Roderick Murchison Collection, MS 2262/2/2/2.

networks to augment their benefits. Ironically, and perhaps most importantly, the traditional historiography of State relationships with the clans and vice versa as defined by a language of antagonism is reductionist in its approach. Indeed, the terminology of cooperation and symbiosis, as ends rather than means, and even if imposed and fortuitous, should transcend the debate and not be underplayed.[56] As such, the Crown promoted the diffusion of Renaissance ideals which partially reformed the character and behaviour of a number of the clan elite and others. The military co-optation allowed this middling sort (at the State level) both in exile and on their return to Britain to position itself for the promotion of their own interests and that of the clan. The State reformed the northern communities but not single-handedly. Social transformations came from below too perhaps most visibly and profoundly at the cultural level. To some extent, what the Crown tried with difficulties to impose in the so-called "civilizing" of the far north was somewhat accomplished almost imperceptibly by cultural influences. One of the agents for this evolution lay in the exile and return of far northerners which brought not only new material culture but also innovative visions and ideas into the region. Because of the vast power exercised by the clan elite within their sphere of influence, be it socio-economic, administrative, judicial, and cultural, the impact of these changes on the ground was significant in a pattern of hybridizing or bicultural integration. The result is a picture less of a retrograde, stultified, and monolithic society, though with some elements of this remaining, but more of a slowly moving and diverse one engaged in and selectively responding to a pre-existing but amplified early-modern bicultural process.

In that sense, the clan military force and network survived by its transposition into an official body, equally military in its nature. This institutionalization of the private sphere into the public sphere resulted in an actual geographical displacement in terms of the military with soldiers in foreign service. The experiences brought back by returning soldiers remoulded both individuals and communities in a process of social regulation which was most visible at the material level but with an inkling of substantial psychological impacts too.

A corresponding phenomenon is discernible in the exile and return of members of the clan elite and others to Europe for educational and cultural purposes which (re)shaped, *mutatis mutandis* and in a more pronounced way, their native culture into a pre-existent hybrid society in their integration into a Lowland and British genteel model. The response

---

56. Witzenrath, *Cossacks*, especially ch. 3; Witzenrath, "Literacy"; H. H. Nolte, "Internal Peripheries: From Andalucia to Tatarstan", *Review*, vol. XVIII (1995), pp. 269–70.

of the northern Highlanders, as *homo peregrinator*, to the push and pull factors of exile and return was to adapt and utilize the opportunities forced onto or presented to them by the State or which arose from *Rinascimento* culture. They used their various kinship ties and other networks to the full for a constant re-alignment according to their respective interests. The concomitant participation of far northerners in patterns of military and educational exile projected the image of the Highlanders and their society abroad, even if indirectly. In Scotland itself, it helped redefine and re-assess the perception of an immovable and immutable society solely immersed in clan warfare. The phenomenon further testified to the partial integration of the clan elite into the wider Scottish and British society which was gradually taking place and which percolated through to the lower orders of these boreal communities. *In fine*, this remained an ongoing process best studied over the *longue durée* and with significant variations both in terms of geography and, within communities, within clans and families themselves.

Bibliography

Primary sources

Manuscript sources:
Aberdeen University Library, Special Collections, Aberdeen:
    volume shelf-marked "BK Rud [1–6]".
Edinburgh University Library, Edinburgh:
    Sir Roderick Murchison Collection, MS 2262.
Lyon Office, Edinburgh:
    Kings and Nobilities Arms II, MS21.
National Archives of Scotland, Edinburgh:
    Commissariot of Edinburgh, Register of Testaments, CC8;
    Glasgow Commissary Court Records, CC9;
    Church of Scotland Records, Register of Presentations to Benefices, CH4;
    Particular Register of Hornings and Inhibitions, Inverness, 1st ser., DI62;
    Exchequer Records, Taxation Papers, E68;
    Reay Papers, GD84;
    Justiciary Records, Books of Adjournal, JC2;
    Calendar of Documents Presented to H. M. General Register House, Edinburgh, by the Rt. Hon. the Baron Reay, ed. C. T. Innes (1929).

National Library of Scotland, Edinburgh:
  Gordons of Gordonstoun and Cummings of Altyre Papers, Dep. 175,
  Acc. 10824;
  Sutherland Papers, Dep. 313.
Scottish Catholic Archives, Edinburgh:
  Colleges Abroad, CA4.

Printed sources:
The Book of Dunvegan, ed. R. C. MacLeod, vol. I, Third Spalding Club,
  1938.
Calendar of State Papers, Domestic Series, of the Reign of Charles I, 1625–49,
  J. Bruce *et al.* (eds), 23 vols, London, 1858–97.
*Collectanea de Rebus Albanicis: Consisting of Original Papers and Documents
  Relating to the History of the Highlands and Islands of Scotland*, W. F. Skene
  (ed.), Iona Club, 1847.
*Duanaire na Sracaire Songbook of the Pillagers: Anthology of Scotland's Gaelic
  Verse to 1600*, W. McLeod and M. Bateman (eds), Edinburgh, 2007.
*The Earl of Stirling's Register of Royal Letters, Relative to the Affairs of Scotland
  and Nova Scotia from 1615 to 1635*, C. Rogers (ed.), 2 vols, Edinburgh,
  1885.
Gàir nan Clàrsach: The Harps' Cry, C. Ó Baoill and M. Bateman (eds),
  Edinburgh, 1994.
GORDON R., *A Genealogical History of the Earldom of Sutherland*, Edinburgh,
  1813.
Highland Papers, J. R. N. Macphail (ed.), 4 vols, Scottish Historical Society,
  1914–34.
MATHESON A., "Poems from a Manuscript of Cathal Mac Muireadhaigh",
  Éigse, vol. XI (1964–66), pp. 1–17.
MONRO R., *Monro His Expedition with the Worthy Scots Regiment (Called Mac-
  Keyes Regiment)*, London, 1637.
*The Munro Tree: A Genealogy and Chronology of the Munros of Foulis and Other
  Families of the Clan, A Manuscript Compiled in 1734*, R. W. Munro (ed.),
  Edinburgh, 1978.
Old Ross-shire and Scotland As Seen in the Tain and Balnagown Documents,
  W. Macgill (ed.), 2 vols, Inverness, 1909–11.
*Origines Parochiales Scotiae: The Antiquities Ecclesiastical and Territorial of the
  Parishes of Scotland*, C. Innes and J. B. Brichan (eds), 2 vols, Bannatyne
  Club, 1851–55.
The Register of the Privy Council of Scotland, J. H. Burton *et al.* (eds), 38 vols,
  Edinburgh, 1877–1970.
Social Life in Former Days: Second Series, Illustrated by Letters and Family Papers,
  E. D. Dunbar (ed.), Edinburgh, 1866.
The Sutherland Book, W. Fraser (ed.), 3 vols, Edinburgh, 1892.

Secondary sources

ASTOUL G., *Les Chemins du Savoir en Quercy et Rouergue à l'Époque Moderne : Alphabétisation et Apprentissages Culturels*, Toulouse, 1999.

BRACEWELL C. W., *The Uskoks of Senj: Piracy, Banditry, and Holy War in the Sixteenth-Century Adriatic*, Ithaca, 1992.

BROUN D. and MACGREGOR M. (eds), Mìorun Mòr nan Gall, *"The Great Ill-Will of the Lowlander"?: Lowland Perceptions of the Highlands, Medieval and Modern*, Glasgow, 2009.

BROWN K. M., *Noble Society in Scotland: Wealth, Family and Culture, from Reformation to Revolution*, Edinburgh, 2004.

BURKE P., *Popular Culture in Early Modern Europe*, 1978, 3rd ed., Farnham, 2009.

CAMPBELL A., "A Closer Look at West Highland Heraldry", *Double Tressure*, vol. XIX (1997), pp. 46–67.

CATHCART A., *Kinship and Clientage: Highland Clanship, 1451–1609*, Leiden, 2006.

DUFFY P. J. *et al.* (eds), *Gaelic Ireland, c. 1250–c. 1650: Land, Lordship and Settlement*, Dublin, 2001.

GAERTNER J. F. (ed.), *Writing Exile: The Discourse of Displacement in Greco-Roman Antiquity and Beyond*, Leiden, 2007.

GLOZIER M., *Scottish Soldiers in France in the Reign of the Sun King: Nursery for Men of Honour*, Leiden, 2004.

GOODARE J., *State and Society in Early Modern Scotland*, Oxford, 1999.

GROSJEAN A., *An Unofficial Alliance: Scotland and Sweden, 1569–1654*, Leiden, 2003.

HOUSTON R. A., *Literacy in Early Modern Europe: Culture and Education, 1500–1800*, 2nd ed., Harlow, 2002.

KIRBY D., *Northern Europe in the Early Modern Period: The Baltic World, 1492–1772*, London, 1992.

MACINNES A. I., *The British Revolution, 1629–1660*, Basingstoke, 2005.

MACLEAN L. (ed.), *The Middle Ages in the Highlands*, Inverness, 1981.

—, *The Seventeenth Century in the Highlands*, Inverness, 1986.

MEIKLE M. M., *A British Frontier?: Lairds and Gentlemen in the Eastern Borders, 1540–1603*, East Linton, 2004.

MURDOCH S., *Network North: Scottish Kin, Commercial and Covert Associations in Northern Europe, 1603–1746*, Leiden, 2006.

— (ed.), *Scotland and the Thirty Years' War, 1618–1648*, Leiden, 2001.

MURDOCH S. and MACKILLOP A. (eds), *Fighting for Identity: Scottish Military Experience, c. 1550–1900*, Leiden, 2002.

PARKES P., "Celtic Fosterage: Adoptive Kinship and Clientage in Northwest Europe", *Comparative Studies in Society and History*, vol. XLVIII (2006), pp. 359–95.

Rackwitz M., *Travels to Terra Incognita: The Scottish Highlands and Hebrides in Early Modern Travellers' Accounts, c. 1600 to 1800*, Münster, 2007.

Selwyn J. D., *A Paradise Inhabited by Devils: The Jesuits' Civilizing Mission in Early Modern Naples*, Aldershot, 2004.

Shuger D., "Irishmen, Aristocrats, and Other White Barbarians", *Renaissance Quarterly*, 1 (1997), pp. 494–525.

Tóth I. G., *Literacy and Written Culture in Early Modern Central Europe*, Budapest, 2000.

Watt D. E. R., "Education in the Highlands in the Middle Ages", in L. Maclean, *Middle Ages*, pp. 79–90.

Withrington D., "Education in the 17th Century Highlands", in L. Maclean, *Seventeenth Century*, pp. 60–9.

Witzenrath C., *Cossacks and the Russian Empire, 1598–1725: Manipulation, Rebellion and Expansion into Siberia*, London, 2007.

Worthington D., *Scots in Habsburg Service, 1618–1648*, Leiden, 2004.

Newspapers, Magazines

Clan Munro Association, *Clan Munro Magazine*, [Perth], 1939–.

Scottish Genealogy Society, *The Scottish Genealogist*, [Edinburgh], 1954–.

Internet resources

The Hunterian Museum, University of Glasgow, GLAHM C.72, available online at <http://www.huntsearch.gla.ac.uk/cgi-bin/foxweb/huntsearch/DetailedResults.fwx?collection=all&SearchTerm=C.72&mdaCode=GLAHM&reqMethod=Link>, accessed 30 April 2010.

"Scotland, Scandinavia and Northern Europe, 1580–1707", S. Murdoch and A. Grosjean (eds), available online at <http://www.st-andrews.ac.uk/history/ssne/index.php>, accessed 19–20 February 2005.

Kathrin Zickermann
University of St Andrews

English and Scottish Exiles in Northwest Germany c. 1683–1709

Research conducted by historians such as Ginny Gardner and Douglas Catterall has shown that the United Provinces became a safe haven for the Scottish Calvinist exiles who left the British Isles in the wake of the restoration of the Stuart monarchy in 1660.[1] The Scottish exile community which established itself in the Dutch towns centred around Scottish and "English" churches which provided aid for fellow countrymen not least through poor relief.[2] The core group of the exiles consisted of a group of ministers who in some cases became incumbents of these Scottish churches. They were joined by a group of approximately 170 laymen as well as by a number of expatriates associated and sympathising with them.[3] Although the group of lay exiles was attached to the Presbyterian faith their motivation to leave the British Isles was not always rooted in their religion but sometimes in political intrigue—albeit the two can be hard to separate. Some men were suspected of being involved in the Bothwell Bridge Rising (1679) or in the alleged Rye House Plot conspiracy to kill Charles II and his brother in 1683.[4]

What remains hitherto unknown is that from 1683 some North West German territories and cities received intensive attention from English and Scottish religious and political exiles who had left or were in the process of leaving the British Isles to take refuge on the continent. Under the leadership of the Englishman William Waller a group of exiles took up negotiations first with the Imperial city of Bremen and then with duke

---

1. Douglas Catterall, *Community Without Borders: Scots Migrants and the Changing Face of Power in the Dutch Republic, c. 1600–1700* (Leiden / Boston / Cologne, 2002); Ginny Gardner, *The Scottish Exile Community in the Netherlands 1660–1690* (East Linton, 2004).

2. Ginny Gardner, *The Scottish Exile Community*, pp. 1–2, 29–30. Although being called "English" the congregations of these churches were often predominantly Scottish. A publication on English exiles in the United Provinces which could mirror Catterall's or Gardner's analysis of the Scots is so far missing.

3. *Ibid.*, pp. 9–24.

4. *Ibid.*, pp. 17–8.

Georg Wilhelm of Braunschweig-Lüneburg who granted extensive privileges to individuals and families of the "reformed faith" regardless of their nationalities. These freedoms led not only to English and Scottish but also to French and Dutch migration of religious and political exiles as well as economic opportunists. This essay analyses the aims of the English and Scottish exiles, their negotiations with the local authorities in North West Germany as well as the success and failure of the set up of the communities in Bremen and Lüneburg and their lasting impact on individual exiles. It also examines whether the diverse migration of individuals of several nationalities resulted in the formation of a single British or multi-ethnic religious community or whether the migrants organised themselves in several groups, divided by nationality or other criteria.[5]

Since the Restoration of 1660 the United Provinces provided a relatively safe environment for religious exiles. However, the Treaty of Breda (1667) between Charles II and the Dutch government stated that those Britons accused of regicide could be extradited without formal demand from London and that political exiles were to be banished on the request of the Stuart Court.[6] Although the Dutch authorities tended to be slow to comply with demands, the climate in the United Provinces became more insecure in the aftermath of the Rye House Plot, as the capture and subsequent execution of the suspect Sir Thomas Armstrong in 1684 demonstrated.[7] From November 1683 the Englishman and Calvinist William Waller negotiated with the senate of the Imperial city of Bremen for the settlement of English and Scottish exiles.[8] The latter had been a London JP (1678–1681) and Westminster MP (1679–1681) during which time he had been demonstrably anti-Catholic in behaviour. Waller was temporarily arrested for debts in 1681 and left the British Isles shortly after his release in the increasingly hostile climate of Stuart Britain.[9] He was accompanied to Bremen by the Scot George Melville (the future 1st Earl of Melville) and the latter's Scottish servant Adam Freer. As a suspect of the Rye House Plot George Melville had been forced to leave

---

5. This article will thus complement existing studies on Scottish migration and community building during the early modern period. An overview over these is given in Christopher Smout's foreword in Alexia Grosjean and Steve Murdoch (eds), *Scottish Communities Abroad in the Early Modern Period* (Leiden/Boston, 2005). Significant works which have been published since include Steve Murdoch, *Network North: Scottish Kin, Commercial and Covert Associations in Northern Europe 1603–1746* (Leiden/Boston, 2006) and David Worthington (ed.), *British and Irish Emigrants and Exiles in Europe, 1603–1688* (Leiden/Boston, 2010).

6. Ginny Gardner, *The Scottish Exile Community*, pp. 104–6.

7. Richard L. Greaves, "Sir Thomas Armstrong", *DNB* (online publication).

8. His presence is briefly noted in Steve Murdoch, *Network North: Scottish Kin, Commercial and Covert Associations in Northern Europe 1603–1746* (Leiden/Boston, 2006), pp. 111–2.

9. Alan Marshall, "Sir William Waller (c. 1639–1699)", *DNB* (online publication).

the British Isles for the United Provinces, where he was joined by his son David Melville, the Earl of Leven.[10] The Melvilles certainly met with other exiles in the Netherlands—including William Waller—and attached themselves to the court of the Prince of Orange.[11]

On 14 December 1683 Freer informed Andrew Russell, the Scottish factor at Rotterdam and sympathiser with the Scottish exile community, of the proceedings in Bremen. He stated that William Waller had informed him that "any person, that thinks themselves not secure enough in Holland may come here to Bremen, where they will be assured of all the protection which this state is capable to give"[12] revealing that it was indeed safety issues which motivated the exiles to turn to North West Germany for sanctuary. Although it did not feature any pre-existing Scottish or English expatriate communities, Waller's choice of the city of Bremen for his project rather than another location is not too surprising. The local authorities had for many years previously been open to receiving individuals of the reformed faith coming in the Calvinist city.[13] For example, in 1620 they had seriously considered the application of a group of Presbyterian English merchants who had previously settled in Hamburg.[14] Moreover, Bremen's confession had attracted some Scottish ministers and students who may or may not have been religious exiles themselves as evidenced, in August 1668, by a Scot called John Ruthven who sat his divinity exam in the city.[15] Also, a D. Niclas Rolandus, who was styled Scoto-Britannus, conducted a service on behalf of a local minister on 29 September 1682.[16] It may have been him who liased with Robert Hamilton, the Scottish agent of the United Societies, a union of various radical Cameronian groups with bases in Leuwaarden and Groningen, who received a sum of eighty "ducatoons" from Bremen's ministry.[17] Although no evidence has yet come to light it is inconceivable that Rolandus did not help with Waller's negotiations in 1683.

---

10. Margaret D. Sankey, "David Melville, Third Earl of Leven and Second Earl of Melville (1660–1728)", *DNB* (online publication); John R. Young, "George Melville, Fourth Lord Melville and First Earl of Melville (1636–1707)", *DNB* (online publication).

11. *Ibid.*

12. NAS, Russell Papers, RH15/106/494, Adam Freer to Andrew Russell, Bremen, 14 December 1683.

13. Anne E. Dünzelmann, *Vom Gaste, den Joden und den Fremden: Zur Ethnographie von Immigration, Rezeption und Exkludierung Fremder am Beispiel der Stadt Bremen vom Mittelalter bis 1848* (Berlin/Hamburg/Münster, 2001), pp. 132–3.

14. *Ibid.*, p. 134. The settlement of these Englishmen failed for reasons which are hitherto unknown.

15. Staatsarchiv Bremen, Acta Venerandi Ministerii 1667–1707, 2-T.2.b.4.c., p. 6, 2 August 1668.

16. *Ibid.*, p. 86, 14 and 29 September 1682.

17. I would like to thank Mark Jardine for providing this information. Michael Shields, *Faithful Contendings Displayed* (Glasgow, 1780), pp. 207–8. The donation of this sum is not listed in the records of the ministry in Bremen. Staatsarchiv Bremen, Acta Venerandi Ministerii 1667–1707, 2-T.2.b.4.c.

The latter made extensive requests to the senate, including the foundation of a church with two ministers to be paid by the city as well as the permission for the congregation to have its "own discipline" in church matters. In addition, he requested citizen rights and privileges for the migrants as well as admission to the guilds at only half the usual payment. Furthermore, Waller planned to encourage the opening of a wool factory, requesting the right to employ poor children for seven years of their lives and demanding an exemption from excise and consumption taxes for a duration of thirty years. Also, Waller asked for the granting of building sites for houses which the incomers were to keep tax free for forty years.[18] Thus Waller attempted to create a community big enough to justify and sustain its own congregation and elders, probably based on the model of the Scots and English churches in the United Provinces. In terms of economic and political advantages, however, he aspired to an integration of the incomers with the indigenous population through the acquisition of citizen rights with long-term economic privileges. For his own benefit and to secure a livelihood Waller asked to be made commandant, and the community would certainly have benefited from Waller's employment in this capacity which would have placed one of their own in a powerful position within the city.[19] Waller's demands reveal that economic opportunities were crucial to him and that he intended to attract a large group of exiles and expatriates to Bremen. This group which would be commercially beneficial to the city was without doubt intended to shelter a smaller group of political exiles such as George Melville whose presence alone would presumably not have been acceptable to the authorities.

Waller's requests were met more than half way by the local authorities, demonstrating their willingness to receive the foreigners in their midst. On 1 December 1683 Waller was employed by the city at a salary of 1,000 Imperial dollars by a contract which made him commander-in-chief of the local militia.[20] In addition, Bremen's officials approved the use of a local church *(Klosterkirche)* at certain times by the immigrants as well as the employment of two ministers who were to be paid by the congregation.[21] Furthermore, they granted free citizen rights to those arriving within the following three years as well as the exemption from

18. Staatsarchiv Bremen, Wittheitsprotokolle 1683–1684, 2-P.6.a.9.c.3.b.14, pp. 473–4, 23 November 1683.

19. *Ibid.*, p. 481, 30 November 1683.

20. Staatsarchiv Bremen, Offiziere des Stadtmilitärs, 2-R.5.d.13.a.19, Appointment, William Waller, 1 December 1683; See also Steve Murdoch, *Network North*, pp. 111–2.

21. Stadtarchiv Lüneburg, Gewerbesachen, G3e No. 2, Privileges granted to the English Manufacturers by the City of Bremen (copy), Bremen, 1 December 1683.

direct taxes for twenty years. Moreover, the incomers were offered building sites for houses and were said to be allowed to keep their houses tax free for a period of ten years. However, they were expected to pay consumption taxes. In order to facilitate the establishment of factories, the privileges stated further that both male and female children in the poor houses would be urged to work in the factories for seven years in return for board and lodgings. In addition, the admission of craftsmen was permitted in principle (and for a fee) but only if it did not violate the rights of the local guilds.[22]

Notably, these privileges were given to "families of true reformed religion" thus subsuming not only Scots and Englishmen but also other nationals. In his letter to Andrew Russell, Freer stated that Waller had promised to send for a minister for "any Scots or English" who would settle in Bremen revealing that the community was envisaged as "British" from the outset.[23] Without doubt Waller had either initiated or was at least content with the permission for all nationals to profit from the new rights as this would enhance the chances of inviting a profitable community to Bremen. In fact, it was probably Waller himself who tried to attract a particular French entrepreneur. The latter (who has not yet been identified) had arrived in Amsterdam from France and aimed to open a wool and silk factory in Bremen, to which end he was accompanied by twenty skilled employees.[24] His request was entered into the council's minute book under the headline "English families" revealing Waller's involvement and his endeavour to establish a multi-ethnic community. Freer approved of the favourable conditions offered by the city of Bremen and informed Russell of the possibility of acquiring citizen rights as well as the cheap prices for food and houses.[25] In addition, he stated that the place would be attractive to students as it featured a college with thirteen to fourteen professors.[26]

Despite the positive outcome of Waller's negotiations the reformed community in Bremen never materialised due to external pressure on the local authorities. The English resident at Hamburg, Sir Bevil Skelton, informed Charles II and other Stuart diplomats about the developments.

22. *Ibid.* Anne E. Dünzelmann has transcribed (another version of) this document and mentions Waller's negotiations. However, she fails to identify him or to contextualise his discussions with the senate. Dünzelmann, *Vom Gaste*, pp. 135–6.

23. NAS, Russell Papers, RH15/106/494, Adam Freer to Andrew Russell, Bremen, 14 December 1684.

24. Staatsarchiv Bremen, Wittheitsprotokolle 1683–1684, 2-P.6.a.9.c.3.b.14, p. 501, 25 January 1684.

25. NAS, Russell Papers, RH15/106/494, Adam Freer to Andrew Russell, Bremen, 14 December 1684.

26. *Ibid.*

Sir Richard Bukstrode passed on the following information from Skelton to Lord Preston:

> Sir William Waller plays the devill at Bremen, which is like to be the nest of all those persons accused of the last conspiracy, that my Lord Mevin (Melville) and many more of that stamp, are there, as also Armstrong[27] and Ferguson[28], and that they expect the Duke of Monmouth there very speedily; they speak most scandalously of the King and Duke and style Waller a second Cromwell.[29]

It was also probably Skelton who advised Charles II in March 1684 that Waller was "drawing to him all the disaffected persons he can under pretence of setting up a woollen manufacture" trying to ship whole families from Yarmouth to Bremen—an action which was to be hindered at all costs.[30] This direct linking of groups of Scottish and English exiles and the attempts to take still more Englishmen directly out of England again confirms the pan-British nature of the Bremen exiles and their projected community. On the receipt of communication from Charles II the senate of Bremen decommissioned William Waller in order not to jeopardise trade relations with the British Isles.[31]

The city's magistrates were eager to declare that only three Englishmen had arrived after December 1683, of whom two had married in the city and one had died, indicating that no large group of dissenting individuals had been welcomed there.[32] However, Skelton's accusations of Waller attracting suspected conspirators to Bremen were not unfounded. We know that George Melville and Adam Freer were present in the city along with Melville's son David, the Earl of Leven. Leven was certainly in Bremen in January 1684, from where he communicated with

---

27. Sir Thomas Armstrong was a suspect of the Rye House Plot and—as previously stated—was captured executed in 1684. See Greaves, "Sir Thomas Armstrong", *DNB* (online publication).

28. Robert Ferguson, son of William Ferguson of Badifurrow in Aberdeenshire, moved to London in the 1650s where he became active in Whig politics by the late 1670s. After becoming a suspect he fled to the continent, initially to Amsterdam. He was one of Monmouth's main advisors and took part in the invasion. Thereafter he managed to escape once again to the continent. Melinda Zook, "Robert Ferguson (d. 1714)", *DNB* (online publication).

29. *HMC, Seventh Report* (London, 1879), p. 386, Richard Bulstrode to Lord Preston, Brussels, 13 March 1684.

30. *CSPD*, 1684, p. 327, Secretary Jenkins to the Earl of Yarmouth, Whitehall, 15 March 1684.

31. Staatsarchiv Bremen, Wittheitsprotokolle 1683–1684, 2-P.6.a.9.c.3.b.14, pp. 543–4, 2 and 7 May 1684; Offiziere des Stadtmilitärs, 2-R.5.d.13.a.19, Charles II to Bremen Senate, Windsor, 7 April 1684; Offiziere des Stadtmilitärs, 2-R.5.d.13.a.19, Release of William Waller, 2 May 1684; Offiziere des Stadtmilitärs, 2-R.5.d.13.a.19, Bremen Senate to Charles II, Bremen, 2 May 1684.

32. Staatsarchiv Bremen, Offiziere des Stadtmilitärs, 2-R.5.d.13.a.19, Bremen Senate to Charles II, Bremen, 18 January 1684.

Russell under the pseudonym David Barclay.[33] Furthermore, the Scot Major George Low, who was later to support the cause of the Duke of Orange, resided in the city until his death in 1699 and commanded the local infantry there, thus working closely with Waller as commandant.[34] He certainly accommodated the dissident Adam Freer in his house and it is likely that George Melville and his son also found shelter there. The latter was certainly in communication with Low in 1689 and it is probable that both men had either established contact in Bremen or before their stay there.[35] Furthermore, George Melville was financially supported by a "friend" whom he expected to arrive in Holland soon in order to receive repayment for what he had spent on Melville. It is likely that this acquaintance was the Scottish merchant Gilbert Spence who resided in Bremen from the early 1670s. His contact with Freer can be proven as he sent his regards to Andrew Russell in one of his letters. The merchant's contacts with and occasional business trips to the Netherlands make this connection all the more likely particularly given the known link with the Bremen exiles.[36] That we cannot identify Spence for sure is not surprising given that he would have wanted any assistance to the exiles be kept a secret due to his strong business links with the British Isles. If Spence was the benefactor, he was only one of several sources of income for Melville. Russell himself took care of some of Melville's business transactions which also involved the second Scottish agent in Rotterdam, James Gordon and after his death in early 1684, the latter's son.[37] Also, a Mr Dick frequently appears in Freer's and Leven's correspondence as being present in Bremen but it is highly likely that this name was used as a false identity for George Melville himself.[38] There is no further proof that Melville's fellow conspirators Thomas Armstrong and Robert Ferguson or indeed the Duke of Monmouth moved to Bremen during the months

---

33. NAS, Russell Papers, RH15/16/532/9, David Baclay alias Leven to Andrew Russell, Bremen, 26 January 1684; For more information on Leven see Margaret D. Sankey, "David Melville, Third Earl of Leven and Second Earl of Melville (1660–1728)", *DNB* (online publication).

34. Staatsarchiv Bremen, Offiziere des Stadtmilitärs, 2-R.5.d.13.a.19, Petition, Ilsa Sprado to Bremen Senate, Bremen, without date. Ilsa Sprado petitioned the Bremen senate to continue payment of her late husband's salary for another two or three months to cover his funeral costs. Low had died in April 1699.

35. NAS, Russell Papers, RH15/106/689, George Low to Andrew Russell, Bremen, 3 August 1689.

36. Steve Murdoch, *Network North*, p. 152.

37. NAS, Russell Papers, RH15/106/532/8, Adam Freer to Andrew Russell, Bremen, 11/21 January 1684; Gardner, *The Scottish Exile Community*, p. 77.

38. NAS, Russell Papers, RH15/106/532/8, Adam Freer to Andrew Russell, Bremen, 11/21 January 1684. This is further confirmed by a letter from George Low who asked Russell in May 1685 about Mr Dick's well-being. As George Melville was likely to be in the Netherlands at this point it is probable that the name was continuously used as his pseudonym. NAS, Russell Papers, RH15/106/576/10, George Low to Andrew Russell, Bremen, 13 May 1685.

before Waller's eviction although Skelton seems emphatic they were there. In any case the presence of Waller and the Scottish exiles proves that a small but significant Anglo-Scottish network operated in the city and maintained important links to sympathisers in the United Provinces.

After Waller's dismissal the city of Bremen was no longer the hub of the exile community in North West Germany despite Low's and Spence's continued presence there. Instead the exiles' interest shifted to another territory whose ruler had previously proven himself to be sympathetic to Calvinist exiles. This was the Welfenian duchy of Braunschweig-Lüneburg under Georg Wilhelm, who governed from his residency in Celle. The Lutheran duke had taken the Huguenot Eléonore Desmier d'Olbreuse as his wife. Her influence and favour drew a number of her fellow-believers to Georg Wilhelm's court, where they were allowed to hold reformed services in her private rooms in the castle.[39] At the same time a number of Huguenot officers found employment in Georg Wilhelm's army, whose military strength was dependent on the intake of foreigners.[40] Among his military leadership was also the Scot and Major-General Andrew Melville who acquired an influential position at the court in Celle and within the French reformed community.[41] Andrew Melville was a kinsman of George Melville, whose acquaintance he had perhaps made as early as 1651 when he received help from a relative of that name in London as a refugee after the battle of Worcester.[42] Furthermore, Andrew Melville was in contact with George Melville's son, the Earl of Leven, who assisted him in acquiring a Scottish birth brief in 1683.[43] These connections linked Andrew Melville to William Waller and it is more than likely that it was the Major-General who initiated—or at least assisted in—talks between the Englishman and duke Georg Wilhelm.

The latter granted a privilege on 9 August 1684 to foreign families and individuals of reformed faith who were willing to settle in the Lutheran town of Lüneburg[44] regardless of their nationality. By so doing he hoped

---

39. Andreas Flick, "„Der Celler Hof ist ganz verfranzt": Hugenotten und französische Katholiken am Hof und beim Militär Herzog Georg Wilhelms von Braunschweig-Lüneburg", *Hugenotten*, vol. 72, no. 3, 2008, pp. 102–6.

40. *Ibid.*

41. *Ibid.*, p. 95. A visible sign of Melville's standing is provided by the seating order of the first official French reformed church in Celle in 1700 which reserved the first bench left of the chancel to "the old General-Major von Melville" and his family.

42. Torrick Ameer-Ali (ed.), *Memoirs of Sir Andrew Melville* (London, 1918), p. 135; Steve Murdoch, *Network North*, p. 25.

43. *RPCS, Third Series*, 1683–1684, pp. 114–5, Supplication, Sir Andrew Melville, without date/place.

44. Lüneburg lay within the duchy of Braunschweig-Lüneburg at the river Ilmenau, a side arm of the river Elbe.

to populate his territory and to enhance his economy.[45] In this edict the duke gave extensive rights to the foreigners in religious, economic and political terms. He permitted both public and private reformed worship, promising the establishment of a church in the event that the reformed community was to increase in size. The migrants were to be allowed to propose two ministers whose salaries were to be paid by the duke for the first two years and, additionally, a reformed school was to be established. The incomers were to receive citizen rights free of charge under the condition that they swore the usual oath of citizenship, after which they would be allowed to trade, to open factories or to work as craftsmen without any hindrance from the local guilds. Additionally, if the foreigners so wished they were to be received into the guilds for a small fee. Moreover, the new entrepreneurs were to be assisted in the establishment of factory houses. They were also allowed to employ children for the duration of seven years in return for the provision of cloth and victuals or other conditions which the entrepreneurs were to negotiate with the children's relatives. In order to promote the sales of products from the factories their goods were to be given preference within the duchy, especially at court and in supplying the militia. Furthermore, the foreigners were exempted from tolls on imported and exported goods transported by land or water to or from Lüneburg (with the exception of the Elbe tolls at Hitzacker and Schnackenburg) as well as from consumption taxes for the following twenty years. However, they were to pay excise as well as some other minor local taxes. As a further incentive, the foreigners were exempted from quarters and other citizen duties as well as from direct taxes for twenty years. Nevertheless, in order to avoid complaints from the local citizens they were to pay a voluntary contribution in relation to their standing and income.[46]

The timing and the content of this edict leave no doubt that it was initiated by William Waller who had not given up on his aim of establishing a multi-ethnic reformed community in North West Germany. Indeed Waller himself was put in charge of the settlement of foreigners at the Lutheran town of Lüneburg in 1684, where he acquired the position of governor with an annual salary of 1,500 Imperial dollars.[47] This offer

---

45. Various copies of this document exist, including a French translation. The privilege has been printed in several secondary studies, for example in Thomas Klinebiel, *Die Hugenotten in den welfischen Landen. Eine Privilegiensammlung* (Bad Karlshafen, 1994), pp. 47–52. An original copy can be found in Stadtarchiv Lüneburg, Gewerbesachen G3e No. 2, Privileges issued by Georg Wilhelm, Celle, 9 August 1684.

46. *Ibid.*

47. Stadtarchiv Lüneburg, Gewerbesachen, G3e No. 2, Appointment, William Waller, Celle, 30 July 1684; Wilhelm Reinecke, Geschichte der Stadt Lüneburg, vol. 2 (Lüneburg, 1933), p. 35.

was conditional and only made on the provision that Waller was successful in attracting profitable migrants to the duchy.[48]

Interestingly, the privileges issued by Georg Wilhelm have hitherto been misunderstood by historians such as Andreas Flick, Walter Mogk, Hartwig Notbohm or Arnulf Siebeneicker. They assumed that Georg Wilhelm aimed to establish a Huguenot colony in Lüneburg and that the freedoms granted on 9 August 1684 must thus be seen as privileges primarily or exclusively granted to French reformed exiles *(Hugenottenprivileg)*.[49] These scholars conclude that Georg Wilhelm had been informed of the deteriorating situation for adherents of the reformed faith in France in the years prior to the revocation of the Edict of Nantes (1685) and that the duke issued his privilege in order to attract rich and skilled Huguenots from France.[50] This position has been challenged by Thomas Klingebiel, who has stated that the privilege did not primarily aim to attract French religious exiles but to draw reformed entrepreneurs regardless of their origin to the city, who could be found in the Netherlands, England, the Hanseatic cities and Danish Altona (Holstein).[51] Klingebiel argues that due to the persecution suffered by members of the reformed religion in England (and thanks to his close connections to the Netherlands) Georg Wilhelm expected refugees primarily from these locations. Klingebiel also points out that the general superintendent of Celle specifically protested against religious concessions for the foreigners from England. He thinks that it is possible that the French version of the privilege was only written when the French-reformed community was founded in Lüneburg in 1685.[52] Klingebiel's analysis was critically examined by Andreas Flick who doubts the later date of the French translation of Georg Wilhelm's privilege and initially stated that a larger group of exiles could only be expected to come from France and not from England. He conceded that the privilege was perhaps deliberately formulated without naming a particular nationality in order to allow the ingress of reformed Scottish,

---

48. Stadtarchiv Lüneburg, Gewerbesachen, G3e No. 2, Appointment, William Waller, Celle, 30 July 1684.

49. Andreas Flick, "„Der Celler Hof ist ganz verfranzt": Hugenotten und französische Katholiken am Hof und beim Militär Herzog Georg Wilhelms von Braunschweig-Lüneburg", *Hugenotten*, vol. 72, no. 3, 2008, p. 95; Walter Mogk, "Zur Geschichte der Evangelisch-Reformierten in Lüneburg vom 17. bis zum 19. Jahrhundert", *Niedersächsisches Jahrbuch für Landesgeschichte*, vol. 55, 1983, pp. 382–4; Hartwig Notbohm, *Geschichte der Französisch-reformierten Gemeinde — Hugenotten — in Lüneburg 1684–1839* (Lüneburg, 2001), pp. 6–8; Arnulf Siebeneicker, "Das Lüneburger Privileg", in Sabine Beneke and Hans Ottomeyer (eds), *Zuwanderungsland Deutschland: Die Hugenotten* (Berlin, 2005), pp. 252–3.

50. *Ibid.*

51. Thomas Klingebiel, *Die Hugenotten in den welfischen Landen*, p. 11.

52. *Ibid.*, pp. 11–2.

English or Dutch individuals in addition to the French into the city.[53] However, after further reflecting on the subject for a decade he later concluded that it was apparently "Englishmen" and not Frenchmen who were primarily expected in Lüneburg.[54]

From the above it becomes evident that none of these historians have fully grasped the importance of William Waller and his goal of establishing a multi-ethnic community. The freedoms granted on 9 August 1684 were frequently described by contemporaries as the "English privileges" and the foreigners were at least in one case said to have been under the protection of the "English nation". This confirms (similarly to the terminology used in the minute book of Bremen's senate) that it was the Englishman Waller (variously mistaken as a Scot or as a French Huguenot by some historians[55]) who had negotiated the deal with the duke. Notably, Waller's own position in the duchy also depended on the successful settlement of profitable individuals. Thus we have to assume that he again welcomed the duke's decision not to exclude any nationalities from his privilege.

It has already been indicated that Georg Wilhelm himself primarily pursued economic interests with his edict in addition to secondary confessional ones. However these may have been complemented by political motivations. On 23 November 1684 it was reported that Georg Wilhelm was resolved to protect Waller and his adherents regardless of Skelton and any pressure he might attempt to bring to bear. The Duke reported that, unlike Bremen's officials, he was not intimidated by English envoys.[56] This indicates that Georg Wilhelm was fully aware of the fact that he was welcoming individuals to his duchy who were seen as political dissidents in Britain. Georg Wilhelm's rhetoric against Skelton is easier to make sense of than the stance taken by the senate of Bremen. Direct trade connections with the British Isles were barely developed, and so English threats were of limited importance. Georg Wilhelm personally communicated with the city of Bremen to demand payment of Waller's outstanding salary providing both a sweetener to Waller and revealing

---

53. Andreas Flick, "Muss das „Lüneburger Hugenottenprivileg" neu bewertet werden?", *Der Deutsche Hugenott*, vol. 59, 1995, pp. 54–5.

54. Andreas Flick, "Hugenotten in Norddeutschland", in Evangelisch-Reformierte Gemeinde Braunschweig (ed.), *Öffentlich und Ungehindert: 300 Jahre Ev.-reformierte Gemeinde Braunschweig* (Braunschweig, 2004), p. 80.

55. See for example Wilhelm Beuleke, *Die Hugenotten in Niedersachsen* (Hildesheim, 1960), p. 137; Walter Mogk, "Geschichte der Evangelisch-Reformierten", p. 387.

56. Stadtarchiv Lüneburg, Gewerbesachen, G3e No. 2, Printed Journal Article, "Novelles Choisis et Veritables", 23 November 1684.

the Duke's esteem for the Englishman.[57] This was also reflected by the ducal council. As early as 25 July 1684 this highest administrative institution in Braunschweig-Lüneburg informed the senate of Lüneburg that several foreign individuals, predominantly Englishmen persecuted at home, were willing to settle, trade and open factories in their city provided that they were given the previously mentioned freedoms.[58] The first of these Englishmen arrived before October 1684 when the ducal council reported their difficulties in receiving personal goods and merchandise from England due to the resistance of the English company of Merchant Adventurers in Hamburg.[59] Although the Adventurers did not hold any authority within Braunschweig-Lüneburg they could influence the Hamburg authorities to enforce their privileges which prohibited the transport of goods belonging to Englishmen outside their company through the city to and from the North Sea. In order to assist the English incomers the ducal councillors thus resolved to re-address their goods from England as though they belonged to a senator of Lüneburg called Johann von Cölln. They could then be shipped through Hamburg via a straw man there.[60] On the surface this seems to confirm Klingebiel's and (to a certain extent) Flick's hesitant statements that it was indeed mainly "Englishmen" who were expected in the city. Furthermore, contemporary reports mention an "English" assembly house in the market place and the presence of an "English" company in Lüneburg.[61] However, due to the lack of demographic registers such as registers of new citizens—which are lost for the vital years between 1674 and 1700—it is impossible to establish the number and nationality of foreigners arriving in Lüneburg after 9 August 1684.[62] The only individual we can positively identify (apart from Waller) is the dyer Paul Hearne whose business in the

---

57. Staatsarchiv Bremen, Offiziere des Stadtmilitärs, R.5.d.13.a.19, Georg Wilhelm to Bremen Senate, Celle, 16 February 1685.

58. Stadtarchiv Lüneburg, Gewerbesachen, G3e No. 2, Ducal Councillors to Lüneburg Senate, Celle, 25 July 1684.

59. Stadtarchiv Lüneburg, Gewerbesachen, G3e No. 2, Ducal Councillors to Lüneburg Senate, Celle, 21 October 1684. The city of Hamburg was a staple city on the river Elbe which linked Lüneburg with the North Sea. Any goods traded between Lüneburg and England thus had to be transported through Hamburg—at least in theory.

60. *Ibid.*

61. Stadtarchiv Lüneburg, Gewerbesachen, G3e No. 2, Heinrich Meyer to Lüneburg Senate, Harburg, 18 March 1685. Meyer, an inhabitant of Harburg, petitioned the Senate of Lüneburg to omit his son, who was to settle as a nail smith in their city, from citizen duties referring to the privileges Georg Wilhelm had granted to the "English Company".

62. In addition a file of applications for citizen rights does not contain any entries for the years between 1683 and 1685. However a handful of applications for citizenship survive in the files relating to the settlement of foreigners in Lüneburg. Stadtarchiv Lüneburg, Acta von Bürgerschaften 1652–1699, B4 No. 71.

duchy caused some complaints to the local authorities.[63] Yet while these two Englishmen can definitively be identified, other foreigners were certainly also attracted to the duchy. Among them were several enterprising Scots. For example, Joseph Moseson was reported as one of the first foreigners to arrive in Lüneburg after the edict. He opened a small business selling tobacco, pipes and "distilled water" and was variously described as a Scot or as an English national. Notably he applied for citizen rights as an "Englishman".[64] This was probably in order to make full use of Waller's growing influence in the city.

Another Scot drawn to the city by Waller was the entrepreneur Robert Hog, who had left Scotland in the early 1660s with his father, the exiled minister John Hog, himself an incumbent of the Scots church in Rotterdam.[65] Waller and Hog established contact in Amsterdam where they were located before their move to Braunschweig-Lüneburg. Both men visited the ducal council in Celle in September 1684 in order to negotiate the establishment of a cloth factory in Lüneburg with a plan to produce fine cloth worth 40,000 Imperial dollars annually.[66] Hog opened his business later the same year with his Dutch business partner Anton de Pau. The enterprise was located in the so-called *Wandhaus* (cloth house) and included a mill as well as a place where finished cloth could be dyed. Soon after their arrival Hog and Pau sought to expand into other buildings and the senate discussed offering them the Marstall (city stables) or the house of a Mr Elwer for their enterprise.[67] In addition to this, both entrepreneurs successfully urged the senate to provide a hall for the sale of cloth.[68] The production depended largely on the use of child labour and the senate had obliged itself to find at least 150 young male and female workers aged between twelve and fourteen who were to stay in the factory for seven years to be replaced thereafter.[69] Nevertheless, Hog and

---

63. Stadtarchiv Lüneburg, Gewerbesachen, G3e No. 2, Report of Complaints, Lüneburg Senate, Celle, 28 July 1685.

64. Stadtarchiv Lüneburg, Gewerbesachen, G3e No. 2, Confirmation of Privileges applying to Joseph Moseson, 24 October 1684; G3e No. 2, Complaints, Lüneburg Senate to Ducal Council Lüneburg, 29 August 1685.

65. NAS, Leven and Melville Papers, GD26/13/492, Robert Hog to the Earl of Leven, Lüneburg, 20 January 1709; Gardner, *The Scottish Exile Community*, p. 31.

66. Stadtarchiv Lüneburg, Gewerbesachen, G3e No. 2, Minutes of the Ducal Chamberlain Albrecht Ramdohr's proposition concerning Hog's factory, Celle, 26 September 1684.

67. Stadtarchiv Lüneburg, Gewerbesachen, G3e No. 22, Memorial, Robert Hog/Anton Pau to Lüneburg Senate, Lüneburg, 12 June 1685 and 7 September 1685.

68. *Ibid.*

69. Stadtarchiv Lüneburg, Gewerbesachen, G3e No. 2, Minutes of the Ducal Chamberlain Albrecht Ramdohr's proposition concerning Hog's factory, Celle, 26 September 1684; G3e No. 2, Lüneburg Senate to Georg Wilhelm, Lüneburg, 29 September 1684; G3e No. 22, Record of the Ducal Council concerning Robert Hog, Celle, 10 October 1684.

Pau also employed a number of skilled adult workers from the Netherlands. For example, at least four Dutchmen were working as chief servants *(Meisterknechte)* in the factory, their tasks lying mainly in supervising the children's work.[70] Furthermore, the entrepreneurs drew at least seven cloth processors *(Tuchbereiter)* to the city, who were to receive their own guild roll in 1686 and who in turn employed a number of apprentices from the Netherlands, the cities of Lübeck and Bremen and other neighbouring places.[71] Another person in a trusted position was Paul Behrenberg who was to administer the business and to act as master of the sales hall from October 1685 but it is unclear where he originated from.[72] In November 1684 Hog's sister Margaret arrived in Lüneburg and was supposed to run the business side of the factory. Her brother planned to direct the factory from Amsterdam and to base himself there in the long term.[73] The latter confirms that Hog was in no immediate danger in the Netherlands and that his move to Lüneburg was due to the economic opportunities offered by Waller and Georg Wilhelm's edict. Nevertheless, his exile background made Hog sympathetic to the Scottish religious exiles' cause and he became involved in one of their financial networks on at least one occasion. On 2 November 1685 the Scottish exiled minister James Brown asked Andrew Russell to remit money via Robert Hog to the Scottish merchant in Königsberg, Mr Andrew Marshall, showing his trust in the entrepreneur.[74]

From the above it becomes clear that several foreigners of different nationalities were directly or indirectly attracted to Lüneburg. Their number also included French Huguenots like the entrepreneurs Vincent du Bois and Jean Rossier Sorans who tried to establish their own enterprises in the city, but who were ultimately unsuccessful.[75] Although the foreigners adhered to the reformed faith, differences existed in their confessions and it is thus not clear if they worshipped together or if several private churches were established. Fortunately there is evidence

---

70. Stadtarchiv Lüneburg, Gewerbesachen, G3e No. 36, Chief Servants to Lüneburg Senate, Lüneburg, 27 March 1686.
71. Stadtarchiv Lüneburg, Gewerbesachen, G3e No. 36, Lübeck Senate to Lüneburg Senate, Lübeck, 20 January 1686; G3e No. 36, List of Cloth Processors, without date/place.
72. Stadtarchiv Lüneburg, Gewerbesachen, G3e No. 22, Robert Hog to Lüneburg Senate, Lüneburg, 7 October 1685.
73. Stadtarchiv Lüneburg, Gewerbesachen, G3e No. 22, Ducal Council to Lüneburg Senate, Celle, 24 November 1684.
74. NAS, Russell Papers, RH15/106/576, James Brown to Andrew Russell, Danzig, 2 November 1685; Steve Murdoch, *Network North*, p. 113.
75. Walter Mogk, "Geschichte der Evangelisch-Reformierten", p. 387.

that Waller aimed to set up a church in his own house.[76] An estimate he obtained of the costs of church furniture from a local craftsman allows for some conclusions to be drawn on the size and social structure of the reformed congregation Waller envisaged for Lüneburg. The furniture was to include a special seat for Waller himself with a baldachin *(Himmel)*, as well as benches which could seat 55 members of the gentry and nobility as well as 21 additional ordinary benches reserved for common people.[77] This suggests that the congregation was to accommodate well over 100 individuals with Waller himself taking a prominent position within it. Nevertheless, we do not know who exactly was to worship within this church nor does the cost estimate prove that the church ever materialised in this form. However, in 1686 Waller requested half of the salary offered by the duke for the two reformed ministers to be paid to a Scot, William Douglas, indicating the presence of a British congregation similar to the ones which can be found in other places such as Elbing.[78]

By a process of elimination we can demonstrate that the English and Scottish exiles worshipped almost exclusively in their own church rather than with other foreigners. On 16 March 1685 a French reformed church was established under the guidance of the French minister Joseph de Casaucau, who arrived from Copenhagen.[79] It was almost certainly he who received the other half of the minister's salary provided by the duke. The church book of the French congregation partially survives and has been analysed by Beuleke who—in correlation with other documents—identified 33 men and 30 women as belonging to the French community between 1685 and the beginning of the eighteenth century.[80] As no English, Scottish or Dutch names appear in the registers—apart from two exceptions[81]—we can conclude that exiles of these nationalities continued to worship in their own private church, giving credit to the notion

---

76. Stadtarchiv Lüneburg, Gewerbesachen, G3e No. 2, Bill Relating to Church Pews, Lüneburg, 4 November 1684; Protocoll Curiae 1684–1685, P7 No. 17, p. 65, 18 November 1684.

77. Stadtarchiv Lüneburg, Gewerbesachen, G3e No. 2, Bill Relating to Church Pews, Lüneburg, 4 November 1684. The German text does not differentiate between gentry and nobility but uses the term *Adlige*. However, it has to be assumed that Waller anticipated attracting members of the gentry primarily. The senate was prepared to give Waller some chairs for the nobles/members of the gentry. Stadtarchiv Lüneburg, Protocoll Curiae 1684–1685, P7 No. 17, p. 65, 18 November 1684.

78. Henri Tollin, "Geschichte der hugenottischen Gemeinde in Celle", *Der deutsche Hugenott*, 5, 1899, p. 6. Tollin got his information from a document in the state archives in Hanover from a file which could so far not be localised. (The old reference states Staatsarchiv Hannover, Celle Br. Arch. Des. 55, Lüneburg No. 682.)

79. Andreas Flick, "Hugenotten in Norddeutschland", p. 80; Walter Mogk, "Geschichte der Evangelisch-Reformierten", p. 389.

80. Wilhelm Beuleke, *Die Hugenotten in Niedersachsen*, pp. 134–7.

81. *Ibid.* Waller's daughter Catherine married the Frenchmen Richard de Courtenay on 19 November 1685. Also Mary Taylor from London married in the French church on 15 August 1685.

that Waller's was in fact built. It is unclear who the 55 members of the nobility and gentry were that Waller hoped to draw to Lüneburg. It is possible that they included the entrepreneurs Hog and Pau, both of whom carried the prefix "de" in their name indicating their high ranking status.[82] However, as argued previously, Waller's main target lay not solely in the establishment of a reformed exile community but in the creation of a safe haven for political dissidents who were in immediate danger in the United Provinces. These were mainly members of the nobility and gentry and they were probably meant to form the majority of high ranking individuals in Waller's church.

One of these exiles, the Scot Sir John Cochrane, arrived in Lüneburg in October 1684 together with his son as well as several other unnamed adherents.[83] After having established links with the earl of Argyll and the inner circle of the duke of Monmouth in early 1683, Cochrane had become suspected of involvement in the conspiracy to overthrow Charles II—an accusation of which he was found guilty in May 1685 with the result that his estates were foreited. In addition the Scottish Privy Council had directed the king's advocate on 16 August 1683 to charge Cochrane with treason for his involvment in the Bothwell Bridge rising. Thus Cochrane had been forced to escape to the Netherlands, from where he moved to the duchy of Cleves and then on to Lüneburg via Hanover.[84] However, his stay was only short as he played an active part in the ill-fated Argyll Rebellion in 1685 and it is likely that the individuals he had brought to Lüneburg followed him back to the British Isles.[85]

Apart from Cochrane (and Waller) it is not possible to identify other exiles or suspected anti-Stuart conspirators in Lüneburg, but this of course does not mean that they were not there. We know that Waller continued in his endeavours to attract entrepreneurs to the city. In the end of 1685 he as well as an (unnamed) Englishman inspected possible locations for a serge factory. In addition to 500 local children, a considerable number of 100 to 200 skilled workers from England and other places were to be employed in this factory.[86] However, negotiations with the senate proved difficult and Waller threatened that the entrepreneur had already

---

82. For evidence that Scots used this device to highlight their status abroad see Steve Murdoch, "The Pearl Fisher Robert Buchan 'de Portlethin' in Sweden", *Northern Studies* (2007), pp. 51–70.

83. Stadtarchiv Lüneburg, Gewerbesachen, G3e No. 2, Johan Halfe to Lüneburg Senate, 11 October 1684.

84. Richard L. Greaves, "Sir John Cochrane (1662–1695)", *DNB* (online publication).

85. *Ibid.*

86. Stadtarchiv Lüneburg, Gewerbesachen, G3e No. 7, Privileges Demanded by the Manufacturers, 11 December 1685.

received a better offer in East Frisia.[87] Although the senate eventually granted privileges to the Englishman there is no further proof that the factory ever materialised.[88] Furthermore, at least one source states that William Waller took his leave from Lüneburg on 15 June 1686, apparently to return to Bremen where he would receive another military command—giving further evidence that the establishment of the serge factory failed.[89]

Waller's departure from the city must have had a profound impact on the exiles. Developments in the political situation of the British Isles negated the need for an exile community and most British exiles left the continent after the Williamite Revolution (1688/1689). However, there were exceptions. Robert Hog remained in production in Lüneburg until at least 1709. The fact that he decided to stay in Lüneburg perhaps confirms that he was primarily concerned with economic matters and not overtly emotionally attached to the exiles' cause. Alternatively, he may have simply found the financial gains of his enterprises abroad too rewarding to give up at that juncture. Furthermore, he may have integrated into Lüneburg's society through marriage or other links which he was perhaps not prepared to surrender. Nevertheless, Hog maintained an interest in his home country despite his long-term absence. This was expressed in 1709 when Hog recommended his son John to the Earl of Leven, stating that he had sent him to his native country to learn the language.[90] Furthermore, Hog—as a "true Scot"—praised the effects which the parliamentary Anglo-Scottish Union of 1707 could potentially have on Scotland if people knew how to make use of the liberty of freely using Irish and English wool. He described his comfortable life in Lüneburg but stated that he was willing to return to Scotland after his 46 years abroad provided that the monarch would allow him a small pension. He further implied that he would then use his expertise to the benefit of the country's economy stating that he "brogt the Lunenburg manufactory to perfection" and that "al my countrymen in Scotland know there could be no better man to give directions".[91] It is not clear why Hog waited for almost two years after the Union before sending this letter. It is possible that he wanted to confirm that the Union was secure as evidenced by the

---

87. Stadtarchiv Lüneburg, Gewerbesachen, G3e No. 7, William Waller to Georg Wilhelm, Celle, 3 February 1686.

88. Stadtarchiv Lüneburg, Gewerbesachen, G3e No. 7, Lüneburg Senate to Ducal Council, 26 January 1686.

89. Wilhelm Beuleke, *Die Hugenotten in Niedersachsen*, p. 137.

90. NAS, Leven and Melville Papers, GD26/13/492, Robert Hog to the Earl of Leven, Lüneburg, 20 January 1709.

91. *Ibid.*

failure of the 1708 Jacobite uprising.[92] His revived interest in Scotland may have been partially financially motivated. However, his position in Lüneburg (unless exaggerated in his letter) suggests that Hog felt genuinely attached to Scotland, perhaps simply wishing to retire there.

Waller's negotiations with the senate of Bremen and Georg Wilhelm of Braunschweig-Lüneburg demonstrate that the interest of British exiles was not limited to the United Provinces. When life in the Dutch cities became too dangerous for some political exiles new places were sought to establish multi-ethnic reformed communities which could provide shelter to a smaller number of endangered individuals. The Imperial city of Bremen and the duchy of Braunschweig-Lüneburg provided obvious choices for the establishment of these communities as they either embraced or at least tolerated Calvinist churches. However, both communities envisaged by Waller were faced with severe difficulties. In Bremen these seemed to come from the outside. It was the pressure from Charles II and Bevil Skelton in Hamburg which forced the Bremen authorities to release Waller and to give up the proposed "British" community. In Lüneburg incomers like Hearne faced complaints and resistance from the local population who feared their competition. This was especially so as the decision to attract foreigners had not been made by the city's authorities but by the ducal authorities at Celle. Despite these difficulties individuals like Hog were successful in the long term. He remained in Lüneburg after the Williamite Revolution revealing that to some exiles mercantile considerations were just as important as spiritual or political concerns. However, the Scottish entrepreneur was an exception in that most exiles left the continent after the Stuart regimes had ended. Nevertheless, for a short time, the duchy of Braunschweig-Lüneburg (and to a lesser extent the city of Bremen) had offered them support and the opportunity of building a reformed community in a mutually beneficial relationship with fellow refugees of other nationalities.

---

92. Daniel Szechi, *The Jacobites: Britain and Europe, 1688–1788* (Manchester, 1994), pp. 56–7.

Marion Amblard
Stendhal University, Grenoble 3

The Scottish painters' exile in Italy in the eighteenth century

In the eighteenth century, a visit to Italy was considered by many as essential in the career of a painter. Although contemporary Italian painting was not as prestigious as before, Rome was still the artistic centre of continental Europe and attracted many artists eager to complete their training and to find patrons among the aristocrats on the Grand Tour.[1] As President of the Royal Academy, Joshua Reynolds (1723–1792) stressed the importance of a stay in Italy to enable young painters to study the works of the Renaissance masters.[2] Not all English artists agreed with Reynolds; William Hogarth (1697–1764), for instance, staunchly opposed the idea of going abroad to copy and imitate foreign artists.[3] For Scottish painters,

---

1. For more on the British and the Grand Tour, see Jeremy Black, *The British Abroad: The Grand Tour in the Eighteenth Century*, New York, Saint Martin's Press, 1992 and Christopher Hibbert, *The Grand Tour*, London, Thames Methuen, 1969. To know more specifically about the Scots in Italy, see Basil Skinner, *Scots in Italy in the 18th Century*, Edinburgh, Scottish National Portrait Gallery, 1966 and Richard Adam Marks, "The Scots in the Italian Peninsula during the Thirty Years' War", *The Ulster Earls and Baroque Europe: Refashioning Irish Identities, 1600–1800*, Thomas O'Connor and Mary Ann Lyons (eds), Dublin, Four Courts Press, 2009, pp. 336–8.

2. Reynolds told the students of the Royal Academy: "study […] the great works of the great masters, for ever. Study as nearly as you can, in the order, in the manner, and on the principles, on which they studied." (Sir Joshua Reynolds, *Discourses on Art*, New Haven–London, Yale University Press, 1975, p. 113.)

In the discourses he delivered at the Royal Academy, Reynolds often praised the Renaissance masters. He admired above all Raphael and Michelangelo as he wrote that "these two extraordinary men […] certainly have not been excelled, nor equalled since". (Sir Joshua Reynolds, *Discourses on Art*, p. 84.)

3. According to Hogarth, painters should be inspired by nature and not by the works of their illustrious predecessors. In his *Analysis of Beauty* he explained: "It is […] evident that the painter's eye may not be a bit better fitted to receive these new impressions, who is in the like manner too much captivated with the works of art. […] This mistake happens chiefly to those who go to Rome for the accomplishment of their studies, as they naturally will, without the utmost care, take the infectious turn of the connoisseur, instead of the painter: and in proportion as they turn by those means bad proficients in their own arts, they become the more considerable in that of a connoisseur. […] It has ever been observed at all auctions of pictures, that the very worst painters sit as the most profound judges." (William Hogarth, *The Analysis of Beauty, Written with a View of Fixing the Fluctuating Ideas of Taste*, London, 1810, p. 5.)

travelling to Italy was of prime importance as this was the means to complete the basic training acquired in their native country. Indeed, before 1798, there was no permanent fine art academy in Scotland; thus to get thorough artistic training they had to leave Scotland, so they either went to London or they studied in Italy. This was not a phenomenon confined to Caledonian artists. Indeed most eighteenth-century Irish and English painters undertook similar journeys to the Continent. Like the Scots, Irish painters did not have access to comprehensive training in their native country: until the middle of the eighteenth century, there was no art school in Ireland, so young Irishmen aspiring to an artistic career trained with craftsmen or went to England to work in the studio of a painter.[4] The first Irish fine art institution was a drawing school opened in Dublin by Robert West (died 1770) in 1746. The school was taken over by the Dublin Society in 1750 and by 1759 two other schools had been set up—the Landscape and Ornament School and the Architectural School—in order to further develop the fine arts in Ireland. In England, painters had several options for training. In London they could join the studio of a famous artist and they could study in one of the fine art schools. Sir Godfrey Kneller (1646–1723) opened the first academy of painting in London in 1711; in 1720, Louis Chéron (1660–1725) and John Vanderbank (1694–1739) founded their own academy in Saint Martin's Lane and, from 1735, painters could study at the Saint Martin's Lane Academy set up by Hogarth with a group of artists. In addition, from 1768 onwards, artists could also become students at the Royal Academy. Yet most English painters still felt the need to go to the Continent because they believed, as did the majority of Western European artists, that their training could not be complete without a visit to Italy. Thus, on the Continent, Irish, English and Scottish painters worked side by side with artists from all over Europe.[5]

This article will investigate the role of the period of "exile" these Scottish painters spent in Italy during the eighteenth century and, through their return, underline the contribution of Italian art to the development of painting in Scotland. Until the publication of *Scottish Painters at Home and Abroad 1700–1900* by David and Francina Irwin in 1975, Scottish art historians had reaffirmed the isolated position of Scottish painting vis-a-vis

---

4. For instance, Nathaniel Hone (1718–1784) was apprenticed to an enamellist whereas Charles Jervas (c. 1675–1739) went to London to become the pupil and assistant of Sir Godfrey Kneller.

5. According to David Irwin, the majority of painters who went to Italy in the eighteenth century came from the British Isles, France and Germany (David Irwin, *Neoclassicism*, London, Phaidon, 2000, p. 13). If Italy was the country they visited the most, John Wraight has shown that Switzerland was also a popular destination for British painters (Sir John Wraight, *The Swiss and the British*, Salisbury, M. Russell, 1987, p. 42–8).

mainstream European art by downplaying or denying foreign influences.[6] Because of commercial and cultural bonds between Scotland and the Dutch Republic dating back to the medieval period, Scottish painting has usually been compared with Dutch painting.[7] The affinities between Scottish art and Dutch art were highlighted in the exhibition entitled *Dutch Art and Scotland: a Reflection of Taste* which was held at the National Gallery of Scotland in 1992. In the exhibition catalogue, Lindsay Errington claimed that:

> Scottish painters have looked towards and learnt from Dutch artists over a long period of time. In the seventeenth and early eighteenth centuries, before romanticism fostered the idea of a national school of painting that might reflect national history and cultural identity, those Scottish painters who had learnt their skills from Dutch examples produced paintings with little to distinguish them from works produced in Holland.[8]

Indeed, the influence of Dutch art is particularly noticeable in seventeenth and early eighteenth-century Scottish paintings. Several Dutch portrait painters worked in Scotland in the seventeenth century and their style deeply impressed Scottish painters: King James VI (1566–1625) sat for two Dutch portraitists, Arnold Bronckorst (active 1565/1566– 1583) and Adrian Vanson (active 1581–1602). At the time, Scotland was not lacking in native painters, but as most of them were trained as craftsmen they specialised in decorative painting and were unable to

---

6. David and Francina Irwin, *Scottish Painters at Home and Abroad 1700–1900*, London, Faber and Faber, 1975. The Irwins were the first scholars to set Scottish painting in a broader British and European context. In their study, they denounced "the chauvinistic tendency of Scottish writers around 1900 and since to see it as an isolated phenomenon" (David and Francina Irwin, *Scottish Painters at Home and Abroad 1700–1900*, p. 35).

Before 1975, art historians shared Brydall's opinion who wrote: "In England, almost to the present day, the influence is felt of Vandyke, Kneller, and other foreigners; but in Scotland there is little indication of foreign influence, except in some of the works of Jamesone, prior to the year 1630." (Robert Brydall, *Art in Scotland. Its Origin and Progress*, Edinburgh, William Blackwood and Sons, 1889, p. 218.)

Scottish painting is also studied in a European context in Marion Amblard, "The Scottish School's Contribution to the Development of European Painting: Exchanges and Interactions between Scottish and European Painters in the Eighteenth Century", *Scotland and Europe, Scotland in Europe*, Gilles Leydier (ed.), Newcastle, Cambridge Scholars Publishing, 2007, pp. 56–68.

7. For detailed studies on the links between Scotland and the Dutch Republic, as well as on the Scottish communities in the Dutch Republic, see Douglas Catterall, *Community Without Borders: Scots Migrants and the Changing Face of Power in the Dutch Republic, c. 1600–1700*, Leiden, Brill, 2002 and Alexia Grosjean and Steve Murdoch (eds), *Scottish Communities Abroad in the Early Modern Period*, Leiden, Brill, 2005, especially the chapters by Douglas Catterall, Ginny Gardner, Andrew Little and Esther Mijers.

8. Lindsay Errington, "Gold and Silver in Shadow. The Dutch Influence on Nineteenth-Century Scottish Painting", *Dutch Art and Scotland. A Reflection of Taste*, Julia Lloyd Williams (ed.), Edinburgh, the Trustees of the National Galleries of Scotland, 1992, p. 49.

paint official portraits of the monarch.[9] The influence of another Dutch painter, Adam de Colone (active 1622–1628) who worked in Edinburgh for several years, can also be seen in the works of George Jamesone (1589/1590–1644), the first major Scottish portraitist.[10] Further, the influence of Dutch painting is also visible in still-lifes painted by early eighteenth-century Scottish painters such as Thomas Warrender (active 1673–1713) and Richard Waitt (active 1708–1732), who had certainly seen Dutch still-lifes imported by Scottish aristocrats.[11] Several art historians have also stressed the influence of Flemish and French arts on Scottish painting. Among others, Sir David Wilkie (1785–1841) has often been compared to the Flemish painter David Teniers (1610–1690) and some of the Glasgow Boys' paintings are reminiscent of the works of the French naturalist painters.[12] In 2009, the influence of Spanish art on nineteenth-century Scottish painters was stressed by the exhibition *The Discovery of Spain. British Artists and Collectors: from Goya to Picasso* held at the National Gallery of Scotland.[13] However, so far, the influence of Italian art on eighteenth-century Scottish painting has been overlooked.

The first part of this article deals with the need for Scottish painters to take voluntary exile abroad in order to complete their training. By drawing up a list of Scottish painters who travelled to Italy in the eighteenth century and of the places they visited, we can see that the majority of Scottish painters trained in Italy. To study Italian painting, they travelled around the country which was then divided into several duchies and kingdoms.

---

9. For a detailed account on painting in seventeenth-century Scotland, see Duncan Thomson, *Painting in Scotland 1570–1650*, Edinburgh, The Trustees of the National Galleries of Scotland, 1975. See also Michael R. Apted and Susan Hannabuss, *Painters in Scotland, 1300–1700: A Biographical Dictionary*, Edinburgh, Edinburgh Scottish Record Society, 1978.

10. Thomson demonstrated that several features of the portraits of Mary Erskine, Countess of Marischal (1626, National Gallery of Scotland, Edinburgh) and of James Graham, 1st Marquess of Montrose (1629, the Earl of Southesk) derive from the influence of de Colone (Duncan Thomson, *Painting in Scotland 1570–1650*, pp. 61–2).

11. These paintings were imported from the Dutch Republic or from London, where several Dutch still-life painters worked. Waterhouse has explained that "Lord Lothian seems to have been a particular patron of this kind of painting, for there remain at Newbattle Abbey examples of Roestraeten and Collier and the solitary signed 'Flower Piece' of B. Ferrers dated 1695." (Ellis Waterhouse, *Painting in Britain 1530–1790*, New Haven–London, Yale University Press, 1994, p. 116.)
Thomas Warrender's *Still Life* (1708, National Gallery of Scotland, Edinburgh) is particularly redolent of Collier's still-lifes.

12. Harry Mount, "'Our British Teniers': David Wilkie and the Heritage of Netherlandish Art", *David Wilkie. Painter of Everyday Life*, Nicholas Tromans (ed.), London, Dulwich Picture Gallery, 2002, pp. 30–9.
Roger Billcliffe, *The Glasgow Boys. The Glasgow School of Painting 1875–1895*, London, John Murray, 2002.

13. *The Discovery of Spain. British Artists and Collectors: from Goya to Picasso*, exhibition held at the National Gallery of Scotland from 18 July to 11 October 2009. The exhibition especially stressed the fact that Wilkie was deeply impressed by the paintings of Velázquez (1599–1660).

Artistic styles varied from city to city and artists had to study the works of the major schools which required a visit to Florence, Bologna, Venice and Rome. Of all the cities they visited, Rome was the place where they spent most of their time. The second part of this article will be devoted to Scottish painters' activities in Rome. In the city, young artists had various opportunities to study. They could attend classes at the French or Italian academies and they could enrol in the studio of a fashionable painter. They were also able to study the works of art displayed in churches and in private collections, which were easily accessible. Then we shall see the impact of Italian art on eighteenth-century Scottish painters. By focusing on a few paintings and drawings the deep and lasting impact of these Italian journeys on Scottish artists will become evident. Unlike, their English contemporaries, we will see that Scottish painters were not only impressed by the Italian Renaissance masters, indeed some of the major portraitists were influenced by the works of Caravaggio (1571–1610) and his followers. However, the Scots were also inspired by some of the most popular eighteenth-century Italian painters.

Pictorial art only began to develop in Scotland after 1745. The consequences of the Reformation and the Union of Crowns had deprived artists of their main patrons, the Catholic Church and the monarch. As in the other reformed kingdoms, the establishment of the Presbyterian Church in Scotland led to the proscription of religious themes in painting which until then had been the most fruitful field of subject matter for painters in Europe.[14] Furthermore, the development of painting in Scotland was somewhat hampered by the Kirk as it objected to the opening of public life classes in fine art institutions, which meant that young artists could not draw from nude models and could not gain a sound knowledge of anatomy. Access to patronage became even more hampered when in 1707 the Union of the Parliaments led to the departure of many Scottish aristocrats for London. The demand for paintings was very limited until the beginning of the nineteenth century and, as a result, very few painters opened a studio in Scotland, preferring to work in London. Painters were not the only ones to leave Scotland for England, as in the eighteenth century several leading Scottish literary figures also moved to London in order to have a successful literary career: James Thomson

---

14. Ian Finlay claimed that: "in the Low Countries Calvinism brought painting down to earth and [...] it created [...] a great school of landscape painting, fully in accord with Calvin's pleasure in Nature as a design of God's creation" (Ian Finlay, *Scottish Art*, London, Longmans Green and co., 1939, p. 5). In Scotland, landscape painting only began to develop at the end of the eighteenth century.

(1700–1748) published his *Seasons* (1730) in London, and it was also in this city that Tobias Smollett (1721–1771) wrote his novels. Others, like James Boswell (1740–1795) and the portraitist Allan Ramsay, travelled regularly between London and Edinburgh.[15] The painters who decided to remain in Scotland could not live on their artwork alone. With the exception of Raeburn (1756–1823), who had a very successful practice as a portraitist, most painters had to work as decorative painters or they had to sell illustrations to publishers. At the end of the eighteenth century, painters such as Alexander Runciman (1736–1785) and David Allan (1744–1796) also had the option of teaching at the fine art academy in Edinburgh. As very few painters worked in Scotland throughout the eighteenth century, the young Scots aspiring to an artistic career did not often have the possibility to study under a painter and most of them began their training working with a craftsman. Thus the landscape painter Alexander Nasmyth (1758–1840) was apprenticed to a coach painter before studying with Allan Ramsay (1713–1784) in London; Henry Raeburn trained with the jeweller James Gilliland.

Throughout the eighteenth century more and more drawing academies and academies of fine arts were opened on the European continent.[16] Compared with continental Europe, the creation of such establishments occurred at a much later date in Great Britain: the Royal Academy was opened in 1768 whereas the *Académie Royale de peinture et de sculpture* had been created in Paris in 1648. However, the Royal Academy was not the first academy of fine arts in Britain. Three art schools had already been established in Scotland, but two of them were short-lived. The Academy of Saint Luke, founded in Edinburgh in 1729, was based on the Roman Academy of the same name. It was created by a few "Painters, and Lovers of Painting […] for the encouragement of these excellent arts of Painting, Sculpture, Architecture".[17] This establishment closed down in 1731 and, twenty-two years later, the second Scottish fine art school was opened in Glasgow. The Foulis Academy was created in 1753 by publisher Robert Foulis (1707–1776) with the help of his brother Andrew (1712–1775). The academy's funding being dependent on a few patrons, it had to close down in 1775 following the death of one of the investors in 1770 and the death of Andrew Foulis in 1775. The first permanent Scottish art school, called the Trustees' Academy, was opened in Edinburgh in 1760.

---

15. Allan Ramsay opened a studio in his father's house in Edinburgh.

16. For more on the development of fine art schools in Western Europe, see Nikolaus Pevsner, *Academies of Art: Past and Present*, Cambridge, Cambridge University Press, 1940.

17. Quoted in Robert Brydall, *Art in Scotland. Its Origin and Progress*, p. 110.

Using John Ingamells' *Dictionary of British and Irish Travellers in Italy 1701–1800*, and the archives of the *Accademia di San Luca* in Rome, as well as Jacob More's correspondence and John Ramsay's journals at Edinburgh University Library,[18] I have been able to draw up a list of the Scottish painters who went to Italy in the eighteenth century.[19] I have included painters in oil, pastellists as well as miniaturists. Among the most prominent Scots to make the journey were Ramsay, Hamilton (1723–1798), Martin (1737–1797), More (1740–1793), Raeburn, Nasmyth and the Runciman brothers. In most cases, they travelled at the beginning of their career before opening their studio, but some of them were already working as professional painters when they went to Italy, as in the case of Henry Raeburn and Alexander Nasmyth. Generally only one visit to Italy was made but there are a few exceptions. Allan Ramsay went to Italy four times. He stayed there from 1736 to 1738, from 1754 to 1757, from 1775 to 1777 and from 1782 to 1784. However, only his first two visits had a decisive impact on his art.[20] Following Ramsay's example, Hamilton went twice to Italy. He studied painting in Rome from 1748 to 1750; back in Britain, he tried to work as a history painter but failed to find patrons and, in 1756, he settled permanently in Italy where he had a successful practice. Hay (d. 1754), Irvine (1757–1831) and Patoun (active 1761–1783) all made a first trip to Italy to study painting, however, when they returned to the Continent, it was no longer as painters—they worked as art dealers or guides for grand tourists.

Travelling and living on the Continent was expensive and not all painters could afford to study abroad for several years. Sometimes they did not hesitate to part with their possessions to go to the Continent:

---

18. John Ingamells, *A Dictionary of British and Irish Travellers in Italy: 1701–1800*, New Haven–London, Yale University Press, 1997.

These are the references of the archives consulted at the Accademia di Luca in which are mentioned Scottish painters. Archivio Storico dell'Accademia di San Luca [hereafter ASASL], *Libro originale delle Congregazioni o Verbali delle Medesime*, vol. 52, ff. 14, 136 and 139 references to James Byres.

ASASL, *Libro originale delle Congregazioni o Verbali delle Medesime*, vol. 52, f. 16, about Gavin Hamilton at the Academy.

ASASL, *Libro originale delle Congregazioni o Verbali delle Medesime*, vol. 54, ff. 136–38, f. 6/b, several references to Jacob More.

ASASL, *Libro originale delle Congregazioni o Verbali delle Medesime*, vol. 55, f. 71, reference to Jacob More. See also Angela Cipriani and Enrico Valeriani, *I Disegni di Figure nell' Archivio Storico dell'Accademia di San Luca*, vols 2–3, Rome, Quasar, 1989 and 1991.

Among the documents consulted at Edinburgh University Library, the letters of Jacob More, La. IV. 20, M. 13 ff. 1–44 "Letter Book, 1786–87" and the journals of John Ramsay, son of the painter Allan Ramsay, Mss. 1833–4, "Journals of John Ramsay (11 Dec. 1782 to 5 May 1784)" have been particularly useful.

19. The list is reproduced at the end of this article.

20. His last two trips were entirely devoted to excavations near Tivoli, since Ramsay had injured his right arm in 1773 and he could no longer paint.

for instance, William Aikman (1682–1731) sold the family estate he had inherited. After the deaths of his father and brother, Aikman became Laird of Cairnie; his relatives wanted him to become a lawyer but instead he was determined to work as a painter. In Edinburgh, he had been a pupil of Sir John Medina (1659–1710) then he moved to London to study in a fine art school. To support himself in London he used the rents from his property in Scotland and from the lands he owned in the British colonies on the Atlantic coast of North America. He also sollicited his uncle Sir John Clerk. To finance his journey to the Continent, he chose to sell his property of Cairnie which enabled him to travel comfortably accompanied by his servant. Aikman arrived in Italy in 1707 and returned to Scotland four years later.[21] Most painters however had to rely on their patrons to pay for their training abroad. Thanks to the generosity of the Cathcart family, David Allan was able to stay ten years in Italy; in order to go to Rome, Alexander Runciman committed himself to complete, on his return, decorative paintings at Penicuik for his patron Sir James Clerk.

In the eighteenth century, travelling to Italy was a long and hazardous undertaking.[22] Most travellers approached Italy through France. Once they reached Lyons, they could either cross the Alps and descend to Turin or they could go over land to Marseilles or Nice then they sailed to Genoa or Leghorn. Nevertheless, neither travelling by land nor by sea was an attractive prospect. The crossing of the Alps was dependent on seasonal factors and by sea there was the risk of storms, the risk of Barbary pirates, as well as the inconvenience of contrary winds. Thanks to the journals of Alexander Cunyngham, who travelled with Allan Ramsay, we know that the painter's first continental journey was particularly difficult. Cunyngham gives us a very detailed account of their misfortunes on their way to Rome and explains that in Genoa, in an inn where they stopped for the night, they were robbed by a servant and, shortly after that, while sailing to Rome, their boat was overturned by a storm and they nearly drowned.[23] Travelling conditions and the number of Scottish painters

---

21. For an overview of Aikman's career, see James Holloway, "William Aikman, 1682–1731", *Scottish Masters*, no. 9, Edinburgh, The Trustees of the National Galleries of Scotland, 1988.

22. Travels to the European Continent were not uncommon before the eighteenth century. In the seventeenth century, France and the Dutch Republic were popular destinations with British travellers. For an account of seventeenth-century British travellers in France, see John Lough, *France Observed in the Seventeenth Century by British Travellers*, Boston, Oriel Press, 1985. For more on seventeenth-century British travellers in the United Provinces, see C. D. Van Strien, British Travellers in Holland during the Stuart Period, Leiden, Brill, 1993.

23. See Mrs Atholl Forbes, *Curiosities of a Scots Charta Chest 1600–1800 with Travels and Memoranda of Sir Alexander Dick, Baronet of Prestonfield, Midlothian Written by Himself*, Edinburgh, William Brown, 1897.

going to Italy were also influenced by political events.[24] During the Napoleonic wars it became extremely hazardous to travel. The war made Italy as unsafe as the French Revolution had already made France and as a result the number of Scottish painters visiting Italy decreased sharply at the beginning of the 1790s. Even though he left Rome before the French invasion, the pastellist Archibald Skirving (1749–1818) had difficulties in returning to his native Scotland. With Britain and France at war, Skirving's boat was captured by the French off the Straits of Gibraltar and suspected of being a spy, he was jailed nine months in Brest.[25] Even in peacetime, travelling around Italy was long and tedious given the fragmented nature of the various Italian states and travellers were often delayed by the complicated formality of obtaining passports.

The traditional tour of Italy made by eighteenth-century Scottish painters was identical to that undertaken by other foreign artists. They mainly visited Naples, Venice, Bologna and Florence, cities noted for their artistic treasures. In Naples and Florence, British painters were easily granted access to private collections thanks to the diplomacy of Sir William Hamilton (1731–1803), ambassador to the court of Naples from 1764 to 1800, and of Sir Horace Mann (1706–1786), British consul at the court of Tuscany from 1738 to 1786. Thus in Florence, painters could study the works of art on display in the Grand Duke's Gallery at the Pitti Palace and in the Uffizi. It was from the second half of the eighteenth century, with the discovery of Herculaneum in 1738 and Pompeii in 1748, that Naples began to attract many artists and tourists from all over the Continent. The unearthing of these two ancient Roman towns, as well as the excavations carried out on other antique sites in the Italian peninsula and in the Middle East, led to a heightened awareness of classical antiquity and stimulated a classical revival in the arts. Many books dealing with ancient history, literature and art were published: among others, the Scots James Stuart (1713–1788) and Nicholas Revett (1720–1804) wrote *The*

---

24. Thus Jeremy Black has shown that during the conflicts from 1739 to 1748 which led to war between Britain and both France and Spain, as well as during the Seven Year's War (1756–1763) the number of British aristocrats and painters visiting Italy decreased (Jeremy Black, *The British Abroad: The Grand Tour in the Eighteenth Century*, pp. 8–9). In time of war, tourists sometimes had to modify their itinerary to reach the Italian peninsula. During the Napoleonic Wars, it became almost impossible to travel and the conflict disrupted the Grand Tour.

25. Skirving's sight seemed to have been deeply affected by the months he spent in jail. In 1802, in a letter he sent to his brother, the painter referred to his eyesight problems. He wrote: "What I meant of my sight was, that both eyes were equally strong, for you remember I complained of the right one, but small objects appear forked. At Brest after getting out of prison my companion who would buy some pins at the gate remarked that they were all split; he never dreamed the defect was in his sight, and I cannot make a pen tolerable. Glasses would remedy this but they do not well to paint, for painting requires to see different distances." (Quoted in Stephen Lloyd, *Raeburn's Rival. Archibald Skirving 1749–1819*, Edinburgh, The Trustees of the National Galleries of Scotland, 1999, p. 22.)

Antiquities of Athens and Other Monuments of Greece (five volumes were published between 1762 and 1830), Piranesi (1720–1778) published *Antichità Romane* (1756) and, in France, Comte de Caylus (1692–1765) published seven volumes of *Recueil d'Antiquités Égyptiennes, Étrusques, Grecques, Romaines* from 1752 to 1767. But the most influential writings were undoubtedly those of the German Johann Joachim Winckelmann (1717–1768), *Reflections on the Imitation of the Painting and Sculpture of the Greeks* (1755) and *The History of Ancient Art* (1764). Indeed, Winckelmann was the leading classical scholar in Europe and when he worked for Cardinal Albani (1692–1779) in Rome he was visited by many tourists and artists. His artistic theories shaped tastes in Western Europe and defined the tenets of neoclassicism, which was the dominant artistic movement in Europe from the second half of the eighteenth to the beginning of the nineteenth century.[26] Thus many painters, like David Allan, made the journey to Naples to draw from classical sculptures and bas reliefs. Bologna was worth a visit to study the paintings of Reni (1575–1642), the Carraccis and Guercino (1591–1666) which were scattered about the churches and palaces of the town. Quite a lot of Scottish painters also visited Venice to see the works of Titian (1488–1576) and of the other great sixteenth-century Venetian painters. Some, like Katherine Read (1723–1778), travelled to Venice in order to meet Rosalba Carriera (1675–1757), who was then one of the most famous pastellists in Western Europe. However, of all the Italian cities, Rome was the focus of the Scottish painters' tour, given that the greatest number of ancient, classical sculptures and the masterpieces of Michelangelo (1475–1564) and Raphael (1483–1520), who were then considered as the greatest painters of all time, were concentrated there. Rome also attracted Scottish painters because there was already a Scottish community established in the city.[27] Since its founda-

---

26. In painting the first representatives of neoclassicism were Gavin Hamilton and Anton Raphael Mengs. At the end of the eighteenth century, the French Jacques-Louis David became the most influential neoclassical painter. The Venetian Antonio Canova, the Dane Bertel Thorvaldsen and the Englishman John Flaxman (1755–1826) are considered as the most famous neoclassical sculptors. As for architecture, Robert Adam (1728–1792) was the leader of neoclassical taste in Britain. There exist several historical and critical overviews of neoclassicism: see Hugh Honour, *Neo-Classicism*, Harmondsworth, Penguin, 1968 and David Irwin, *Neoclassicism*.

27. In the eighteenth century, Scottish communities were established in various parts of Continental Europe—in Holland, France, Scandinavia and Poland among others—as well as in the British Empire. Indeed, Smout has written that: "from at least as early as the Hundred Years War, [...] the Scots were a people quick to seek their fortunes abroad by temporary or permanent migration. It was a national propensity only checked after 1945 by the collapse of the British Empire." (T. C. Smout, "Foreword", *Scottish Communities Abroad in the Early Modern Period*, Alexia Grosjean and Steve Murdoch (eds), p. v.)

To know more about Scottish communities in Northern and Eastern Europe, see Thomas Fischer, *The Scots in Eastern and Western Prussia*, Edinburgh, Schulze, 1903 and Jonas Berg and Bo Lagercrantz,

tion in 1600 by Pope Clement VIII (1536–1605), the Scots College had been the focal point of the community.[28] Furthermore the number of Scots living permanently in Rome had increased in 1719 with the arrival of the exiled Stuart court.[29] Thus visiting Scottish painters had a network of compatriots to connect with if they so desired.

Rome had long attracted foreign artists. In the eighteenth century, the role of the city as artistic capital of Western Europe was further strengthened by the growing interest in classical antiquity and, until the French invasion in 1796, an increasing number of painters came to finish off their training. Rome was a cosmopolitan city with tourists and artists coming from all over Europe. Although most artists settled near *Piazza di Spagna* but, as Olivier Michel underlined in his article entitled "La Vie quotidienne des peintres à Rome au dix-huitième siècle", painters tended to live within their own national communities.[30] English and Scottish painters met regularly at the *Caffè degli Inglesi*, but they stayed in different streets, most Scottish painters lived in the *Strada Felice*. This street lay in the heart of the Scottish community, being the location of the Scots College; it was also very close to the Palazzo Muti, where the exiled Stuart family lived.

The Scots formed a very close-knit artistic community. During the second half of the eighteenth century, young Scots arriving in Rome sought the help and advice of Gavin Hamilton and Jacob More, who had very successful practices in the city. Hamilton was engaged in various activities: he worked as an art-dealer, he carried out excavations on the ancient sites of Ostia, Tivoli, Tor Colombaro and Monte Cagnolo, and

---

Scots in Sweden, Stockholm, the Swedish Institute, 1962. The articles published in *Scottish Communities Abroad in the Early Modern Period*, Alexia Grosjean and Steve Murdoch (eds), deal with various Scottish communities in Swedish, Polish, Lithuanian, Dutch and Germany cities in the seventeenth century. The presence of Scottish Jacobites in France has been studied in Edward Corp (ed.), *A Court in Exile: the Stuarts in France, 1689–1718*, Cambridge, Cambridge University Press, 2004.

To know more specifically about the Scottish community in Bordeaux, see Steve Murdoch, "The French Connection: Bordeaux's 'Scottish' Networks in Context, c. 1670–1720", *Scotland and Europe, Scotland in Europe*, Gilles Leydier (ed.), pp. 26–55.

28. Adam Marks, "The Scots in the Italian Peninsula during the Thirty Years' War", pp. 336–8.

29. Edward Corp has explained that many Scots left Britain after the failure of the Jacobite uprisings in 1715, 1719 and in 1745. The composition of the exiled Stuart court evolved after each of these rebellions and it included an increasing number of Scots. The composition and the life of the exile Stuart court has been studied extensively by Professor Corp. See Edward Corp (ed.), *The Stuart Court in Rome: the Legacy of Exile*, Aldershot, Ashgate, 2003; Edward Corp (ed.), *A Court in Exile: the Stuarts in France, 1689–1718*; see also Edward Corp, *The Jacobites at Urbino: an Exiled Court in Transition*, Basingstoke, Palgrave Macmillan, 2009.

30. Olivier Michel, "La Vie quotidienne des peintres à Rome au dix-huitième siècle", *Vivre et Peindre à Rome au XVIIIᵉ siècle*, Rome, École française de Rome, 1996, p. 42.

he was also a renowned painter.[31] He specialised in history painting and was able to find patrons among the British grand tourists for a series of paintings inspired by Homer's *Iliad*. With his rival Anton Raphael Mengs (1728–1779), Hamilton was the leading history painter in Rome, whose paintings helped establish a taste for Neoclassicism in Western Europe. Indeed, his works were praised by Winckelmann and influenced many artists such as Jacques-Louis David (1748–1825) as well as the sculptors Antonio Canova (1757–1822), Bertel Thorvaldsen (1770–1844) and Tobias Sergel (1740–1814).[32] As for More, he became one of the most fashionable landscape painters after settling down in Rome in 1771.[33] His classical landscapes were sought after by British aristocrats and impressed several Scottish painters who met him. When Ramsay stayed in Rome, he was visited by many of his fellow countrymen too.[34] It was Ramsay who asked his pupil and assistant David Martin to come to Rome in 1755 and, in 1783, it was probably thanks to his former master Ramsay that Nasmyth met More with whom he went drawing landscapes in the countryside. This meeting was extremely important in Nasmyth's career as it encouraged him to give up portraiture for landscape painting. Ann Forbes (1745–1840), Henry Raeburn, James Nevay (c. 1730–after 1811), Nasmyth, John (1744–1768/1769) and Alexander Runciman and David Allan frequented Hamilton's studio. Among all these painters, Alexander Runciman and Allan were the most deeply impressed by Hamilton and when they returned to Scotland they both longed to work as history painters. Thus, the successful career of Hamilton and More and the contact with these artists in Italy encouraged young Scottish painters to specialise in genres other than portrait painting and it helped diversify Scottish painting, which until the end of the eighteenth century was limited to portraiture.

As previously mentioned, whilst in Rome Scottish painters had the option of attending classes at the two prestigious fine art academies of Rome: the *Académie de France* and the *Accademia di San Luca*. The French academy in Rome was established in 1666 by Colbert to welcome promi-

---

31. David Irwin, "Gavin Hamilton: Archaeologist, Painter and Dealer", *The Art Bulletin*, June 1962, pp. 87–102.

32. See Robert Rosemblum, "A Source for David's 'Horatii'", *The Burlington Magazine*, May 1970, pp. 273–4. See also Ellis Kirkham Waterhouse, "The British Contribution to the Neo-Classical Style in Painting", *Proceedings of the British Academy*, no. 150, 1954, pp. 57–74.

33. For an overview of More's career, see Patricia R. Andrew, *Jacob More 1740–1793*, unpublished Ph.D. thesis, University of Edinburgh, 1981.

34. Aikman of Ross wrote: "Hamilton is what the Italians call the *Premiero*, and we students call him the Principal, in the Academy of Painting at Rome all the students apply to him for Direction and instruction in their Studies." (Quoted in Julia Lloyd Williams, "Gavin Hamilton, 1723–1798", *Scottish Masters*, no. 18, Edinburgh, The Trustees of the National Galleries of Scotland, 1994, p. 16.)

sing young French artists, winners of the *Prix de Rome*, in order to study art and architecture. Along with the students, foreign artists could attend the daily life classes provided by the French academy from 1725. Apart from a few classes held during the summer by the *Accademia di San Luca*, the French academy classes were the only public life classes in Rome before 1754, when Pope Benedict XIV (1675–1758) decided to open the *Accademia del Nudo* under the supervision of the *Accademia di San Luca*. These life classes, which consisted in drawing from live nude male models, were popular with Scottish painters, for instance, when in Rome, Ramsay regularly attended the classes of the French academy; Alves (1738–1808) and Maxwell, who studied at the *Accademia del Nudo*, won a prize for their drawings. Before 1836, painters in Scotland had no access to public life classes, while classes held at the Trustees' Academy only used plaster casts of antique sculptures. If artists wanted to draw from a live nude, they could either hire a model or, as David Wilkie used to do, they could draw their own body. Scottish painters were also admitted to the *Accademia di San Luca*. This academy had been founded in 1593 and was one of the oldest fine art institutions in Western Europe. Unlike the French academy, it did not consistently provide classes before 1754 but painters could copy the collection of paintings and of plaster casts of antique sculptures belonging to the academy. If they were introduced by an academician, painters could also take part in the *concorso Clementino* and the *concorso Balestra*, the two competitions organised by the academy. In the eighteenth century, two Scots won these competitions: in 1707 John Taylor was awarded a medal at the *concorso Clementino* for a drawing and, in 1773, David Allan won the *concorso Balestra* with his painting entitled *Hector's Farewell to Andromache*.[35] Winning a prize at the *Accademia di San Luca* was very prestigious and generally ensured a painter gained important commissions in Rome, however, for Allan this did not seem to have been the case. Being a member of the Academy also helped to find patrons. Gavin Hamilton and Jacob More were the only two Scottish painters to be elected members of the *Accademia di San Luca*, in 1761 and 1781[36] respectively, and it was probably for this reason that Marcantonio Borghese (1730–1800) hired them to paint one room each in his villa.

Besides the life classes at the academies, many Scottish painters decided to complete their training by working as pupils in the studio of a famous painter. Thanks to the recommendations of the Jacobite Andrew Lumisden

---

35. David Allan, *Hector's Farewell to Andromache*, 1773, Accademia di San Luca, Roma.

36. For the election of Hamilton, see ASASL, *Libro originale delle Congregazioni o Verbali delle Medesime*, vol. 52, f. 16. For the election of More, see ASASL, *Libro originale delle Congregazioni o Verbali delle Medesime*, vol. 54, ff. 136–7.

(1720–1801), Byres (1734–1817), Morison (1732–1810), Cunningham (c. 1741–1793), Nevay and Willison (1780–1848) studied under the neo-classical painter Anton Raphael Mengs. Hamilton and Provan worked with Masucci (c. 1691–1758); Mosman (c. 1700–1771) and Ramsay enrolled as pupils in the studio of Francesco Imperiali (1679–1740). The main tasks of young pupils were to improve their drawing technique, to help their masters with their paintings and to copy the works of the great Italian painters. They generally went to copy paintings in churches and some had the permission to study the works of Michelangelo in the Sistine Chapel and of Raphael in the *Stanze*. Then they often went to study the collection of classical sculptures displayed in the Capitoline Museum and in the Pio-Clementino Museum, which were opened in 1734 and 1771 respectively. The importance of drawing and painting from classical sculptures to their training as is represented in the por-trait of Allan[37] painted by Corvi (1721–1803). Allan, who may have been Corvi's pupil, is shown painting from a cast of the *Borghese Gladiator*.

As the Scots copied Italian paintings and worked side-by-side with Italian artists in the fine art academies or in their studios for several years, they were naturally influenced by Italian painting.

In the eighteenth century, artists believed in the superiority of Italian Renaissance painting and worshipped Michelangelo and Raphael. In the hierarchy of genres of painting history painting was at that time consi-dered the noblest form of art; young artists who wanted to become successful history painters had to draw their inspiration from the greatest Italian Renaissance and Baroque masters. In addition to Raphael and Michelangelo, they had to study carefully the works of Titian and Correggio (1489–1534) as well as the paintings of Annibale Carracci (1560–1609), Guido Reni and Domenichino (1581–1641), who were the leaders of the baroque style. Thus, in Italy, many Scottish painters made copies after these masters; the work of Raphael and Michelangelo was the most studied by these painters, closely followed by the painting of Carracci and Reni.[38]

The Scots were also interested in other painters who were not pop-ular during the eighteenth century. For instance, Raeburn preferred to study the works of Caravaggio and his followers. In his Ph.D. thesis on

---

37. Domenico Corvi, *David Allan*, 1774, Scottish National Portrait Gallery, Edinburgh.

38. Thus, Willison copied the *Madonna della Sedia* and the *Self-portrait* by Raphael; Morison and John Alexander copied the *School of Athens* and *Parnassus* by Raphael. John Runciman studied care-fully Michelangelo and showed his admiration for this Italian master by representing Michelangelo's figure of *Day* in the background of his self-portrait.

Raeburn, David Mackie explained that "Raeburn arrived in Rome a virtual beginner [and] he left [Italy] with a mastery of the art of portraiture that was acquired in a surprisingly brief time".[39] Raeburn's two-year stay in Italy proved very profitable both technically and stylistically as is evident when the portraits he painted before and after his journey are compared. Little is known about Raeburn's activities in Rome, but he painted a *David with the Head of Goliath*[40] after Romanelli (1610–1662), a follower of Reni. The scene represented in Romanelli's painting was one of the favourite subjects of Italian baroque painters and the chiaroscuro reminds us of the first paintings of Caravaggio, who produced three paintings representing the victory of David. We do not know if he copied some of his works but he certainly saw paintings by Caravaggio, the inventor of chiaroscuro whose art was at the origin of an aesthetic revolution at the beginning of the seventeenth century. During his lifetime, Caravaggio's works were controversial but he had many followers in Italy, Spain and the Netherlands. In the eighteenth century he was not generally considered as an example to be followed by young artists, yet quite a few Scottish painters copied his paintings: Skirving copied *The Cardsharps* and *the Fortuneteller*.[41] Throughout his career, Raeburn was interested in lighting effects and the use of dramatic contrast between light and shadow apparent in many of his portraits reveals the influence of the Caravaggisti in his works. In the portrait of Patrick Moir,[42] painted when Raeburn was in Rome, we already find a distinctive interplay of suffused light and deep shadow in small areas which presages Raeburn's interests in the 1790s, when he devised original lighting schemes. A portrait such as *Sir John and Lady Clerk of Penicuik*[43] reminds us of the Caravaggisti's paintings because of the intermingling of strong illumination and deep shadow defining shapes. Owing to the range of colours and to the stark contrast between the intense dark of the background and the shaft of light falling from high on the sitter's right, the portrait of

---

39. David Mackie, *Raeburn Life and Art*, vol. 1, unpublished Ph.D. thesis, University of Edinburgh, 1994, p. 43.

40. Sir Henry Raeburn after Giovanni Francesco Romanelli, *David with the Head of Goliath*, c. 1785–1786, location unknown.

41. For several centuries, the majority of artists and art historians shared Nicolas Poussin's point view concerning Caravaggio. Félibien, who personally knew Poussin (1594–1665), wrote that: "Mr Poussin nous en parloit un jour avec grand mépris. Mr Poussin [...] ne pouvoit rien souffrir du Caravage, & disoit qu'il étoit venu au monde pour détruire la Peinture." (André Félibien, *Entretiens sur les Vies et sur les Ouvrages des Plus Excellens Peintres Anciens et Modernes*, vol. 3, Amsterdam, 1706, p. 128.) If Caravaggio was not popular with artists and grand tourists, it was because the realism of his paintings was contrary to the idealised beauty advocated by Winckelmann and neoclassical artists.

42. Sir Henry Raeburn, *Patrick Moir*, c. 1784–1785, National Gallery of Scotland, Edinburgh.

43. Sir Henry Raeburn, *Sir John and Lady Clerk of Penicuik*, 1792, National Gallery of Ireland, Dublin.

Margaret Macdonald[44] is redolent of the paintings of the Caravaggisti. Some of Raeburn's portraits, as well as the works of his countrymen, show that the Scots were also impressed by some the most popular eighteenth-century Italian painters.

The most famous Italian painters working in Rome during the eighteenth century were: Masucci (c. 1691–1758), Chiari (1654–1727), Pozzi (c. 1700–1768), Luti (1666–1724), Imperiali, Benefial (1684–1764), Conca (c. 1680–1764), Trevisani (1656–1746) and Batoni (1708–1787). Today, apart from Batoni who has recently been rediscovered, all these painters have fallen into oblivion. Batoni is best known for his numerous portraits of travellers. Back in the second half of the eighteenth century, he was the most fashionable portraitist in Rome. His main rival was the German Mengs but he was by far the favourite painter of British grand tourists.[45] At the beginning of his career, Batoni was not specialised in portrait painting. Born in Tuscany, he moved to Rome at the end of the 1720s and worked in the studios of Conca, Masucci and Imperiali. His reputation was first founded on his drawings and on his history paintings. He completed many altar pieces and devotional pictures for various churches in Rome; he also painted scenes taken from classical history and mythology. From 1754, he produced many portraits of travellers; British tourists were particularly fond of Batoni's portraits representing his sitters with a fashionable air of nonchalance among the most celebrated antiquities of Rome. These portraits particularly influenced Scottish painters. When Gavin Hamilton painted the portrait of the Duke of Hamilton,[46] he certainly had Batoni's paintings in mind. Indeed, the Duke's pose and the background showing the forum and the Colosseo are reminiscent of Batoni's work. Raeburn's portrait of Moir also seems to have been influenced by Batoni, whom Raeburn may have met thanks to James Byres. This portrait displays smoothness and a degree of finish unusual for Raeburn at the time but which reminds us of Batoni. Batoni's influence is even more obvious on Allan Ramsay. The two portraitists had been friends since the 1730s, when Ramsay met him in the studio of Imperiali and, whenever he was in Rome, Ramsay saw Batoni regu-

---

44. Sir Henry Raeburn, *Margaret Macdonald, Mrs Scott Moncrieff*, c. 1814, National Gallery of Scotland, Edinburgh.

45. Batoni's popularity with British aristocrats has been stressed by the exhibition entitled *Pompeo Batoni 1708–1787. The Europe of Courts and the Grand Tour* held at the Palazzo Ducale of Lucca from 6 December 2008 to 29 March 2009. Liliana Barroero and Fernando Mazzocca, *Pompeo Batoni 1708–1787. L'Europa delle Corti e il Grand Tour*, Milano, Silvana Editoriale, 2008.
See also Edgar Peters Bowron and Peter Björn Kerber, *Pompeo Batoni: Prince of Painters in Eighteenth-Century Rome*, New Haven–London, Yale University Press, 2007.

46. Gavin Hamilton, *Douglas Hamilton, 8th Duke of Hamilton and 5th Duke of Brandon, with Dr John Moore, and Sir John Moore*, 1775–1777, National Gallery of Scotland, Edinburgh.

larly. Ramsay admired his colleague and, in 1782, he sent his son John to study drawing under Batoni. Moreover, it is very likely that Ramsay recommended his former pupil Gabriel Matthias to enrol in the studio of the Italian painter. During his first two visits in Rome, Ramsay copied several of Batoni's drawings and it is in Ramsay's preparatory drawings that the influence of Batoni can best be seen. Indeed Ramsay's studies dating from the 1730s and the 1740s are so reminiscent of Batoni's that art historians had long attributed some of Batoni's drawings to Ramsay.[47] Ramsay used the same technique as Batoni and their drawings have the same degree of finish and the same delicacy. In *A Man's Hand with a Stave*,[48] which is a typical drawing by Ramsay, he, like Batoni, used red and white chalks to convey the play of light and shadow. The parts of the hand on which light is falling are slightly enhanced with white chalk which defines shape; the shadow is represented by intertwining hatchings. Both painters also used red chalk to draw the outlines.

Many, if not most eighteenth-century Scottish painters chose to go into voluntary exile in Italy in order to further their careers. They could not get thorough artistic training in their native country, so if they wanted to become accomplished painters they had no other option but to leave Scotland. Their self-imposed exile generally lasted from one to three years, but thanks to the financial support of their patrons a few painters were able to remain abroad for a longer period. Only two Scottish painters, Jacob More and Gavin Hamilton, decided to settle permanently in Italy. It is possible that they opted for this permanent exile because they had been unable to find patrons for their work in Great Britain, let alone Scotland. Indeed, very few of the Scottish painters who returned to Britain after their sojourn in Italy were able to work in Scotland because of the lack of patronage. In fact most of them went into another exile in order to open a studio in London, the main artistic centre of Great Britain. This time it is debatable as to whether they were in anyway abroad as Scotland formed one component of the British state. However the fact remains that they were forced to work outside Scotland and so involuntary, albeit commercially lucrative exile is still probably the most appropriate term to describe their relocation.

---

47. For instance, Batoni's drawings *Studies of a Child's Head, Left Arm and Right Hand* (D 2145, prints and drawings collection, National Gallery of Scotland, Edinburgh) and *Studies of Child's Legs, Drapery and a Profile Head of Christ* (D 2146, prints and drawings collection, National Gallery of Scotland, Edinburgh) were attributed to Ramsay: Indeed, they are particularly redolent of Ramsay's drawing for the head and shoulders of Prince George (D 1908, prints and drawings collection, National Gallery of Scotland, Edinburgh).

48. Allan Ramsay, D 2144, prints and drawings collection, National Gallery of Scotland, Edinburgh.

Returning from their exile in Italy, these migrants transformed the Scottish artistic world despite the fact that the majority settled in England rather than "home". Their training abroad contributed to the development and diversification of Scottish painting through the influence it had on other British painters and upon the new academies which were developed in Scotland in the later eighteenth century. These painters had not only improved technically, they were also deeply influenced stylistically by ancient and contemporary Italian art, and their return to Britain ensured future generations would be exposed to both the styles and techniques they picked up abroad. Today, Scottish painting is very often compared with Dutch painting, but until the end of the eighteenth century the influence of Italian painting is clearly visible on Scottish art, and that is in no small part due to the return of the artistic exiles.

List of Scottish painters (including miniaturists and pastellists) who visited Italy between 1701 and 1800

AIKMAN William (birth: 1682–death: 1731): *in Italy from 1707–1711*.
ALEXANDER Cosmo (1724–1772): *1747–1752*.
ALEXANDER John (1686–c. 1766): *1711–1719*.
ALLAN David (1744–1796): *1767–1777*.
ALVES James (1738–1808): *1762–1771*.
BROWN John (1747–1789): *1771–1780*.
BYRES James (1734–1817): *1758–1790*.
CHALMERS George (c. 1723–1791): *c. 1750–1753*.
CLERK James (c. 1745–1800): *1768–1800*.
CLERK Alexander (fl. 1729–1737): *1736–1737*.
COCHRAN William (1738–1785): *c. 1761–1766*.
COCKBURN Patrick: *1726–1727*.
COOPER Richard (c. 1740–1814): *1771–1776*.
CUNNINGHAM Edward Francis (c. 1741–1793): *c. 1745–1765*.
DAY John "MacGilp" (c. 1736–1807): *1756–c. 1765*.
ERSKINE Colin (Nicholas) (c. 1705–1740): *1733(?)–1740*.
ERSKINE David: *1775–1780*.
FORBES Anne (1745–1840): *1767–1771*.
FOULIS James (1770–1842): *1790–1794*.
GRAHAM John (c. 1706–c. 1775): *1726–1727*.
GUTHRIE: *1735*.
HAMILTON Gavin (1723–1798): *1748–1750 / 1756–1798*.
HAY Andrew (d. 1754): *1716–1717 / 1718 / 1720–1722*.
IRVINE James (1757–1831): *1780–1791 / 1797–1798*.

MacLauchlan Archibald (fl. 1762–after 1770): *c. 1762.*

Marshall George (d. 1732).

Martin David (1737–1797): *1755–1757.*

Maxwell James: *1758.*

Moir John (1775–1859): *1792–1797.*

More Jacob (1740–1793): *c. 1773–1793.*

Morison Colin (1732–1810): *1754–1810.*

Mosman William (c. 1700–1771): *c. 1733–1740.*

Nasmyth Alexander (1758–1840): *1783–1784.*

Nevay James (c. 1730–after 1811): *1755–1811.*

Patoun William (fl. 1761–d. 1783): *1761–1763 / 1763–1764 / 1768–1769 / 1773–1774 / 1777.*

Provan Samuel: *1748.*

Raeburn Henry (1756–1823): *1785–1787.*

Ramsay Allan (1713–1784): *1736–1738 / 1754–1757 / 1775–1777 / 1782–1784.*

Read Katherine (1723–1778): *1751–1753.*

Ross George (birth c. 1691?): *1713–1720.*

Runciman Alexander (1736–1785): *1767–1771.*

Runciman John (1744–1768/1769): *1767–1768/1769.*

Skirving Archibald (1749–1818): *1787–1794.*

Smibert John (1688–1751): *1719–1722.*

Taylor John: *c. 1707.*

Willison George (1741–1797): *1760–1767.*

Wilson Andrew (1780–1848): *1799–1803.*

Christian Auer
University of Strasbourg

The transportation of the "Scottish Martyrs" in 1793: a particular form of exile?

Thomas Muir and his companions in misfortune, who later became famous as the Scottish Martyrs, were among the prominent figures of the vast movement for reform that emerged in Britain at the end of the eighteenth century. What makes their case particularly interesting is that these men were sentenced to transportation, a form of exile that needs to be included in any consideration of the themes of exile and return. Drawing on the example of Thomas Muir, this article will investigate the specific nature of political exile. Does the "time" (in the sense of temporality) of political exile differentiate itself from the "time" of other forms of exile? Is political exile characterized by a state of "fundamental discontinuity"?[1] Does the political, intellectual or ideological dimension of political exiles enable them overcome, maybe more than other exiles, the essential sadness of exile? These are some of the questions I propose to address in this paper.

In the seventeenth century the English and Scottish governments viewed the colonies, for example America, as perfectly appropriate places to send miscreants of all kinds, criminals, vagrants, prostitutes or political prisoners. Transportation constituted an instrument of social control whose function was to deter people from resorting to criminal acts. Andrew Fletcher of Saltoun, who was one of the most determined opponents of the Union of 1707, thought, like many of his contemporaries, that the system of transportation was the panacea for solving the endemic problem of vagrancy:

> There are at this day in Scotland [...] two hundred thousand people in Scotland begging from door to door. These are not only no way advantageous, but a very grievous burden to so poor a country [...] in all times there have been about one hundred thousand of those vagabonds who have lived without any regard or subjection either to the laws of the land or even those

---

1. E. Said, *Reflections on Exile and Other Essays*, Cambridge, Harvard University Press, 2000, p. 177.

of God or nature [...] in years of plenty many thousands of them meet together in the mountains, where they feast and riot for many days; and at country weddings, markets, burials, and other the like publick occasions they are to be seen both men and women perpetually drunk, cursing, blaspheming and fighting together. These are such outrageous disorders, that it were better for the nation they were sold to the gallies or West Indies, than that they should continue to be a burden and like upon us.[2]

After the Transportation Act of 1718 was passed, the number of people sentenced to transportation increased regularly: between 1718 and 1755, 700 people were sentenced to transportation by the Scottish courts. This means of sentencing was halted by the American War of Independence of 1776 but resumed in 1787 with a new destination: Australia. Transportation was now seen as a more serious punishment than imprisonment, since it involved exile to a distant land and made return to the home land very difficult. The first convicts (about 750) arrived in Botany Bay in Australia on 20 January 1788, marking the beginning of the most extensive system of forced exile ever to be undertaken by the British government. 80,000 convicts were deported to New South Wales between 1787 and 1840 and 60,000 to Van Diemen's Land in Tasmania between 1803 and 1852. The limited number of Scottish convicts (about 8,000 in total) can be accounted for by the fact that the Scottish legal system of the eighteenth century differentiated from its English counterpart. It was common in England to transport convicts found guilty of minor criminal offences whereas in Scotland the sentence was reserved only for serious offences.

The system of transportation was not unanimously approved of though, and some specialists in criminal law believed that it failed to deter crime and did not lead to the reformation of the convicts. Jeremy Bentham was one of those who wrote extensively about the flaws of the system:

> The main object or end of penal justice is example [...]. Of this property, transportation is almost destitute: this is its radical and incurable defect [...]. The second end or object of punishment is reformation [...]. Under this head, what has been done in the colony of New South Wales? By referring to facts, we shall find, not only that in this respect it has been hitherto radically defective [...]. The third object or end of punishment is incapacitation [...]. The convict, whilst in New South Wales, cannot commit crimes in England; the distance between the two places in a considerable degree precludes his

---

2. A. Fletcher of Saltoun, *The Political Works of Andrew Fletcher*, London, J. Bettenham, 1737, pp. 145–6.

illegal return, and this is the sum of the advantage. Whilst the convict is at Botany Bay, he need not be dreaded in England: but his character remains the same, and the crimes which are mischievous in the mother country are mischievous in the colony; we ought not, therefore, to attribute to this punishment an advantage which it does not possess.[3]

The term Scottish Martyrs is something of a misnomer, as only two of the five convicts who were sent to Australia were Scottish (Thomas Muir and William Skirving, the secretary of the Scottish branch of the National Convention of the Friends of the People). Most historians who have written about the Scottish Martyrs tend to use the term with inverted commas: this is for example the case of Thomas Devine who, in his book about the *Scottish Empire*, refers to the "Scottish Martyrs".[4] Some historians seem to use the notion with even more care, which is the case of Malcolm Prentis who speaks of "the so-called 'Scottish Martyrs'",[5] a process which casts doubts as to the validity of the notion. Yet other historians seem to be less critical of the notion, such as Clive Emsley, who uses the words *Scottish martyrs*,[6] or Frank Clune, the author of a monograph on Muir and his companions, who uses *Scottish Martyrs* without inverted commas.[7]

The political context is obviously most important in understanding the nature of the sentence that was pronounced against this group of Scottish radicals. In the 1790s the British ruling classes were concerned that the revolutionary ideas that had overthrown the French monarchy might spread to Britain and, in their view, contaminate its population. Societies demanding better and fairer political parliamentary representation were created all over Britain. Demonstrations were organised, trees of liberty were planted and some of the protesters went as far as burning effigies of Henry Dundas, the political figure who they felt represented all the evils of a corrupted system. Thomas Muir's trial can only be understood in this context of political instability and social unrest. Thomas Muir was greatly influenced by the French revolutionary ideas and actively militated in favour of parliamentary reform. In October 1792 he was elected to the vice presidency of the Glasgow Associated Friends of the

3. J. Bentham and J. Bowring, *The Works of Jeremy Bentham*, vol. 1, Edinburgh, W. Tait, 1838, pp. 491–5.

4. Th. Devine, *Scotland's Empire and the Shaping of the Americas 1600–1815* (2003), Washington, Smithsonian Books, 2004, p. 277.

5. M. Prentis, *The Scots in Australia*, Sydney, UNSW Press, 2008, p. 47.

6. Cl. Emsley, "Repression, 'Terror' and the Rule of Law in England during the Decade of the French Revolution", *The English Historical Review*, vol. 100, no. 397 (October 1985), p. 832.

7. Fr. Clune, *The Scottish Martyrs: their Trials and Transportation to Botany Bay*, London, Angus and Robertson, 1969.

Constitution and of the People. At the general convention of the Scottish Societies of the Friends of the People in December 1792 Muir read a message from the United Irishmen of Dublin:

> We rejoice that the spirit of freedom moves over the face of Scotland: that light seems to break from the chaos of her government; and that a country so respectable in her attainments in science, in arts and in arms [...] now rises to distinction, not by a calm contented secret wish for a Reform in Parliament, but by openly, actively and urgently willing it, with the unity and energy of an imbodied [sic] nation.[8]

This speech was to have wide-reaching consequences: Muir was accused of propagating seditious ideas undermining the security of the state. He was arrested in January 1793 and released on bail. As he was in Paris at the time of his trial, he was declared an outlaw and struck from the Bar. His trial took place on 30 and 31 August 1793. Muir was accused of taking part in seditious meetings, of accusing the government and the judicial authorities of corruption, of exhorting people to read Thomas Paine's *The Rights of Man* and of reading a message from the *Society of United Irishmen*. Muir rejected all these accusations:

> The Criminal Libel is false and injurious; so far from exciting the people to riot and insurrection, it can easily be proved by a numerous list of witnesses, that, upon every occasion, the Panel exhorted them to pursue measures moderate, legal, peaceable and constitutional. The charge of distributing seditious publications, and of advising the people to read them, is equally false and calumnious.[9]

It appears from the proceedings of the trial that the judges feared that reformers such as Muir might propagate their ideas of reform to the "gullible" working-classes, or to use Lord Braxfield's own words to the "knots of ignorant labourers and herds of poor manufacturers".[10] After a sixteen-hour long trial Thomas Muir was unanimously found guilty and sentenced to 14 years transportation. As Lord Henderland made it clear, Thomas Muir and his unacceptable seditious ideas had to be sent as far away as possible: "What security could we have against his future operations, but a removal from his country, to a place where he could do no further harm."[11]

---

8. Quoted in Fr. Clune, *The Scottish Martyrs*, p. 5.
9. Th. Muir, *The Trial of Thomas Muir, Esq. Younger of Huntershill*, Edinburgh, Alexander Scott, 1793, p. 14.
10. *Ibid.*, p. 45.
11. *Ibid.*, p. 67.

Muir had spoken for about three hours at his trial and had declared that he was convinced his ideas would triumph in the end:

> I can look danger, and I can look death in the face, for I am shielded by the conscience of my rectitude. I may be condemned to languish in the recesses o a dungeon. I may be doomed to ascend the scaffold. Nothing can deprive me of the recollection of the past. Nothing can destroy my peace of mind, arising from the remembrance of having discharged my duty.[12]

Muir could not have been more explicit about one of the essential components of the process of exile, namely the indissoluble attachment to the past, even if Muir did not know when he pronounced these words that he was going to be sentenced to transportation. It is possible to extract a person from their natural geographical environment by force but it is much more difficult to deprive them of their past, of everything that has formed or shaped them. This is exactly what Muir indicated in one of the letters he wrote to his lawyer:

> I leave you and Mrs Moffat perhaps for ever, but your remembrance never shall be effaced from my mind [...] in the remotest corner of the world your remembrance and that of Mrs Moffat will soothe me in my affliction , but my tears shall flow over the remembrance. I am really unwell.[13]

Muir's words clearly express the utter importance of the past for those who are cut from their roots. Incidentally it is interesting to note that Muir did not totally rule out the possibility of going back to Scotland, as exemplified by the words "perhaps for ever". Edward Said, one of the leading figures of post-colonial studies, argues that exile is first and foremost characterised by a state of "fundamental discontinuity".[14] Yet to put the stress on discontinuity, which is undoubtedly a central component of the process of exile, is equivalent to relegating to the background everything that enables the exile to carry on with their trajectory, to establish some continuity between the realities of the past, the dislocation of the present and the uncertainties of the future. The connection between exile and identity has been discussed by numerous critics and historians.[15] Gillian Bourras has written that "exile affects identity since

---

12. Quoted in Fr. Clune, *The Scottish Martyrs*, p. 11.
13. Quoted in Fr. Clune, *The Scottish Martyrs*, p. 14.
14. E. Said, *Reflections on Exile and Other Essays*, p. 177.
15. See for example M. Harper's works such as *Adventurers and Exiles: The Great Scottish Exodus*, London, Profile, 2003 or *Emigrant Homecomings: the Return Movement of Emigrants, 1600–2000*, Manchester, Manchester University Press, 2005.

the past becomes myth and the present reality".[16] It seems to me that associating the past with the notion of myth is equivalent to rejecting the past in some kind of artificial or fictitious place, which is exactly what the past is not for the person in exile. There is no doubt that the exile is bound to idealise the past but it is also true that the exile's past remains an indisputable reality that furthermore enables the exile to confront better the difficulties of the present.

Let us now turn our attention to some of the characteristics of political exile. The counts of indictment against Thomas Muir leave no doubt as to the fact that rather than Thomas Muir as a person, it was his subversive, radical ideas and their potential threat to the authorities and society that were targeted:

> Inciting a spirit of disloyalty and disaffection to the King and the established government,
> Wickedly advising and exhorting persons to purchase seditious publications,
> Wickedly distributing seditious writing,
> Wickedly producing and reading aloud a seditious and inflammatory writing.[17]

Thomas Muir's exile did not concern just the individual himself but all those who shared or were likely to share his political ideas and who thus represented or were likely to represent a threat to the regime. It was a multiple form of exile or a "synecdoche form of exile", the individual Muir representing a body of people united around common values of social change and political reform. The political exile is subjected to a double form of exile, geographical-spatial and ideological. The political discourse and propaganda cannot exist without an audience, which is necessarily absent in a distant and isolated land. The political exile is thus cut from what constitutes their essential being. Robert Hughes has written that "[the dissenter] slipped off the map into a distant limbo, where his voice fell dead at his feet. There was nothing for his ideas to engage, if he were an intellectual [...]. He could preach sedition to the thieves or the cockatoos, or to the wind. Nobody would care".[18] Yet it is precisely the political exile's commitment to a noble cause that enables him to overcome the tragedy inherent to any form of exile. The political exile, like any other exile, is dispossessed of his geographical belonging

16. G. Bourras, "Memories of Living In-between", in A. Luyat and Fr. Tolron (eds), *Flight from Certainty, The Dilemma of Identity and Exile*, Amsterdam, Rodopi, 2001, p. 17.

17. Quoted in Fr. Clune, *The Scottish Martyrs*, pp. 7-8.

18. R. Hughes, *The Fatal Shore: a History of Transportation of Convicts to Australia, 1787–1868*, London, Collins Harvill, 1987, pp. 175–6.

but not of his political ideas: there is a clear discontinuity between being and place but not between being and ideas. The specificity of political exile becomes apparent when compared to other forms of exile. One example that could be given here is that of the thousands of Highlanders who left for America, Canada or Australia in the middle of the nineteenth century; they were the victims of the clearances and the policies of improvement undertaken by the landowners.[19] The newspapers which supported the landed elite and the authorities who were in charge of the emigration schemes insisted on the fact that the emigrants were under no obligation to leave. The *Skye Emigration Society*, the structure that was created at the end of 1851, presented the multiple advantages of the landlords' emigration policies:

> They [the measures] benefited the people they sent out by relieving them from a state of despondency and deprivation, and placing them in a position where they might attain to prosperity and comfort by their own industry; they conferred a benefit on those that remained by relieving them from the incubus of a superfluous population which was now pressing them down; and they also benefitted in the highest degree those colonies which he believed were destined to add to the greatness and wealth of our empire.[20]

Yet numerous peasants of the Highlands decided to leave their lands because they had no real choice. For them exile was all the more traumatic since their homes represented the centre of their world, their point of reference. As Pierre Bourdieu and Abdelmalek Sayad have noted:

> The peasant spirit cannot resist for long to uprooting: the peasant, who is possessed by his land more than his land possesses him, is defined by his attachment to his field and his animals.[21]

For a peasant, the familiar world is his birth place and his whole habitus is based on his surroundings; that is why the uprooted peasant is deeply hurt, so deeply that he can neither understand what is happening to him nor express his confusion. For the Highlander the land also represented the symbolical link between generations: leaving one's land amounted to leaving and betraying one's ancestors. Nobody would deny

---

19. Thomas Muir's political exile and the Highland peasants' socio-economic exile are obviously different in nature; yet the comparison with the Highland peasants' exile seems particularly relevant since a large part of the Highlanders who emigrated in the middle decades of the nineteenth century were directly or indirectly forced to leave their country. Furthermore, studies of Scottish emigration often fail to take into account the specificity of the Highland experience.

20. "Highland Emigration", *The Inverness Courier*, 4 March 1852.

21. P. Bourdieu and A. Sayad, *Le Déracinement*, Paris, Éditions de Minuit, 1964, p. 112.

that the Highlanders left full of the wealth of their past, their culture and their language but their departure represented a tragic dissociation with their environment, a journey towards the "perilous territory of not belonging"[22] that left them in a state of profound existential uncertainty. If one compares the conditions of existence of the Scottish Martyrs to those of the exiled peasants of the Highlands, one realises that the term "exile" can have very different meanings. The Scottish Martyrs, and Thomas Muir in particular, lived in quite comfortable conditions in Australia, if we go by a letter Muir wrote to one of his friends in London:

> I am perfectly well; I am pleased with my situation as much as a person can be who is for ever separated from all they loved and from all they respected […]. I have a neat little house here, and another two miles distant, at a farm across the water.[23]

The situation was radically different for the exiled Highland peasants. Most of them arrived completely destitute, as exemplified by this account of the arrival of a group of emigrants in Canada in November 1851:

> A number of these poor creatures arrived, during last week, in Woodstock. It is truly lamentable to see them trudge along the road, each carrying a heavy load of articles, which, generally speaking, are entirely useless. Many of the females were bare-foot and poorly clad, while the children exhibited much suffering and misery […] the fact of turning them adrift, penniless, on a foreign shore, is a species of cruelty and injustice which should not be permitted to exist.[24]

Thus Thomas Muir was not an exile like other exiles. Contrary to most others he could project himself into the future; he could hope to see his ideas triumph, as Muir explicitly said during his trial:

> Were I to be led this moment from the bar to the scaffold, I should feel the same calmness and serenity which I now do. My minds tells me that I have acted agreeably to my conscience, and that I have engaged in a good, a just and a glorious cause—a cause which sooner or later must and will prevail.[25]

The political exile's ideas serve as a form of connection between the past and the future and enable them to go on constructing their identities. Although *The Telegraph: A Consolatory Epistle* was actually not written

22. E. Said, *Reflections on Exile and Other Essays*, p. 177.
23. Quoted in Fr. Clune, *The Scottish Martyrs*, p. 76.
24. "How forced emigrants fare in America", *The Inverness Advertiser*, 25 November 1851.
25. Th. Muir, *The Trial of Thomas Muir*, p. 70.

by Thomas Muir the poem is interesting to consider since its content is very similar to the letters Muir wrote while he was in exile.[26] The poem is pervaded by sadness and melancholy and conveys the image of helpless convicts:

> From this remote, this melancholy shore;
> Round whose bleak rocks incessant tempests roar:
> Where sullen Convicts drag the clanking chain,
> And desolation covers all the plain;
> My heart, dear DEAN, with anguish turns to you,
> And mourns the scenes, just opening to your view.[27]

The poem also demonstrates that Muir did not renounce his commitment to liberty and democracy:

> Like me you fall—"a martyr in the cause,
> Of *truth*, of *justice* and of *injur'd laws*".[28]

The rebel spirit cannot be vanquished, whatever the circumstances may be:

> The best and noblest privilege in hell
> For souls like ours is, boldly to rebel;
> To rear the standard of revolt, and try
> The happy fruits of lov'd democracy.[29]

This constant and unbending commitment to democracy can also be perceived in the different letters Muir wrote in 1796 while he was in Monterey. In a letter written to the Earl of Stanhope, Muir reaffirmed his attachment to justice and constitutional rights:

> My mind, firm and erect, rises superior to affliction, and that when I descend into the tomb, my enemies will be unable to impeach my consistency.[30]

---

26. Some historians attribute the poem to Th. Muir; see for example T. Devine who writes that "Thomas Muir in *The Telegraph: A Consolotary* [*sic*] *Epistle*, a long poem to his friend Henry Erskine, began by describing the landscape of exile" (Devine, *Scotland's Empire*, p. 277) or R. Hughes who mentions the "lengthy poem Thomas Muir addressed to his fellow reformer Henry Erskine in Scotland" (R. Hughes, *The Fatal Shore*, p. 178). Yet the catalogue of the National Library of Scotland clearly indicates that the poem was actually written by George Hamilton, a minister of Gladsmuir.
27. G. Hamilton, *The Telegraph: a Consolatory Epistle*, Edinburgh, 1796, p. 2.
28. *Ibid.*, p. 3.
29. *Ibid.*, p. 8.
30. Quoted in Fr. Clune, *The Scottish Martyrs*, p. 117.

In another letter written to MP Charles James Fox, Muir indicated that he intended to do everything he could to save his country and to bring democracy to his country.[31]

Let us briefly mention some elements of the remaining part of Thomas Muir's life journey. Muir managed to flee from Botany Bay in February 1796 thanks to the help of the captain of an American ship. Muir then went to Monterey, Havana and Cadiz; he arrived in Paris in December 1797 where he died on 26 January 1799. Muir managed to come back to Europe but his return from exile was only partially achieved since he never returned to his country of origin.

To conclude, it would seem that political exile is different from other forms of exile; the political exile can perhaps retain a fundamental part of their identity more than other exiles. By establishing an ideological bridge between past, present and future, political exiles can transcend the sorrow inherent to any form of exile and up to a certain point continue to develop themselves without losing all of their roots. Two other examples taken from the same historical period tend to confirm the view that the transfer from one place to another cannot totally destabilise the political exile. Thomas Paine was charged with sedition in 1792 because of the anti monarchical views he had expressed in the *Rights of Man* and he was forced to flee to France to avoid prosecution. It was in exile that he completed his last major work, *The Age of Reason* (1794–1796). William Cobbett, who was forced into exile to the United States between 1817 and 1819, managed to continue his political activity through the publication of the *Political Register*. It would be hard to deny that the judges who sentenced Thomas Muir to transportation reached their goal, i.e. to prevent Muir from "poisoning" society through his subversive ideas. But if we keep in mind the following words by Emmanuel Levinas, who argues that exile is a form of violence that "consists less in hurting or annihilating than in interrupting, in making people play parts in which they find themselves lost or in making them betray their commitments or their own substance",[32] then it would seem that the judiciary authorities that condemned Muir to exile did not succeed totally in their aim since Muir never betrayed his commitment to values of reform, freedom, justice and democracy.

---

31. *Ibid.*, p. 118.
32. Quoted in M. H. Alaoui, "Rupture et incertitude, deux invariants des trajectoires d'exil", *Euroorient*, no. 29, 2009, p. 6.

Bibliography

ALAOUI Myriam Hachimi, "Rupture et incertitude, deux invariants des trajectoires d'exil", *Euroorient*, no. 29, 2009, pp. 7–22.

BENTHAM Jeremy and BOWRING John, *The Works of Jeremy Bentham*, vol. 1, Edinburgh, W. Tait, 1838.

BOURRAS Gillian, "Memories of Living In-between", in Anne Luyat and Francine Tolron (eds), *Flight from Certainty, The Dilemma of Identity and Exile*, Amsterdam, Rodopi, 2001, pp. 17–25.

BRIGGS John, *Crime And Punishment In England An Introductory History*, London, UCL Press, 1996.

BOURDIEU Pierre and SAYAD Abdelmalek, *Le Déracinement*, Paris, Éditions de Minuit, 1964.

CLUNE Frank, *The Scottish Martyrs: their Trials and Transportation to Botany Bay*, London, Angus and Robertson, 1969.

DEVINE Thomas, *Scotland's Empire and the Shaping of the Americas 1600–1815* (2003), Washington, Smithsonian Books, 2004.

EMSLEY Clive, "Repression, 'Terror' and the Rule of Law in England during the Decade of the French Revolution", *The English Historical Review*, vol. 100, no. 397 (October 1985), pp. 801–825.

FLETCHER OF SALTOUN Andrew, *The Political Works of Andrew Fletcher*, London, J. Bettenham, 1737.

HAMILTON George, *The Telegraph: a Consolatory Epistle*, Edinburgh, 1796.

HARPER Marjory, *Adventurers and Exiles: The Great Scottish Exodus*, London, Profile, 2003.

—, *Emigrant Homecomings: the Return Movement of Emigrants, 1600–2000*, Manchester, Manchester University Press, 2005.

HUGHES Robert, *The Fatal Shore: a History of Transportation of Convicts to Australia, 1787–1868*, London, Collins Harvill, 1987.

MUIR Thomas, *The Trial of Thomas Muir, Esq. Younger of Huntershill*, Edinburgh, Alexander Scott, 1793.

PRENTIS Malcolm, *The Scots in Australia*, Sydney, UNSW Press, 2008.

SAID Edward, *Reflections on Exile and Other Essays*, Cambridge, Harvard University Press, 2000.

Gordon Pentland
University of Edinburgh

Radical Returns in an Age of Revolutions

In 1795, James Kennedy, a Paisley weaver and Assistant Secretary to the British Convention held in Edinburgh in 1793–94, published a collection of verse entitled *Treason! Or Not Treason! Alias the Weavers Budget*. Poems such as "Common Sense" and "Swinish Gruntings" and dedications to "The Majesty of the People" bore the unmistakable imprint of Painite ideology and of the intense debate surrounding the French Revolution. Kennedy also wrote consciously from the authorial perspective of a "Scotch Exile" and provided a prefatory stanza for the reader:

> Chas'd from my calling to this hackney'd trade,
> By persecution a poor Poet made—
> Yet favour court not—scribble not for fame;
> To blast Oppressors is my only aim.
> With pain I started from a private life;
> In sorrow left by Children and my Wife!
> But though fair Freedom's foes have turn'd me out,
> At every resting place I'll wheel about,
> And charge the Villains!

Kennedy was not, however, enduring his exile at the penal colony of Botany Bay nor even "across the water" in Europe or North America. He was, in fact, in London, having fled Edinburgh on the discovery of the Pike Plot in 1794. In London he seems to have become part of a small knot of Scottish émigrés orbiting round the radical publisher, Daniel Isaac Eaton (Harris, 2008, pp. 104–5). What Kennedy's versifying does indicate is the centrality of ideas of "exile" to the language and symbolism of popular politics.

There are a number of very good reasons as to *why* exile was such a prominent theme in radical movements and an obvious reference point for men like Kennedy. First, it was admirably suited to the rhetorical resources of popular culture. Many of Kennedy's verses, along with those of other Jacobin poets, were set to Jacobite tunes, which evoked similar themes of exile and loss. Others, such as "Skirving's Farewell to his Country", were set to popular songs dealing with these themes, in this case Allan Ramsay's "Farewell to Lochaber" (One of the Herd, 1794, p. 10).

Second, and more importantly, exile, following on from trial, dramatized the conflict between the state and radical reformers (Epstein, 1996, pp. 22–51; Davis, 2005, pp. 148–58). Part of what Kennedy was doing in styling himself as a "Scotch Exile" in London was joining in a critique which was being levelled against Scottish institutions by opposition Whigs as well as Paineite radicals in the 1790s. Their argument was that Scottish institutions, Scottish law in particular, were more draconian and more tyrannical than their English equivalents. The debates surrounding the sentences of transportation passed on Thomas Muir and Thomas Fyshe Palmer gave parliamentary Whigs such as Charles Fox an opportunity to denounce this evidence of "the infamous fabric of Scottish persecution", while Charles Grey claimed that "Scotland had no more liberty, than it had under the race of the Stuarts" (*Parliamentary History*, 1817, cols. 1300, 1563). Similarly, Kennedy suggested he was little different from those displaced by persecution and despotism elsewhere in Europe—he had fled the tyranny of Scottish law for the relative freedoms afforded by "exile" in England.

Dwelling on the theme of exile proved politically useful at different times and in different contexts. For example, in a radical movement of dwindling numbers in the mid-1790s the exile of Muir and his companions galvanized the existing membership of the reform societies and attracted new recruits (Harris, 2008, pp. 99–100; McFarland, 1994, p. 105). Later, in the period surrounding the first reform bill in the 1830s and the emergence of the Chartist movement, exile was dwelt on as a characteristic crime of unreformed and arbitrary Tory government (Tyrell, 2004, pp. 25–56). This flexibility made exile a central concern to radicals.

This centrality is reflected in the historiography, which privileges those "martyrs" exiled from their country. The exiles of the 1790s, in particular, are the celebrities of the historiography, the worthy subjects of both academic and populist biographies and even operas (Bewley, 1983; Macmillan, 2004; Scottish Opera, 2004). While all histories of radicalism make much of trial and exile as transformative moments in the *internal* histories of their subject, even studies that have followed the "martyrs" into exile have not followed them on their return.

This essay addresses the neglected flipside of this privileged theme of "exile" and explores the idea of radical "return". There were two episodes of multiple transportations from Scotland during the period preceding the Reform Acts: first, the "Scottish Martyrs" transported in the 1790s (three of whom, of course, were not Scottish); and second, the nineteen men who were transported for their involvement in the abortive "general rising" of 1820. Both of these episodes provide only a limited sample of radical returnees. Of the Scottish Martyrs of the 1790s only one returned to Britain. Of the nineteen transported after 1820, only two returned. Nevertheless, the experiences of these three men provide a useful insight into how the ideas of exile and return featured in radical political culture.

The Scottish Martyrs[1] of the 1790s were transported to Botany Bay for sentences of between seven and fourteen years for their involvement in radical politics and, in particular, their participation in a series of Conventions that met in Edinburgh between 1792 and 1794 (Pentland, 2004, pp. 340–60). Only one man returned to Britain and he was not one of those who had been born or lived in Scotland. Maurice Margarot had played a prominent role as chairman of the radical London Corresponding Society, formed in 1792. He was selected as one of the Society's delegates to attend the British Convention in Edinburgh, which sat between November and December 1793 before it was dispersed by the authorities and its leadership (including Margarot himself) arrested. Margarot had flamboyantly arrived at the High Court of Justiciary for his trial dressed as a French Revolutionary and walking underneath a triumphal arch of a "liberty tree" in the shape of an "M" (Cockburn, 1888, II, p. 23–4). He was deliberately confrontational throughout his trial and carried this into his experience of exile. In New South Wales, Margarot quickly gained a reputation as a trouble maker. When, for example, Joseph Holt, a prominent United Irishman exiled after the rising of 1798, arrived in the colony it was to Margarot's house that he was first invited. The following morning, Holt was warned by Captain Johnstone that "you lodged in the most seditious house in the colony" (*Memoirs*, 1838, II, p. 73).

On his return from exile in the middle of 1810 Margarot re-engaged with radical politics (Roe, 1958, pp. 75–6). He was afforded an opportunity to give evidence to the select committee on Transportation and denounced a system of corruption and arbitrary punishment, peculation and monopoly in the stores (*Report*, 1812, pp. 52–5). 1812 seems to have been the turning point, at which Margarot's activities took on something of their old character and he became, once again, a figure of considerable interest to those in authority. This was a year of profound crisis

1. The Scottish Martyrs are usually seen as being comprised of five men: Thomas Muir, Thomas Fyshe Palmer, Joseph Gerrald, William Skirving, and Maurice Margarot. Sometimes George Mealmaker (tried and transported in 1798) and Robert Watt (executed in 1794) are also included.

in the British state, which was suffering from a severe recession caused by the dual impact of the Orders in Council and Napoleon's blockade, while government was faced with the escalating disruption associated with Luddism and the aftermath of the only assassination of a British Prime Minister.

Margarot chose this moment to throw himself back into politics with two pamphlets: *Thoughts on Revolution* and *Proposal for a Grand National Jubilee*. Both demonstrated that his radical sentiments remained undimmed. The latter developed the idea of a redistributive jubilee. This was a biblical concept with a key role in the metropolitan ultra-radicalism of the followers of Thomas Spence, and has been characterized as involving a kind of parish-based communism (Chase, 1990, pp. 138–40). Margarot's experience of exile in Australia, where radical land schemes might be seen as applicable, may well have moved him closer to the position held by Spence's supporters. Finally, this one-time exile was not afraid to risk imprisonment again, apparently travelling to France to attempt to encourage Napoleon to invade England and restore the Saxon constitution (Prothero, 1981, p. 89).

Of most interest for this essay, however, is the fact that Margarot made two kinds of return to Scotland between 1811 and 1812. The first involved revisiting his experiences in Scotland. He had returned from exile in penury and part of his activity was a desperate scrabble to make ends meet. At the same time he sought to maintain a rhetoric of manly "independence" for his radical colleagues. He expressed this in a letter to one of them declaring that "I would rather fall with such than live to associate with public Depredation & partake of the public plunder" (HO102/22, f. 533, Maurice Margarot to Arthur Kidder, 26 Nov. 1812). He made these claims in spite of a quite extraordinary letter he addressed to Henry Dundas, first Viscount Melville, the bête noire of Scottish radicals, on 23 May 1811. Margarot had intended to send it but, in the covering letter to Melville's son and heir, he made it clear that he had been rudely interrupted by the death of Lord Melville on 27 May. The letter itself is one of the most brazen of the many begging letters in the Melville papers. It offered Melville, on his death bed, a unique opportunity to atone for his sins in having had Margarot transported:

> Your Lordship may now avail yourself of that timely repentance & in some measure attone [*sic*] for your unjust persecution of an individual unknown & unoffending [...] seize the opportunity my Lord. Let not the Grave enclose you unrepenting or me unredressed—the Vanities of the World now recede both from your Eyes & from mine—futurity open[s] to our view—worldly grandeur falls upon the sense & a just judgement from an all discerning Judge

is at hand—you my Enemy I admonish—be my Enemy no more—you my unjust persecutor redress a part of my wrongs. (GD51/6/1782, ff. 1–2.)

The unrepentant radical asked his persecutors to repent on his return. It does not appear from the papers that any compensation was forthcoming.

The following year, however, Margarot physically returned to Scotland, where he was watched and followed very carefully. There was a flurry of activity to try to get an accurate description of him into circulation. And *because* he was watched so closely, the returned exile affords the historian glimpses of tenacious radical networks it would otherwise be very difficult to identify. So, for example, in Paisley Margarot dined with Archibald Hastie, a baker who had been a delegate to the British convention in 1793 and was the leader of Paisley radicalism for decades (HO102/22, f. 629, John Connell to Lord Sidmouth, 22 Dec. 1812). In Edinburgh one of his contacts was the solicitor William Moffat, a friend of Thomas Muir, who had fled Edinburgh following the suppression of the Convention (Harris, 2008, p. 162). Other contacts, stated the Lord Advocate, "were known to me formerly when I was an active Member of the Committee of the Goldsmiths Hall Association which was formed for supporting the Constitution in December 1792" (HO102/22, f. 556, Archibald Colquhoun to Sidmouth, 2 Dec. 1812). Clearly, Margarot could still rely on the support of radical connections made in the 1790s and apparently reported to his associates in London that: "He found the good old conventional & Republican Party in that part of the Kingdom [Scotland] to be as determined as ever" (HO102/22, f. 537, Sidmouth to Colquhoun, 27 Nov. 1812).

Of more concern for the authorities was exactly what Margarot was doing in Scotland. He was, apparently, unguarded and injudicious in his language. It was reported that "his conversation when he first came from Carlisle in the Stage Coach was open & violent, in censuring every thing here & in praising Bonaparte even for the murder of Captain Wright" (HO102/22, f. 525, Colquhoun to Sidmouth, 22 Nov. 1812). There was concern that Margarot, who had also been touring the disturbed north of England, was attempting to politicize the massive weavers' strike of 1812. And he was certainly working at the publication of his two pamphlets (HO102/22, ff. 455, 509, Colquhoun to Sidmouth, 4 and 15 Nov. 1812). What comes across from the authorities is a sense of panic that this returnee was acting as that bogey of febrile loyalist imaginations, the radical emissary, sent out from London to "poison the minds of the lower orders". The Home Secretary was certainly concerned that "there are at this time in Scotland materials for this Man & his associates to work upon, which are highly favourable to their malignant designs" (HO102/22, f. 537, Sidmouth to Colquhoun, 27 Nov. 1812).

From the point of view of the history of radicalism, the most interesting and the most plausible explanation is the one forwarded by John Connell, the Sheriff of Renfrewshire, following the interrogation of those with whom Margarot had associated and the examination of their papers. He suggested that Margarot was an integral part of Major Cartwright's attempts to reorient and revive the parliamentary reform movement in 1812, through the circulation of printed petitions and the establishment of Hampden clubs. Several of those who Margarot contacted had letters from Cartwright in their possession (HO102/22, ff. 629, 648, Connell to Sidmouth, 22 and 25 Dec. 1812). And Margarot was the obvious choice for this kind of endeavour. The returned exile, the victim of persecution, was the perfect vehicle with which to attempt to revitalize the reform movement. It is likely that those radicals who were visited by Margarot were also those who offered hospitality to Major Cartwright himself on his proselytizing tour three years later in 1815, an event typically seen as kickstarting postwar Scottish radicalism (Roach, 1970, pp. 17–25; *Life and Correspondence*, 1826, II, pp. 110–7).

So, Margarot was a returned radical whose ardour apparently remained undimmed; who could use pre-existing contacts to tour the north of England and Scotland and provides some insight into the tenacity of these radical networks; and whose status as a returned exile proved to be politically useful. Historians know virtually nothing about radical politics in Scotland between 1800 and 1815, but the return of Margarot offers some valuable clues as to where they might look and suggests that it might be necessary to rethink the chronology of Scottish radicalism.

The life histories of the martyrs of the 1790s have been more assiduously researched than those of other transportees. They were wealthier, more literate and better connected than those men who were to follow them to Botany Bay. The abortive general rising across the west of Scotland in April 1820 had the air of a movement of desperation rather than one of aspiration. Indeed, post-war popular radicalism between 1815 and 1820 attracted a social constituency that was more monolithic than had been the case for the movement of the 1790s and the Union Societies of 1819–20 recruited heavily in the weaving communities of the central belt, Tayside and Perthshire. In the historiography of the 1820 rising itself, it is those who were "martyred" in the most obvious sense, by giving up their lives, whose names are indelibly associated with events: Andrew Hardie, John Baird and James Wilson. Besides these three, however, nineteen other men were transported for their involvement. They have attracted some attention—notably from the descendants of one of the men (Macfarlane, 1981). It was only in 1993, after a prolonged restoration in the 1980s, that the names of these transported men were added to the monument that had been raised in 1847 in Sighthill Cemetery in Glasgow (Ellis and Mac a'Ghobhainn, 2001, p. XI). This monument itself, and others, demonstrate that the memory of 1820 played an important role in political culture and language in the nineteenth and twentieth centuries (Pentland, 2008). The two men who came back from Botany Bay—Thomas McFarlane and Andrew White—offer useful case studies of how their own exile and returns contributed to the continuing "usability" of 1820 in radical politics.

The role of McFarlane was particularly prominent. In contradisctinction to his peers, he was not a young man even in 1820. Born in Glasgow in 1775 or 1776 he had played an active role in the radical movement of the 1790s and was residing in Condorrat at the time of the abortive general rising (Macfarlane, 1981, p. 38). He had been one of the men who had gone with Baird and Hardie to Bonnymuir and had faced and engaged the troops. He also had the dubious distinction of being one of the men seriously injured in the affray, having sustained a sabre cut across his face. He was transported to Botany Bay for his offences and, after the King granted an Absolute Pardon in 1836, he returned to Scotland in 1839 (*Caledonian Mercury*, 2 Dec. 1839).

What is interesting is how he was treated when he returned. On 15 January 1840 he was fêted by the Working Man's Association of Airdrie, a Chartist Society, which held its second annual soirée in his honour. The members marched out of Airdrie with a band and banners to meet McFarlane in Glenmavis. There were a number of speeches, which were reported in the press, and the public address from the Association amply demonstrated the purpose of the event. Political movements, of course, always appeal to the past as well as to the future. Parading veterans is one powerful way of achieving this appeal. The Association reminded McFarlane of his involvement in reform since the 1790s, when he had apparently swallowed a compromising piece of paper on which was written an illegal oath. Speakers dwelt, however, on his involvement at Bonnymuir, pointing out that he still bore the scar "a convincing proof of the merciful disposition of a Tory government" (*Scottish Patriot*, 25 Jan. 1840). Interestingly, *all* newspaper reports in which McFarlane featured mentioned his scar—both his physical presence and his damaged body served to dramatize the conflict on which radical rhetoric focused. Entertainment at the soirée was provided by the singing of "Dark Bonnymuir", a composition by one of McFarlane's fellow transportees, Allan Barbour Murchie, which had been published in 1820. The audience was also treated to a performance by the talented Misses Fraser, the daughters of another man who had been "out" in 1820, John Fraser the editor of the *True Scotsman* (Fraser, 1879, pp. 20–9). All told, McFarlane's reception was a consummately "1820" event and demonstrates how the memory of the rising was being used within radical political culture.

This was not the end of McFarlane's involvement in radical politics. 1841 saw an enormous gathering of Chartists in Glasgow to meet Fergus O'Connor, who was visiting the city. "Macfarlane of Condorrat, the aged Bonnymuir martyr" was given pride of place at the table in the evening sitting alongside O'Connor and was presented with "a handsome ebony staff, silver-mounted, and a sovereign to pay his travel expenses" (*Northern Star*, 16 Oct. 1841). McFarlane's presence helped to emphasize a central theme of the rest of O'Connor's visit, during which opportunities were taken not only to mention and draw comparisons with the 1820 rising but physically to escort O'Connor to the sites and relics associated with it. In Stirling, he was taken to the Castle and shown where Baird and Hardie had been executed; he was taken to the dungeon where the prisoners had been held; and he was shown the pikes used by the Radicals, which were held in the armoury (*Northern Star*, 6 Nov. 1841).

In this way, the return of McFarlane allowed Chartists both to confirm the "Radical War" as a foundational moment and to draw parallels with their own conflict with the state. In newspaper reports McFarlane and earlier radicals were co-opted as the "pre-cursors of Chartism" or even more simply as "Chartists". McFarlane contributed to the continuing memory of the events of 1820, which would see the monument raised in Sighthill in 1847. Indeed, "the venerable Macfarlane" with his "sabre wound" was a prominent guest at the dinner commemorating the anniversary of the executions and celebrating the recent erection of the monument (*Glasgow Saturday Post*, 11 Sept. 1847).

The memory of the events of 1819–20 could be used in different ways: to support physical force and insurrectionary violence or to justify resistance or as a warning against the dangers of physical force (Pentland, 2008, pp. 153–7). For it to be usable at all, however, required a stock of memories, images and relics on which to hang these various interpretations. A returned radical provided the perfect foil. McFarlane clearly was not much of a speaker—there are only a couple of mumbled lines of thanks recorded at dinners in his honour. He was not, however, there to speak. He was far more important as a mute physical relic of the rising, his scar and venerability making him an object to be displayed, a peg on which various interpretations could be hanged.

As far as it is possible to ascertain, Andrew White, the other returnee, came back to no mass meeting and there were no soirées in his honour. White, who had been a mere boy of sixteen when he had appeared in arms at Bonnymuir, was a "lucky" transportee. On arrival in Australia he was made a house servant to a progressive master, Dr Douglass, who was interested in the rehabilitation rather than the punishment of convicts. He secured an absolute pardon in February 1824, fully twelve years before his peers, and returned to Britain with his master immediately (Macfarlane, 1981, p. 57–60).

He is harder to trace in the records, but White clearly also became an active Chartist. A very slim notice in the *Northern Star* reports that he addressed a crowd in the People's Hall in Birmingham in 1849 on his involvement in the rising (9 June 1849). Again, there was an obvious political purpose—amidst agitation for a pardon for transported Chartists such as John Frost, who had led the Newport rising of 1839, the political capital of transportees was high.

Perhaps the more interesting facts about White do not concern his life, but rather his death. White died in Glasgow Infirmary in November 1872 and a short notice in the *Glasgow Herald* recorded: "He is to be interred today in Sighthill Cemetery, and in accordance with his dying request his body will be laid in the same grave which contains the remains of Baird and Hardie" (23 Nov. 1872). There has been some dispute as to whether White is, in fact, buried alongside Baird and Hardie (Macfarlane, 1981, p. 60). The intention was, however, clear. This was to be the ultimate physical return, White having his bones mingled with those of Baird and Hardie and asking different generations to contemplate the events of 1820.

This flow of information about the radical war, which has made its reshaping and reimagining possible, was maintained by more than the physical returns of individual transported radicals. Letters were sent back from Botany Bay, which were intended for publication and conveyed subtle political messages. Such letters, like those of other emigrants, often praised their new homes in terms which made unflattering comparisons with the Scotland from which they had been transported. William Smith, for example, was enthusiastic about the economic freedom afforded in New South Wales, where there was "no rent, no taxes, and most part of the land bears two excellent crops every year"; Andrew White could report that he was "more comfortable than when in Scotland" and both he and Thomas McCulloch included positive news about the other transportees (*Copy*, 1821; *Copy*, 1822; *Caledonian Mercury*, 27 Sept. 1824).

Indeed, some of the transported men deliberately sought their freedom by returning items to Scotland. Most notably, John McMillan encouraged the radical journalist Peter Mackenzie to pursue the campaign for their pardon by sending back items which would help him make the case. In 1834, for example, McMillan (having somehow read Mackenzie's account of the "spy system", which had brought disaster for the radicals in 1820) sent Mackenzie his journal, with a view to publication, and a pair of "Radical Boots" or shackles, presumably to help to dramatize the transportees' fate (GD185/1, f. 2, 17 Aug. 1834). McMillan, however, did not himself return to Scotland like McFarlane and White and instead he made a success of his new life in Australia. Tellingly, however, he tried to perpetuate the memory of 1820 in the colony itself. He named one of his farms "Thrushgrove", in conscious salute to Turner of Thrushgrove, who had allowed a monument to be erected to Hardie and Baird on his estate in 1832 (*Manchester Times*, 21 Nov. 1840).

In looking at these few men who did return to Scotland from political exile, it would be difficult to draw any profound conclusions from such a small sample. Exile and return as a theme does, however, speak to two historiographical currents within the study of popular politics. First, the work of James Epstein, Iain McCalman and others has vastly expanded our perceptions of what constitutes the "political" and has encouraged historians to study symbolic practices and what might broadly be called the political culture of popular movements. Exile played an important role in shaping radical culture and examining the activities of returned exiles provides one way of looking at this. In particular, the *historicity* of popular politics—the ways in which radicals looked to the past to create political identities and push agendas in the present—is highlighted by the experiences of these returnees.

Secondly, scholars are increasingly examining various themes within a wider "British world" rather than within narrowly defined national boundaries. There have been recent and convincing calls to "globalize the age of reform". Achieving this would involve not only waving goodbye to exiles as they exit one national historiography and enter another, but also following men such as Margarot, McFarlane and White into exile and exploring those roles they played within popular politics on their return.

Bibliography

Manuscript sources

National Archives of Scotland, Edinburgh, Melville Castle Papers, GD51/6/1782.

National Archives, London, Home Office Correspondence (Scotland), HO102/22.

William Patrick Library, Kirkintilloch, Peter Mackenzie Papers, GD185/1.

Newspapers

Caledonian Mercury.
Glasgow Evening Post.
Glasgow Herald.
Manchester Times.
Northern Star.
Scottish Patriot.

Printed

A SCOTCH EXILE [James Kennedy], *Treason! or Not Treason! Alias the Weavers Budget*, London, 1795.

BEWLEY Christina, *Muir of Huntershill*, Oxford, Oxford University Press, 1983.

CHASE Malcolm, "From Millennium to Anniversary: The Concept of Jubilee in Late Eighteenth- and Nineteenth Century England", *Past & Present*, no. 129, Nov. 1990, pp. 132–47.

COCKBURN Henry, *An Examination of the Trials for Sedition which have hitherto Occurred in Scotland*, Edinburgh, 2 vols, 1888.

Copy of a Very Interesting Letter from Botany Bay, Glasgow, 1821.

Copy of a Very interesting Letter which was received in Glasgow on Wednesday last from Andrew White, Glasgow, 1822.

DAVIS Michael T., "Prosecution and Radical Discourse during the 1790s: The Case of the Scottish Sedition Trials", *International Journal of the Sociology of Law*, vol. 33, no. 3, September 2005, pp. 148–58.

ELLIS Peter Berresford and MAC A'GHOBHAINN Seumas, *The Scottish Insurrection of 1820*, Edinburgh, John Donald, revised edition, 2001.

EPSTEIN James, "'Our Real Constitution': Trial Defence and Radical Memory in the Age of Revolution", *Re-reading the Constitution: New Narratives in the Political History of England's Long Nineteenth Century*, James Vernon (ed.), Cambridge, Cambridge University Press, 1996, pp. 22–51.

FRASER James Roy, *Memoir of John Fraser, Newfield, Johnstone*, Paisley, 1879.

HARRIS Bob, *The Scottish People and the French Revolution*, London, Pickering & Chatto, 2008.

Life and Correspondence of Major Cartwright, F. D. Cartwright (ed.), London, 2 vols, 1826.

McFARLAND E. W., *Ireland and Scotland in the Age of Revolution*, Edinburgh, Edinburgh University Press, 1994.

MacFARLANE Margaret and Alastair, *The Scottish Radicals Tried and Transported for Treason in 1820*, Stevenage, Spa Books, 1981.

MacMILLAN Hector, *Handful of Rogues: Thomas Muir's Enemies of the People*, Glendaruel, Argyll Publishing, 2005.

Memoirs of Joseph Holt, General of the Irish Rebels, in 1798, T. Crofton Croker (ed.), London, 2 vols, 1838.

ONE OF THE HERD, *Husks for Swine: Dedicated to the swine of England, the rabble of Scotland, and the wretches of Ireland*, Edinburgh, 1794.

The Parliamentary History of England, from the earliest period to the year 1803, William Cobbett (ed.), London, T. C. Hansard, 1817, vol. 30.

PENTLAND Gordon, "Patriotism, Universalism and the Scottish Conventions, 1792–94", *History*, vol. 89, no. 295, July 2004, pp. 340–60.

—, "'Betrayed by infamous spies'? The Commemoration of Scotland's 'Radical War' of 1820", *Past and Present*, no. 201, November 2008, pp. 141–73.

PROTHERO Iowerth, *Artisans and Politics in Early Nineteenth-Century London: John Gast and his Times*, London, Methuen, 1981.

Report from the Select Committee on Transportation, London, HMSO, 1812.

ROE Michael, "Maurice Margarot: A Radical in Two Hemispheres, 1792–1815", *Bulletin of the Institute of Historical Research*, vol. 31, no. 83, May 1958, pp. 68–78.

SCOTTISH OPERA, *Friend of the People: An Opera in Three Acts with a Prologue*, London, Boosey & Hawkes, 2004.

TYRELL Alex and DAVIS Michael T., "Bearding the Tories: The Commemoration of the Scottish Political Martyrs of 1793–94", *Contested Sites: Commemoration, Memorial and Popular Politics in Nineteenth-Century Britain*, Alex Tyrell and Paul A. Pickering (eds), Aldershot, Ashgate, 2004, pp. 25–56.

Céline Sabiron
Sorbonne-Paris IV

Homecoming and Liminality
in Walter Scott's *Guy Mannering*[1]

"He cannot deny, that, looking round upon the dreary region, and seeing nothing but bleak fields, and naked trees, [...], he did for some time suffer melancholy to prevail upon him, and wished himself again safe at home" (I, 1: 3): Walter Scott's *Guy Mannering* opens on this epigraph, a quotation from Samuel Johnson[2] which serves as a motto for the whole novel. The idler, the Londoner Will Marvel, feeling estranged and yearning for home, while lost in the wilder and more desolate county of Devonshire, mirrors most of the characters of Scott's fiction. Whether a tourist, like the Englishman Guy Mannering visiting the north of England and extending his "tour into the adjacent frontier of the sister country" (I, 1: 3), or an outcast, like the orphan Brown and the gypsy Meg Merrilies, the exile is temporarily or permanently away from his home—epitomized by a house or a family—or even his homeland. Either internal or external, either involuntary as the result of abduction, expulsion, and banishment,[3] or, in a more figurative sense, self-imposed and prompted by business or curiosity, the exilic journey is accompanied by a feeling of disorientation and homesickness, a "crippling sorrow of estrangement",[4] especially among the Scots in an age marked by the "consolidating of national consciousness".[5] Both displaced and out of place, the exile is an eccentric[6] outsider leading his decentred life outside habitual order,[7] and longing to return home.

---

1. All quotes from Walter Scott's *Guy Mannering, or the Astrologer* are taken from the Edinburgh UP 1999 version, edited by P. D. Garside.

2. S. Johnson, "The Idler", No. 49 (Saturday, 24 March 1759), *The Works of Samuel Johnson*, vol. 2., W. J. Bate and others (ed.), New Haven, Yale UP, 1963, p. 154.

3. "Exile originated in the age-old practice of banishment. Once banished, the exile lives an anomalous and miserable life, with the stigma of being an outsider." (E. Said, *Reflections on Exile and other Essays*, Cambridge, Harvard University Press, 2000, p. 181.) Exile is literally the state of being forced to leave one's own country and live in another, especially for political purposes or as a punishment.

4. E. Said, *Reflections on Exile*, p. 173.

5. A. Lincoln, "Walter Scott and the Birth of Nation", in *Romanticism*, vol. 8, April 2002, p. 3.

6. "eccentric" from Greek *ekkentros*, meaning "out of the centre".

7. "Exile is life led outside habitual order. It is nomadic, decentered, contrapuntal" (Said, p. 186).

Whereas the first pages of *Guy Mannering* deal with emigrations, i.e. outward movements away from home, most of the novel focuses on the counter-journey, i.e. the return home. Homecoming is a concept based on a dynamic motion backward to a former home. No longer homeless outcasts and not yet home owners, homecomers are thus in an inbetween, liminal[8] state, standing at the threshold between home and abroad. Their liminality is symbolized by their transitional position as guests taking refuge at hospitable landlords' before settling back home as their own landowners: "Hospitality [...] identifies the hero as guest in preparation for his own part as host, as landlord; it marks the transition between exile and home."[9] The young English artist Dudley, the Scottish farmer Dandie Dinmont, and even the gypsy Meg Merrilies offer Brown, alias Henry Bertram, both assistance and lodging on his return home.

If Walter Scott chooses to centre his plot on the return rather than the exile, it is owing to the much more liminal, and therefore problematic, status of homecomers: "*Guy Mannering* emphasizes *returning* populations [...]. Though their leaving and the time of their exile might be an occasion for sentiments of loss and sadness, Scott's novel turns to focus on their *return*, precluding, or at least complicating, such nostalgia."[10] Indeed, the feeling of nostalgia does not necessarily fade away with homecoming as both concepts are semantically linked by the Greek word *nostos*[11]; hence the complicated mixed feelings of achievement and longing, of restitution and deprivation experienced by homecomers. Is the return home a restoration, a re-establishment, or even an improvement after the loss and the feeling of regression brought about by the exile? The novel thus raises the question of the relationship between home and abroad, and more largely between the centre and the periphery, by focusing on the liminal concept of homecoming.

Guy Mannering presents different types of homecomers driven by a search for a home and a self. These homeward-bound exiles inhabit a liminal space—at the margin of society and at the edge of the country— and a liminal time between linear and cyclical chronology. And yet, returning home does not lead to homecoming. The latter can only take place within the literary home created by the author.

---

8. "liminality" from Latin *limen*, meaning threshold.

9. I. Duncan, *Modern Romance and the Transformations of the Novel: The Gothic, Scott, Dickens*, Cambridge, Cambridge UP, 1992, p. 120.

10. A. Bardsley, "In and Around the Borders of the Nation in Scott's *Guy Mannering*", in *Nineteenth-Century Contexts*, vol. 24, no. 4, 2002, p. 399.

11. *Nostos* is the Greek word for homecoming: it expresses a yearning for a place, while nostalgia (from Greek *nostos* + *algos* meaning pain, grief, distress) suggests a longing for the past. The concept of homecoming combines these two spatial and temporal notions, with home being a place in time.

Homecomers in Transit through Spatial and Temporal Liminalities

The homeward-bound displaced converging towards one home, the Ellangowan property

Walter Scott's *Guy Mannering* is peopled with homeward-bound exiles, be they individuals or communities, be they rightful or self-proclaimed home owners. Henry Bertram, whose homecoming is at the heart of the diegesis, is early depicted as "a little wanderer" (I, 8: 40; later "a harassed wanderer" [III, 1: 243]) enjoying adventurous rambles around the family home of Ellangowan. As Deborah Epstein Nord has commented: "The miniature exiles and returns of his earliest childhood adventures are replayed in the exile abroad and return to the Scotland of his adulthood."[12] Henry is indeed abducted by a German smuggler and carried away from his Scottish home and homeland ("I left Scotland, which is my native country" [III, 2: 247]) to the foreign country of Holland, and then India. Even though he feels a very instinctive, sentimental, and almost patriotic attachment to Scotland,[13] his homecoming is unintentional and directly linked to his romance with Julia Mannering whom he follows up north to Scotland after she has settled down at Woodbourne with her father, Colonel Guy Mannering. Like Homer's Odysseus, the exiled Henry longs to return home to his Penelope-like Julia after his partaking, not in the Trojan War but, in the Indian war fought to establish an imperial control over the British colony.

The gypsies are also doubly exiled from home, as they are both a Diaspora[14] people, expelled from their alleged fatherland, "the land of Egypt" (II, 18: 231), and an "exiled community" (I, 8: 42) banished from their "city of refuge" (I, 7: 37) after trespassing on the "forbidden precincts" (38) of the Ellangowan property. This fault, akin to the Fall in the *Genesis*, causes the Exodus[15] of these mock Israelites led by their female Moses described as "the wild chieftainess of the lawless people"

---

12. D. E. Nord, "A 'Mingled Race': Walter Scott's Gypsies", in *Gypsies and the British Imagination, 1807–1930*, New York, Columbia UP, 2006, p. 37.

13. "Despite my Dutch education, a blue hill to me is as a friend, and a roaring torrent like the sound of a domestic song that hath soothed my infancy. I never felt the impulse so strongly as in this land of lakes and mountains" (I, 21: 115).

14. "Diaspora, like exile, is a concept suggesting displacement from a center. [...] *Exile* suggests pining for home; *diaspora* suggests networks among compatriots. Exile may be solitary, but diaspora is always collective." (Naficy, p. 20.)

15. For an extensive comparison between the gypsies' exodus and the biblical Exodus, see the parallels between the community's expulsion by the officers (I, 8: 41) and the destruction of the Egyptians by the exterminating angel of the Lord (*Exodus*, 12, 7-13).

(III, 16: 340). Despite their former nomadic[16] habit the gypsies long to return home to Derncleugh where they had settled and erected a few huts: "They had been such long occupants, that they were considered in some degrees as proprietors of the wretched sheelings which they inhabited" (I, 7: 37). The new sedentary lifestyle of "these old settlers" (38) is attested through the lexical field of immobility, with words such as "stationary" (37) and "harboured" (37) which convey the image of a ship finally dropping her anchor at a homely port after endless voyages across the seas. The notion of stasis is further brought forward by the anaphoric repetition of the adverbial pair "still, however": "Still, however, the gypsies made no motion to leave the spot which they had so long inhabited" (I, 7: 39); "Still, however, they showed no symptoms either of submission or of compliance" (I, 8: 41). If the adverb "still" signifies "nevertheless", it is also endowed with the adjectival meaning of "motionless", thus echoing the negative noun phrases referring to the gypsies' inertia ("no motion", "no symptoms").

Not only individuals or communities but also nations as a whole can feel exiled from home. The 1707 Act of Union merging England and Scotland together is interpreted by many Scots as an annexation of their country governed from London. Henceforth, the Scottish people features at the margin of the new kingdom of Great Britain and feels alienated from the centers of British power.[17] The Scottish history of inner-colonization and exclusion is thus replayed in the story of *Guy Mannering*: the Scots' dispossession of their own homeland is indeed re-enacted through the dismembering of the Bertrams' home, a "diminished property" (I, 2: 9) in which the family feel sequestered and exiled after many a reduction of their possessions through the centuries.[18] The part of the invading colonizer is acted by the learned English serviceman, Colonel Guy Mannering, an expatriate "Indian Nabob" (I, 14: 81) who, after making a fortune in Eastern India, now aims to return to Ellangowan and fulfill his early self-proclaimed promise to make the Bertrams' property his home: "'How happily', thought our hero, 'would life glide on in such a retirement! [...] Here then, and with thee, Sophia!'" (I, 4: 22), he

---

16. Contrary to exile, nomadism dispenses with the idea of a fixed home or a centre.

17. For the emergence of a Scottish nationalism and patriotism, see Andrew Lincoln's article entitled "Walter Scott and the Birth of the Nation".

18. Godfrey Bertram's son, Dennis Bertram, "was obliged to mortgage half of the remaining moiety of his paternal property" (I, 2: 8); "The appriser, therefore, (as the holder of a mortgage was then called,) entered upon possession, and [...] cut the family out of another monstrous cantle of their remaining property." (I, 2: 9.) Lewis Bertram, the father of the present owner, "sold parts of the land, evacuated the old castle, where his family lived [...] [and] pulling down part of these venerable ruins, he built a narrow house [...] which was the New Place of Ellangowan" (I, 2: 9).

daringly declares. His feeling of belonging is repeatedly hinted at in the narrative: "It may seem strange, that Mannering was so much attached to a spot which he had seen only once, and that for a short time, in early life" (I, 19: 102), or "he felt a mysterious desire to call the terrace his own" (I, 19: 102). If home can feel outlandish, abroad can also feel like home. Therefore, Walter Scott's novel deals with three joined stories of homecoming, all converging towards the same home, that is to say the Ellangowan property.

Margin and Marginality: From the Periphery to the Centre

While trying to return home, the homeward-bound displaced are in transit, living in a grey area in between two homes. They are marginals confined to the margin of society and the outskirts of the country. "[M]uch estranged from general society" (I, 2: 12), the Ellangowan family stands in between two social castes. No longer part of the landed gentry after his financial difficulties and not yet part of the yeoman class, Godefroy Bertram is a "gentleman farmer": "These occupations encroached, in [...] [the lairds'] opinion, upon the article of Ellangowan's gentry, and he found it necessary gradually to estrange himself from their society, and sink into what was then a very ambiguous character, the gentleman farmer" (I, 2: 9–10). The class title reflects his liminal status as the compound noun is written in a spaced form which brings together the two conflicting nouns "gentleman" and "farmer" without connecting them.

Another inter-class character, Gilbert Glossin is a parvenu, a member of the minority *nouveaux riches* discriminated against by the "Old Money" sects of society for lack of historical and genealogical prestige:

> [H]e was excluded from the society of the gentry of the country, to whose rank he conceived he had raised himself. He was not admitted to their clubs, and at meetings of a public nature found himself thwarted and looked upon with coldness and contempt. Both principle and prejudice co-operated in creating this dislike; for the gentlemen of the county despised him for the lowness of his birth, while they hated him for the means by which he had raised his fortune. (II, 11: 171)

Socially excluded from the gentry, this upstart is also scorned by the working class who deprive him of his home by refusing to acknowledge his new territorial appellation of Ellangowan after his purchase of the property: "With the common people his reputation stood still worse. They would neither yield him the territorial appellation of Ellangowan, nor the usual compliment of *Mr* Glossin;—with them he was bare Glossin" (171).

The most marginalised characters belong to the lowest order of the working castes; they are vagabonds, drifters and criminals. Branded as "the *Parias* of Scotland" (I, 7: 37), the gypsies are both outcasts and out-laws. Meg Merrilies is altogether a "[h]arlot, thief, witch, and gypsey" (I, 3: 15), which sets her four times as much aside from society. Her exotic and iconic turban ("a large piece of red cotton cloth rolled about her head in the form of a turban" [I, 8: 43]) casts her as both out of place and out of time in Enlightened Scotland: "the turban signifies being past one's prime and out of place, if not out of fashion."[19] Neither man, nor fully woman with her gigantic size and her "masculine stature" (II, 2: 123), neither native, nor foreign with her outfit composed of both national and Eastern[20] features, she is the epitome of the liminal character.

Socially but also geographically excluded, the exiles find shelter on the fringe of a territory or on the periphery of a country. They live in limbo, either in desert wastelands or on the wild sea, like the permanent exile, the Dutch contraband trader Dick Hattaraick. The Waste of Cumberland, that English barren stretch of land, that moorish void running up to the border with Scotland, shelters many smugglers, vagrants, and criminals, who make this wild country their home as illustrated by the two armed ruffians' violent attack on Dandie Dinmont (125). Henry Bertram himself falls victim to a gang of "mendicant strollers" (II, 7: 148) as he crosses the Scottish Borders on his way home to Ellangowan: "the thieves shared his property", a "portemanteau contain[ing] various articles of apparel, a pair of pistols, a leathern case with a few papers and some money, &c. &c." (150). Doubly deprived of his identity after the theft, the young outcast hides in the Marches and merges with the blank snow-white landscape around him. Hunted down as an outlaw after injuring Charles Hazelwood he first undertakes to flee to some peripheral coun-tries such as "Ireland or the Isle of Man" (II, 10: 170), before resolving "to escape for the present to the neighbouring coast of England, and to remain concealed there" (III, 1: 237). His crossing and re-crossing of the Solway Firth, a geographical threshold between the two adjacent coun-tries, symbolize the passage from immature youthfulness to unabashed manhood. Too impulsive and vindictive to come home, Henry must first come to term with himself before he can acknowledge his name, accept his lineage, and claim the Ellangowan property as his home. Living on

---

19. J. Lewin, "Legends of Rebecca: Ivanhoe, Dynamic Identification, and the Portraits of Rebecca Gatz", in *Nashim: A Journal of Jewish Women's Studies and Gender Issues*, vol. 10, September 2005, p. 189.

20. She was "[e]quipt in a habit which mixed the national dress of the Scottish common people with something of an eastern costume" (I, 4: 23).

the margin, at the periphery of both the society and the country, home-comers are thus driven by a centripetal force homeward. They move from the periphery to the centre, but come home through "trap-doors and back-doors" (I, 21: 112) as Henry metaphorically puts it.

A Liminal Time Caught between Linearity and Circularity

If homeward-bound exiles live in a liminal space, they also live in a liminal time caught between past and future. The time-flow of the homecoming story is frequently broken up by a shift between fortune-telling, i.e. journeys into a predicted but uncertain future, and anamnesis, i.e. returns to a fixed and homely past. The first few chapters are forward-looking and mostly dedicated to foretelling as the fortune-teller and the astrologer use their occult powers to uncover the destiny of the Laird of Ellangowan's first-born. Spinning a thread and singing incantations, the prophetess Meg Merrilies measures up the loops wound between her forefinger and thumb to predict Henry Bertram's future, while Guy Mannering resorts to his "imaginary science" (I, 4: 20) and studies the position of the main planets to "calculate [...] [the boy's] nativity according to the rule of the Triplicities, as recommended by Pythagoras, Hippocrates, Diocles, and Avicenna" (I, 3: 16). Both predict three misfortunes and the "horoscope" (I, 4: 21) proves right.

The narrative, exiled from its chronological sequence, is left oscillating between its natural course forward and its desperate attempt at turning back time to replay the scene of the Fall and twist the tragic ending. The catastrophic turn of events of volume I, chapter 9 brings the diegesis to a climax and freezes it; hence the recurring allusions to the past scene of Henry's disappearance. This event of olden days keeps looming back throughout the narrative to haunt the characters: Glossin is so tormented by the return of Henry Bertram that at night his mind is assailed by a "mental phantasmagoria" (II, 12: 183) in which the heir is "approaching to expel him from the mansion-house of his fathers" (183). The homely past is also constantly revived through Henry's blurred memories of his youth. The anamnesic process is released by his encounter with the gypsy (II, 1: 123) and above all by his return visit to Ellangowan from volume III onwards. Henry's homecoming is at once intimated by the narrator's renaming of his main character: "Brown, (whom, since he has set foot upon the property of his fathers, we shall hereafter call by his father's name of Bertram)" (III, 2: 243). The recovery of his family name marks the first implacable step towards the restoration of his family home. The confrontation between the returning heir and the new *de facto* landlord emphasizes Henry's symbolic repossession of the Ellangowan property before its legal restitution in volume III, chapter 19. Henry gains ground both literally, by stepping onto the property of his ancestors, and metaphorically, through his gradual recollection of the past. Conversely, Glossin retreats both physically, by "staggering back two or three paces" (III, 2: 245) when encountering Henry, and verbally, by the very short, vague ("extremely cautious in his replies"; "suppressing for obvious reasons the more familiar sound of Bertram"; "evasive answer"; "do not exactly know"; "something of that kind"; "only answered by a nod") and hesitating replies ("N—n—no—not ours"; "—mine is—mine is—"; "compressed muttering") which he makes to Henry's volley of questions:

> Glossing [was] [...] speaking as if his utmost efforts were unable to unseal his lips beyond the width of a quarter of an inch, so that his whole utterance was a kind of compressed muttering, very different from the round bold bullying voice with which he usually spoke. Indeed, his appearance and demeanour during all this conversation seemed to diminish even his strength and stature, so that he withered as it were into the shadow of himself, now advancing one foot, now the other, now stooping and wriggling his shoulders, now fumbling with the buttons of his waistcoat, now clasping his hands together—in short, he was the picture of a mean-spirited, shuffling rascal in the very agonies of detection. (III, 2: 247)

Deprived of a motto ("mine is—") and his name questioned ("Glossin—Glossin?"), the upstart is actually dispossessed of Ellangowan in this very scene. His gradual fading away ("diminish"; "withered"; "shadow of himself") contrasts with Henry's progressive ascendancy and self-assertion. To the closed questions—"your name is Brown?" and "Vanbeest Brown?"—which Glossin puts to Henry, the latter does not reply in the affirmative but only answers with counter-questions—"And what of that, sir?"—as if he did not fully acknowledge the assumed name of Brown as his own any longer. His search for a self comes to an end when the faded black and white picture of the past is eventually coloured in by his final hunt in the caves of Ellangowan:

> The scene, independent of the peculiar moral interest and personal danger which attended it, had, from *the effect of the light and shade* on the uncommon objects which it exhibited, an appearance emphatically dismal. The *light* in the fire-grate was the *dark*-red glare of charcoal in a state of ignition, relieved from time to time by a *transient flame of a more vivid or duskier light*, as the fuel with which Dirk Hatteraick fed his fire was better or worse fitted for his purpose. Now a *dark cloud* of stifling smoke rose up to the roof of the cavern, and then *lighted* into a reluctant and sullen *blaze*, which flashed wavering up the pillar of smoke, and was suddenly rendered *brighter* and *more lively* by some drier fuel, or perhaps some splintered fir-timber, which at once converted

the smoke into flame. By such fitful irradiation *they could see*, more or less distinctly, the form of Hatteraick, whose savage and rugged cast of features, now rendered yet more ferocious by the circumstances of his situation and the deep gloom of his mind, assorted well with the rugged and broken vault, which rose in a rude arch over and around him. (III, 15: 332, my italics.)

The red glow flaming up the black and white hues serves as a metaphor of Henry's homecoming.

Besides, Scott often sets the scenes of his novel between light and darkness, so that the most meaningful episodes take place at twilight, just at the equipoise between sunset and sunrise: Ellangowan is first presented "an hour after midnight" (I, 3: 18). Henry's journey homeward to Scotland happens at night ("spending the whole night upon the firth" [III, 1: 241]), while the scene preceding his return home, the attack on the jail of Portanferry where he is kept prisoner, occurs "at the hour of midnight" (III, 9: 293). If homecomers evolve in a chronological time caught between past and future, day and night, they also evolve in a cyclical time as shown in the myth of the Eternal return (Eliade).

After exiling their tenants from the Ellangowan property the Bertrams are then, in turn, expelled from their home by Gilbert Glossin ("the last of their descendants [...] expelled, a ruined wanderer, from his possessions!" [I, 13: 73]), who is subsequently dispossessed of his newly-acquired home. The last scene of the novel mirrors the first one; the ending meets the beginning; the triple exile from the Ellangowan home leads to a triple return to the property. This cyclical movement is further developed by the constant reference to astronomy. The vocabulary of planetary and astral revolution permeates the narrative: Dominie Sampson is an "unexpected satellite" (I, 15: 83) revolving in "the orbit in which [...] Godefroy Bertram, Esq. J. P. must be considered as the principal luminary" (I, 6: 34), with a pun on the word "luminary" referring to a person of prominence, but also to one of the celestial bodies. This spiral motion suggests the image of the vortex, which is the movement of a flow rapidly and constantly spinning around a centre. The three movements homeward—centripetal, chronological, and above all cyclical—contribute to paving the way for a complete homecoming. And yet, even though the diegesis follows a circular pattern, it does not come full circle: the homecoming topos is a "recovery myth".[21]

---

21. J. Wilt, *Secret Leaves: The Novels of Walter Scott*, Chicago, UCP, 1985, p. 25.

A Return Narrative, or the Composition of a Literary Home

Coming Home without Homecoming

Despite Henry Bertram's re-establishment in his own home as a returned heir ("the creditors did not hesitate to recognise Bertram's right, and to surrender to him the house of his ancestors" [III, 19: 353]), there is no satisfying homecoming at the end of the novel. The Ellangowan property is fully handled by Colonel Guy Mannering, who pays for the family's former debts and "superintend certain operations which he had recommended to Bertram" (III, 19: 353). The latter's home is to be replaced by "a large and splendid house, which […] [is] to be built on the site of the New Place of Ellangowan, in a style corresponding to the magnificence of the ruins in its vicinity" (353). Henry's passivity and effacement in the Ellangowan projects puts his homecoming into question. He is a mere "Scottish pawn"[22] in the hands of an English imperialist who composes Henry's fortune ("[u]pon inspecting this paper, Colonel Mannering instantly admitted it was his own composition" [III, 18: 348]) from his birth by drawing a scheme of nativity. He is a character *in absentia* who leaves Guy Mannering in charge of ending both the Ellangowan tragedy and the novel: "the association of Brown/Bertram's approach to the land with Mannering's […] qualifies any sense that his return home is a restoration."[23] Likewise, with Henry Bertram's legal rights to the property fully recognized, Guy Mannering's return is also challenged as their homecomings are mutually exclusive.

As for Meg Merrilies, she expires in her own bed in her half-destroyed cottage at Derncleugh: "To the Kaim o' Derncleugh—the Kaim o' Derncleugh— the spirit will not free itself o' the flesh but there" (III, 16: 336), the dying gypsy insists, while producing the key to her former home. "In death, Derncleugh is still a place of belonging, but the old relationship with the big house is never re-established",[24] and "there is no textual evidence that her deathbed wish for the reconstruction of Derncleugh, to make amends for earlier 'clearances' by Harry's father, is ever carried out".[25] At the end of the novel Henry has only "gone to plan out a cottage at Derncleugh" (353), and this textual silence makes the gypsy's home-

---

22. J. M. D'Arcy, *Subversive Scott: the "Waverley Novels" and Scottish Nationalism*, Reikjavik, University of Iceland, 2005, p. 83. See the link between Henry's fortune and Scotland's fate: both Ellangowan and Scotland go on being under English imperial rule despite the Scots' nationalist attempt at reclaiming their country and regaining their independence.

23. A. Bardsley, "In and Around the Borders of the Nation", p. 408.

24. J. Reed, *Sir Walter Scott: Landscape and Locality*, London, Athlone Press, 1980, p. 76.

25. J. M. D'Arcy, *Subversive Scott*, p. 82.

coming quite problematic too: "The final un-figuring of Meg would represent a betrayal more devastating in its effects than the elder Bertram's original sin in evicting the Gypsies."[26] If there are returns home, there is no homecoming in *Guy Mannering*. Indeed, home is less a place than a concept.

Home as a Utopia

If home was briefly thought to be a heterotopia[27] embodied by the Ellangowan property sheltering tourists, outcasts, and outlaws, it quickly appears that the Ellangowan home is only a utopia, an imaginary and indefinitely remote place: "Kippletringan was actually retreating before him in proportion to his advance" (I, 1: 5). The position of the village seems subjected to the passersby's judgements as if it were a mere figment of their imagination:

> Kippletringan was distant at first "*a gay bit*". Then the "*gay bit*" was more accurately described, as "*aiblins three miles*"; then the "*three miles*" diminished into "*like a mile and a bittock*"; then extended themselves into "*four miles or there awa*"; and, lastly, a female voice [...] assured Guy Mannering, "It was a weary lang gait yet to Kippletringan, and unco heavy road for foot passengers." (I, 1: 4)

This pattern of physical and psychological estrangement is constantly repeated throughout the novel. The closer to home Henry Bertram moves, the stranger and further away it seems, as if home were a mere chimera. On his first return home to Scotland, the thick layer of snow recovering the country makes the once familiar landscape look totally unfamiliar:

> The scene, which we have already described in the beginning of our first volume, was now covered with snow [...]. A landscape covered with snow [...] has, both from the association of cold and barrenness, and from its comparative infrequency, a wild, strange, and desolate appearance. Objects, well known to us in their common state, have either disappeared, or are so strangely varied and disguised, that we seem gazing on an unknown world. (II, 12: 184)

The strange blend of the familiar and the unfamiliar conjures up the Freudian concept of the "uncanny", *das Unheimliche*, literally "un-home-ly".

---

26. P. Garside, "Meg Merrilies and India", in J. H. Alexander and D. Hewitt (eds), *Scott in Carnival*, Aberdeen, Association for Scottish Literary Studies, 1993, p. 168.

27. M. Foucault, "Dits et écrits, *Des espaces autres*" (conférence au Cercle d'études architecturales, 14 March 1967), in *Architecture, Mouvement, Continuité*, 5 October 1984, pp. 46–9.

Ellangowan[28] is so barely outlined in the novel that it is even called by the very vague and indefinite name of "the Place" (I, 1: 6), while the two buildings erected on the property are respectively called "the Auld Place" and "the New Place" (I, 1: 7). Dandie Dinmont's home is similarly named "the town": "This was the farm-steading of Charlieshope, or, in the language of the country, 'the town'" (II, 3: 128). Homes and homelands are so indistinct that Scotland is just a mirror image of India: the parias of Scotland, nicknamed the "Maroons of Derncleugh" (I, 8: 41), live "like wild Indians among European settlers" (I, 7: 37). Both Guy Mannering's friend, Mr Mervyn, and Henry Bertram's companion, Dudley, compare themselves to wild Indians: "I am as free as a wild Indian" (I, 21: 115), the artist claims.

Neither here nor there, neither fully real nor utterly unreal, home is ungraspable and indefinable; it is the ultimate non place. To be able to return home the characters must first confront reality and history; hence Henry Bertram's short visit to the historic Roman Wall (II, 1: 118) on his way back to Ellangowan. Yet, the young Scotsman fails to grasp the true meaning of the "celebrated work of antiquity" (118) and only moralizes on the grandeur of the Romans before soon "remember[ing] he was hungry" (118). This ironic punch line brings about Henry's failure at confronting history and foretells that his return home will not be a homecoming.

A Narrative Return and a Paper Home: From Homeland to Homepage

Homecoming can only take place within the homely space of literary writing. *Guy Mannering* offers a narrative return and draws a paper home. The narrative hinges around Henry Bertram's tentative homecoming, so that the actions preceding his return are concentrated in the first eleven chapters. The story even jumps five years ("years had rolled on, and [...] little Harry Bertram [...] now approached his fifth revolving birthday" [I, 8: 40]) and then seventeen years forward to accelerate the pace of the narration: "Our narrative is now about to make a large stride, and omit a space of nearly seventeen years [...]. The gap is a wide one [...]" (I, 11: 59). The large stride, this "chasm in our history" (59) already announced by the epigraph ("I slide / O'er sixteen years, and leave the growth untried / Of that wide gap.—" [I, 11: 59]) and heavily insisted upon in the course of the chapter ("about seventeen years after the catastrophe narrated in the last chapter" [59]), is then followed by a slow tread

---

28. "gowan" is the Scottish generic word for daisy, which is the symbol of innocence and purity, but also of transience.

forward dealing with Henry's homecoming. The decelerated narrative dedicates its remaining three hundred pages to his return, while spanning over only two months, November and December. A final acceleration occurs in the last chapters once Henry has returned home.

Besides, the narrative is constantly brought back home to the heart of the plot dealing with the characters' homecoming: "Our narrative now recalls us for a moment to the period when young Hazelwood received his wound" (III, 1: 237); "we return to the party at Woodbourne" (III, 13: 322); "we must return to Bertram and Dinmont" (III, 14: 327). These anaphoric references to narrative returns are often stressed as they appear in capital letters at the very beginning of a new chapter: "WE RETURN to Portanferry, and to Bertram and his honest-hearted friend" (III, 8: 291), or "WE MUST now return to Woodbourne, which it may be remembered we left just after the Colonel had given some directions to his confidential servants" (III, 10: 296).

Homecoming remains prospective in *Guy Mannering*, and Scott uses this interspace, the liminal space between the homecoming project and the actual but never completed homecoming, to create his own literary home. Names of homely places are erased or invented by Scott to help him build an ideal home for his story: Henry Bertram "reached [...] the village which we have called Portanferry (but which the reader will in vain seek for under that name in the county map)" (III, 1: 237). "The function of many of the actual place names are kidnapped by Scott to create, directly or obliquely, a past space in which his own manufactured toponyms find room and can be accommodated" (Nicolaisen, 141). And the characters are co-writers drawing the outline of their dream homes:

> [Dominie Sampson] was suddenly summoned by Mannering to assist in cal-culating some proportions relating to a large and splendid house, which was to be built on the scite of the New Place of Ellangowan, in a style correspon-ding to the magnificence of the ruins in its vicinity. Amid the various rooms, the Dominie observed, that one of the largest was entitled THE LIBRARY; and snug and close beside was a well-proportioned chamber, entitled, MR SAMPSON'S APARTMENT. —"Prodigious, prodigious, prodigious!" shouted the enraptured Dominie. (III, 19: 353)

Dominie Sampson's home takes the shape of a paper apartment adjoined to a huge library, while Guy Mannering's home is a paper bungalow: "And do you propose to continue at Woodbourne?", the lawyer Pleydell asks. "Only till we carry these plans into effect—see, here's the plan of my Bungalow" (III, 19: 355). Drawing their environment with paper and pencils, they also defend their homes by building barricades of books (II, 10: 166).

To conclude, homecomers—be they long-time owners abducted away from their family home, wandering gypsy communities banished from their temporary home, or homeless tourists moving away from their host's sheltering home—are border-line characters living on the fringe of society, on the edge of the country, and inhabiting a liminal time between past and future, day and night, linearity and circularity. Standing at the periphery, they long to settle back home and move to the centre. Yet, the home of their choice, Ellangowan, is a remote and barely outlined property located on the Borders, at the frontier between England and Scotland. The main centripetal movement is thus threatened by an underlying centrifugal force bringing them back to the periphery. Ellangowan can only become a centre through Walter Scott's creative narrative, which puts this peripheral home at the heart of the plot, and turns it into a literary home for both the characters and the reader.

Caught in a "tale of private life"[29] the reader is drawn away into the very heart of the story, thus inhabiting the literary home created by the author. Made intimate with the characters' private lives and personal thoughts through their correspondence, the reader goes through the looking glass, crosses the story frame to evolve inside the novel along-side the protagonists who become his acquaintances ("the old woman, whom the readers have already recognised as their acquaintance Meg Merrilies" [II, 1: 121]), or even his friends: "our friend Dinmont" (II, 16: 216). Sharing his home with the other characters conjured up by the author's imagination, he has "the privilege of looking over [Guy Mannering's] shoulder as he writes [...]" (I, 12: 68) in the room of an inn at Kippletringan. But is it not Walter Scott's last master stroke that, whereas he aims to write a "return home" story, he ironically ends up exiling his readership to a fictitious and romanticized Scotland?

Bibliography

BARDLEY Alyson, "In and Around the Borders of the Nation in Scott's *Guy Mannering*", in *Nineteenth-Century Contexts*, vol. 24, no. 4, 2002, pp. 397–415.

D'ARCY Julian Meldon, *Subversive Scott: the "Waverley Novels" and Scottish Nationalism*, Reikjavik, University of Iceland, 2005.

DUNCAN Ian, *Modern Romance and the Transformations of the Novel: The Gothic, Scott, Dickens*, Cambridge, Cambridge UP, 1992.

---

29. W. Scott, *Familiar Letters of Sir Walter Scott*, D. Douglas (ed.), Edinburgh, 1894.

ÉLIADE Mircéa, *Le mythe de l'éternel retour : archétypes et répétitions*, Paris, Gallimard, 2001.

FOUCAULT Michel, "Dits et écrits, *Des espaces autres*" (conférence au Cercle d'études architecturales, 14 March 1967), in *Architecture, Mouvement, Continuité*, 5 October 1984.

GARSIDE Peter, "Meg Merrilies and India", in J. H. Alexander and David Hewitt (eds), *Scott in Carnival*, Aberdeen, Association for Scottish Literary Studies, 1993, pp. 154–71.

JOHNSON Samuel, "The Idler", No. 49 (Saturday, 24 March 1759), *The Works of Samuel Johnson*, vol. 2, W. J. Bate and others (ed.), New Haven, Yale UP, 1963, p. 154.

LEWIN Judith, "Legends of Rebecca: Ivanhoe, Dynamic Identification, and the Portraits of Rebecca Gatz", in *Nashim: A Journal of Jewish Women's Studies and Gender Issues*, vol. 10, September 2005, pp. 178–212.

LINCOLN Andrew, "Walter Scott and the Birth of Nation", in *Romanticism*, vol. 8, April 2002, pp. 1–17.

NAFICY Hamid (ed.), *Home, Exile, Homeland: Film, Media, and the Politics of Place*, New York, Routledge, 1999.

NICOLAISEN W. F. H., "Onomastic Interaction in the Waverley Novels", in J. H. Alexander and David Hewitt (eds), *Scott in Carnival*, Aberdeen, Association for Scottish Literary Studies, 1993, pp. 133–44.

NORD Deborah Epstein, "A 'Mingled Race': Walter Scott's Gypsies", in *Gypsies and the British Imagination, 1807–1930*, New York, Columbia UP, 2006, pp. 21–43.

REED James, *Sir Walter Scott: Landscape and Locality*, London, Athlone Press, 1980.

SAID Edward W., *Reflections on Exile and other Essays*, Cambridge, Harvard University Press, 2000.

SCOTT Walter, *Guy Mannering, or the Astrologer* [1815], P. D. Garside (ed.), Edinburgh, Edinburgh UP, 1999.

—, *Familiar Letters of Sir Walter Scott*, David Douglas (ed.), Edinburgh, 1894.

TRUMPENER Katie, *Bardic Nationalism: The Romantic Novel and the British Empire*, Princeton, Princeton UP, 1997, pp. 184–92.

WILT Judith, *Secret Leaves: The Novels of Walter Scott*, Chicago, UCP, 1985.

Lesley Graham
Victor Segalen University, Bordeaux 2

The Displaced Naturalist: W. F. Campbell's life of exile in Normandy

Few would argue that the concept of home is not intimately linked with the notion of place. People are born into and evolve in attachments that are always based in a place and this natural environment is of quite fundamental importance in the formation of a sense of self. Attitudes to these places are socially constructed, and, to some extent, conditioned by a mental hierarchy associated with the movement of capital from place to place. This paper explores one textual example of what comes about when a person is forced for economic reasons from the area in which he has invested his sense of self and slips down the accepted hierarchy of places from home to away: in this case being displaced from the West Highlands of Scotland to Normandy in France.

The work in question is *Life in Normandy*, written by Walter Frederick Campbell (1798–1855). Campbell was the Laird of Islay from 1816 to 1848, the island estate having been in the hands of his family, the Campbells of Shawfield, for some 300 years. He was also the reformist MP for Argyll for most of this period (1822–1832 and 1835–1841). Campbell inherited Islay in 1816 and initiated one of the most revolutionary eras in the history of the island through a bold series of reforms, the effects of which are still evident today.[1] He created new villages, diversified economic activity, extended the internal and external communications network and imposed agricultural reform. When the price of cereal and cattle fell dramatically at the end of the Napoleonic Wars, confronted with overpopulation, depressed agricultural prices and substantial rent arrears among his tenants, Campbell sought to accelerate the transformation of his estate. He was largely successful in meeting his objective which was to "retain tenants on the estate without outright clearance or large-scale emigration."[2] Consequently, Campbell was generally perceived to be a "humane" and "liberal" proprietor.

---

1. For a full account of this period see Storrie, pp. 107–34.
2. National Library of Scotland, *Lamplighter and Story-teller*, p. 23.

By October 1847, however, Campbell's liabilities were colossal. In December of the same year one of the creditors petitioned for formal bankruptcy and the Islay estate was sequestered. In a "state of hopeless embarrassment" (Walker, p. 822), the destitute laird removed to Avranches in Normandy initially to recover his health. There, he spent the final years of his life as an economic exile, aided by an annuity from his friends. Like Boulogne and Dinan, Avranches was a financial haven for numerous Britons. Since the 1820s, many military families had been living on half-pay in the new period of peace with France and Normandy attracted a growing number of financial casualties who found the cost of living in Great Britain unaffordable. The town probably had what Pemble describes as "the threadbare look associated with bankrupts, officers on half pay, penurious spinsters, and families making do with cut price gentility" (p. 10).

Life in Normandy was published anonymously in 1863, eight years after Walter Frederick Campbell's death. His son, John Francis Campbell (1821–1885), the well-known folklorist, edited the two volumes—a fictionalized account[3] of a short trip undertaken by the two main characters from Avranches to Granville further along the coast. Hope and Cross, the protagonists of the narrative, are clearly Campbell's alter egos, both characters being passionately interested in nature, fishing and shooting. Indeed, John Francis Campbell confirms in the preface to the third edition that "those who knew the author [...] know that Hope and Cross think his thoughts and narrate many of his adventures" (vol. 1, p. VI). Cross is described as a man having a small independence who found himself the great man of the quiet little town where he lived, poverty in England being wealth in Normandy.

The fictionalization of the account eliminates the dreary description characteristic of so many nineteenth-century travel narratives while it also allows Campbell to present several subjectivities including that of the "West Highland gentleman", that of the Eton-educated older man, and that of the detached narrator, accommodating an interesting heteroglossia that entwines peasant and bourgeois voices from Scotland, France and England.

Given how much nineteenth-century travel writing on France was characterized by an urge to point out just how much better France could

---

3. Campbell may have been influenced in the literary recycling of life events by his mother Charlotte Campbell Bury (28 January 1775–1 April 1861) after whom he had named Port Charlotte on Islay. Following her second marriage and a period spent as lady-in-waiting in the household of the future Queen Caroline, she became the author of numerous works of light literature, part of a movement that came to be known as the Silver Fork School. Certain of her novels were once extremely popular, the most successful being *Diary illustrative of the Times of George IV* (1838).

be if only it were a little more British, it is surprising to discover that the declared intention of these two volumes as set out in the preface is to suggest ways in which the poorest Scots might find new ways of catching and preparing food by adopting French ways.

> It was suggested that various ingenious foreign devices and engines for ensnaring, growing and gathering food, and making it eatable, might be described as to benefit the poor at home, whose single dish of potatoes might easily be varied at small cost. It was argued that a good cheap dinner would tempt a poor man from bad dear drink abroad, and that a poor Scotchman's wife might be taught to do that which poor wives do elsewhere. (Vol. 1, p. v)

This paternalistic effort to incite Highlanders to improve their way of life by learning from French example has to be understood in the context of the extreme poverty and devastating distress brought about on Islay by the potato blight just two years before Campbell's exile. The declaration echoes several of the very problems at the origin of Campbell's exiled state: the poverty of the people of Islay who could no longer pay him their rent; their dependence on the potato; and their penchant for alcohol. When the potato blight struck in 1846, it was reported that over 5,000 inhabitants of Islay were suffering "pressing wants and impending starvation" (Storrie, p. 133). At the end of October 1846 Campbell sought public assistance for the population on his estate claiming that ninety-five percent of the seventeen thousand individuals under his protection were in "great distress" (Walker, p. 821).

Campbell obliquely suggests that the people of Islay might have found the material resources to overcome this crisis but had neither knowledge nor skill enough to do so. His many propositions for improvements that might be adapted in Scotland range from decks on fishing boats (vol. 2, p. 241), a pulley system for baskets covering food (vol. 1, p. 123), the *four de campagne* (vol. 1, p. 126), an organized market for fish (vol. 1, pp. 218–9), and cooking techniques that might render seabirds edible. The character Hope claims:

> [...] a Frenchman will live in luxury where our people would starve, merely from knowing how to make the most of what falls in his way. I confess I wish that our peasant women in Scotland knew something more of cookery than merely boiling a potato. Certainly our friend the Marquis errs quite as much in the one way as our Highland wives do in the other; still, if he can show us how to convert marrots into good food, the lesson is worth learning, for what myriads of them have I seen on the coasts of Scotland which might benefit our poor, instead of merely destroying the herring fry. So let us go and see how he gets on, and try to teach his method to some of the people at home. (Vol. 1, p. 57)

Campbell's approach is an interesting variation on the customary traveller's prospective transformative project for new lands visited. Instead of considering that the host country is available for improvement, Campbell explicitly directs his suggestions northwards to home, and backwards in time to a catastrophic period for him personally. So that, far from looking forward to the glorious vision of improvement in the country in which he currently resides, the usual trope in 19th C travel narratives (Pratt, p. 61), his suggestions for improvement are sad reminders of lost opportunities at home, his own financial errors and catastrophic natural events.

In an effort to make his exile and this account of it meaningful, Campbell's principal strategy is that of exchange: the exchange of knowledge and experience between Highland Scotland and Normandy with himself as the textual intermediary. However, the exchange is ineffective since few of the potential beneficiaries will ever read his work. It is, rather, an assertion of Campbell's identity as a dignified subject, an expert in both Highland and Norman localities and a useful, if displaced, agent of enrichment through exchange. The account is shadowed by a rumination on the torment occasioned by the motivation for the author's presence in Normandy—financial ruin. I would like to suggest, then, that given Walter Frederick Campbell's personal circumstances, more than merely being a self-help book for distressed islanders, the text can been approached as a reflection on the notion of home and the catharsis of exile, discursively concentrating the author's strategies for coping with an acute sense of both social and cultural dislocation.

As an amateur naturalist, Campbell's observations certainly centre more often than is usual in this type of work on questions of home in the natural environment and more precisely expulsion from home and return to that place of origin: thus as well as learning about flight patterns and plumage and reproduction, we find conjecture about the homing instinct of the salmon, descriptions of digging kingfishers out of their nests in river banks, ruminations on the migration patterns of various birds and comparison of their arrival dates in Scotland and in France, as well as observations on the excavation of the holes inhabited by giant squid and the process of hauling them out of their hiding place with hooks.

Campbell's precarious financial situation and his displacement also resonate in several long passages on natural dangers. The first of these episodes takes place when Hope and Cross are caught out by the tide and find a temporary, uncomfortable home on a rocky island. Fear mounts and a feeling of powerlessness overtakes them until they are saved by a heroic effort from one of the fisher girls who puts her own life in danger to do so. "I went through all the stages, from the cold perspiration of good honest fear to the quiet resignation of despair" admits Hope (vol. 2,

p. 89). An earlier evocation of the sensation of being pulled under involves stories of a kraken dragging whole boats under the sea and an encounter with the minaur or giant squid:

> "How disgustingly ugly and revolting it is!" said Hope [...] "How would you like, Cross, to have that brute clinging round you, sucking you in with all those leech-looking mouths?" (Vol. 1, p. 297)

Fog and walking in circles are the dangers evoked in another pivotal episode that can be interpreted as allegory.

> I felt that death was inevitable, and mine was the calmness of resignation to a certain fate which I could not avert. Fear is most painful while there remains any uncertainty; when doubt ceases, fear in a great measure ceases also, and resignation takes its place. (Vol. 2, p. 89)

A similar passage juxtaposes parallel incidents, one that took place on the sinking sands around the Mont Saint Michel and another on a strand in the West Highlands. "I felt myself slowly going down" (p. 100) writes Campbell, and even as he describes the terrible feeling experienced in Normandy, he harks back to Scotland, its bogs, trembling eyes and well-heads (p. 101). All of these brushes with death—the rising tide; getting lost in thick fog; sea monsters; and sinking sands—are irresistible reminders of the helplessness Campbell must have experienced as he struggled to keep his head above water financially, slowly losing Islay and his livelihood.

> The sensation to me was as if a slight crust had broken under my feet, through which they sank, and then something seemed to suck or drag me down, leaving me not the slightest power to assist myself. (p. 101)

One of the ways that exiles play out the tension created by their displacement is by doing boundary work, that is consolidating the definition of what is "us" and what is "them". Avranches in the mid-nineteenth century surely qualifies as what Pratt in the colonial context has theorized as a contact zone, that is: a social space "where disparate cultures meet, clash, and grapple with each other, often in highly asymmetrical relations of domination and subordination" (Pratt, p. 4). From the very outset of this narrative, Campbell goes about establishing his difference by creating the impression that Normandy is in many ways a hostile environment. The action in Normandy takes place against the background of rumblings from the 1848 Revolution in Paris with one insurgent taking refuge in the inn in which Hope and Cross are lodging in Granville, lending a whiff of ambient menace to the exiles' presence in an unpredictably turbulent foreign land.

In the very first chapter, Hope and Cross are harassed by a group of men from Granville who hurl stones at them and chant "*Sur la France l'Anglais / ne régnera jamais*" (vol. 1, p. 51). The local men in turn are described over the space of thirty-two pages as blackguards, scoundrels, rascals, persecutors, confounded French frogs, vermin, scum of the earth, scamps and tormentors (vol. 1, pp. 51, 53, 58, 59, 82, 83). The altercation comes to a head when a band of around fifty men marches down the road with pitchforks and scythes only to be settled by Cross asserting his economic power by proposing to palm them off with "a few fish hooks and a franc or two" (vol. 1, p. 82).

The jostling to assert social and cultural domination is played out throughout the travel narrative with multiple subtle examples of discourses that promote bourgeois authority and devalue French subsistence ways of life (Pratt, p. 10). In general, the Norman peasants are portrayed as being childlike and social order is reassuringly respected by the young fisher girls:

> in spite of "liberté, égalité", they were shy and respectful, and as soon as they had finished eating, they rose, curtseyed, and left the room. (p. 245)

The maintenance of these class barriers is all the more important in France, where social status less easily perceptible than in Great Britain. The Marquis, for example, sometimes dresses like a peasant and is portrayed as being somewhat limited intellectually and abnormally preoccupied by the preparation and consumption of food. Language is also used to reinforce stereotypes and anchor boundaries. The Marquis' French is transposed into the sort of deficient English that consolidates his portrayal as a somewhat ridiculous character.

Several aspects of Campbell's text reflect interactions based on domination and subordination and serve to remind the reader that although he may be exiled in terms of nation he maintains his social class. Despite reduced circumstances, Campbell seeks to convey his undisputable membership of the upper classes[4] and the narrative dramatizes an unquestioned domination exerted over the peasant population of Normandy. However, he also clearly considers himself a benevolent benefactor and this quality is acted out in his account during an episode in which Cross and Hope use their financial resources to reward the young fisher-girl who had saved them from the rising tide, thereby simultaneously asserting their authority and their economic superiority.

---

4. Indeed, he had even greater aspirations. The Campbell papers in the National Library of Scotland include a draft letter from W. F. Campbell to the Duke of Argyll concerning his desire for a peerage.

The following passage relating Hope's shock at coming upon a rather slovenly house in the Norman countryside serves to maintain several boundaries; that between social classes, that between Celts and everyone else, and that between France and Great Britain.

> "Talk of French civilisation", said Hope; "I will be hanged if this does not beat Celtic indolence. You may see the same sort of carelessness among the lowest orders of Welsh, Irish, and Scottish Highlanders, but not among the better class. The proprietor of this place, you told me, is rich, is in the employment of the government, and considers himself enough of a gentleman to call me out, if I told him what I think of his dirt and ignorance." (Vol. 1, p. 122)

The passage also clearly illustrates the value of fictionalizing the account and including characters with different points of view. Only Hope, the old Etonian, can make such a remark since the character Cross represents West Highland wisdom and tolerance. Cross's response immediately re-establishes the objective voice of reason appropriate to a conspicuously impartial observer: "*C'est la mode du pays*", answered Cross; "and as we are not their schoolmasters, we must take them as we find them" (vol. 1, p. 122). "It is always more agreeable to praise than to censure" he adds.

Cross's innocent stance is typical of many naturalists writing about abroad. Indeed, the "natural" authority exerted by Campbell's protagonists over the local population is reinforced by their status as amateur naturalists. Going beyond the obvious contrast between the local people who live off the land and the exiles taking a dilettante scientific interest in it, Pratt has further examined the relationship between naturalists and locals in the colonial context and identified "an ideological drama essential to the authority of the naturalist, that of validating his way of knowing over others" (p. 55) often involving clashes between peasant knowledge and science. She further claims that the conspicuously innocent stance invariably taken by the naturalist reflects an assumed guilt of conquest and a great longing for a way of taking possession without subjugation and violence (p. 57).

The undeniable otherness of Normandy is typically illustrated by Campbell through descriptions of unfamiliar eating habits and exotic foodstuffs. The two volumes of *Life in Normandy* are peppered with these, notably with enumerations of the various courses in the gargantuan meals prepared by the French Marquis. The detailed descriptions serve to establish the fact that Normandy is decidedly not home but also suggest that the most savoury elements from it might be integrated— indeed ingurgitated—into Campbell's new identity as an exile. These

possibilities, however, are counterbalanced by descriptions of unequivo-
cally alien foodstuffs such as limpets (apparently eaten in Normandy
while periwinkles are not) (vol. 1, p. 191), snails and even slugs (vol. 2,
pp. 16–20), and guillemots (vol. 2, p. 47), as well as bacon that because
of the *gabelle* has to be cured by burying it in the earth for six months
in a modest amount of salt. This last practice provides the author with
the opportunity to voice his rejection of this repugnant element in the
Norman diet while at the same time affirming the superior discernment
of his compatriots by declaring that it gives him "what the Scotch call a
regular scunner" (vol. 2, p. 134).

The preoccupation with a possibly useful "otherness" available for
appropriation is mirrored by a similar preoccupation with "sameness".
For the exiled subject sameness provides stability and comfort. It is a
discursive coping strategy. In this way, numerous parallels are drawn
between Normandy and Scotland or more generally Great Britain:
between the horses, the fields, the roads, the housewives and their collections of linen, girdles, drinking habits, and penny weddings. "The habits
and superstitions which I observe resemble much more those of Scottish
Highlanders than of the English" concludes Campbell (vol. 2, p. 304).
Levi Strauss asks: "What does travel ultimately produce if it is not, by a
sort of reversal, an 'exploration of the deserted places of my memory',
the return to nearby exoticism by way of a detour through distant places,
and the 'discovery' of relics and legends" (quoted by de Certeau, p. 107).
Accordingly, Norman otherness and sameness produces in Campbell a
heightened awareness of the abandoned myths and legends of home
and, at the same time, underlines the sameness of Highland Scotland
and Normandy: original home and adopted home. A single example will
suffice: that of magpies as birds of augury. Hope remarks that in England
it is considered fortunate to see an even number of magpies and unfortunate to see an odd number.

> One is sorrow, two is mirth,
> Three's a wedding, four's a birth.
>
> Ay, that is the English edition, and put together for the sake of the rhyme;
> but our Highland belief agrees with the Norman. We think that the uneven
> numbers are fortunate, and the even unfortunate. In the Highlands the lines
> are—
>
> One is joy, two is grief,
> Three a wedding, four a death. (Vol. 2, p. 221)

Another of the discursive techniques used both to assert the traveller's authority and expertise, and to establish correspondences between

home and here, is that of glossing unfamiliar terms. Glossing provides a way of re-establishing some semblance of order on the natural world since one of the sources of the alienation associated with exile is that the signifier has become severed from the signified, that words no longer stand for things in an unquestionable way. The mission for the expatriate, and to an even greater extent for the exiled naturalist, is thus to supply the "correct words" for foreign terms. Lexical correspondences must be found and pointed out, as in the following explanation provided by the Marquis:

> Bouquets are what you call prawns; chevrettes are shrimps; in Paris and in most parts of France, prawns are called salicoques, and shrimps crevettes, but here they bear the names of bouquets and chevrettes. (vol. 1, p. 141)

Glosses are provided by Campbell for many of the terms associated with the fauna and flora of Normandy although the process can be rather confusing given that the correct word may simply be considered the English word or more rarely the scientific word, but sometimes it may be the Scots word for a Norman term. Thus, in dialogue, familiar words are substituted for strange terms and the otherness is controlled, and sometimes even rendered homely with the substitution of that Scots word. On at least one occasion, Campbell is pleased to note that the Norman word is in fact the same as the Scots word:

> [...] little Matilde held one of the poles with the iron hooks, which she called by the same name as the salmon-fisher in Scotland gives to his landing-hook—namely, a clip. The one Matilde carried was exactly of the same form as those used by the northern salmon-fisher, but was six times as strong, looking more like a short boat-hook, without the spike, than a clip. But a clip it was called. (Vol. 1, p. 285)

The narrative also unselfconsciously contains Scots words such as *burn*, *caller*, *blether*, and *burthen* that are not glossed, suggesting that both W. F. an J. F. Campbell used these terms naturally and expected their readers to understand them too.[5]

Alas, Campbell was never able to take those words back to their natural habitat. There was to be no Scottish homecoming at the end of his life for he died and is buried in Avranches cemetery where the inscription on his gravestone reads: "Where your treasure is there will your heart be also." It is clear that despite a sincere effort to live a useful life in France, Walter Frederick Campbell's sense of self was never completely invested

---

5. Occasionally, however, Scots terms in dialogue are glossed, ostensibly for the benefit of the French Marquis: this is the case for the term "leister and blaze" for example (vol. 2, p. 51).

in his place of exile and that he never entirely came to terms with his displacement. So that even as he wrote about life in Normandy, he was constantly and obsessively reworking thoughts of his home, Islay, and of the circumstances of his expulsion from it. The clues in the text reveal a man as intrigued by similarities between Highland Scotland and Normandy as by differences between the two places and a benevolent individual intent on learning from this experience and transferring the knowledge acquired to those who might benefit from it at home. At the same time, they betray a mind endlessly ruminating on the meaning of home in the natural world, the helplessness that accompanies going under be it financially or literally, the dislocation of exile and the need to maintain and cultivate social barriers as well as cultural differences.

Bibliography

[CAMPBELL Walter Frederick], *Life in Normandy Life in Normandy; sketches of French fishing, farming, cooking, natural history, and politics, drawn from nature*, Edinburgh, Edmonston & Douglas, 1863.

J. F. Campbell Collection, Special Collections, National Library of Scotland, MS. ADV–50–59.

CERTEAU Michel de, *The Practice of Everyday Life*, Berkeley, University of California Press, 1988.

National Library of Scotland, *Lamplighter and Story-teller: John Francis Campbell of Islay, 1821–1885* [exhibition catalogue], Edinburgh, 1985.

STORRIE Margaret C., *Islay: biography of an Island*, Port Ellen, The Oa Press, 1981.

PEMBLE John, *The Mediterranean Passion: Victorians and Edwardians in the South*, Oxford, Oxford University Press, 1988.

PRATT Mary Louise, *Imperial Eyes: Travel Writing and Transculturation*, London, Routledge, 1992.

WALKER Stephen P., "Agents Of Dispossession And Acculturation. Edinburgh Accountants And The Highland Clearances", Critical Perspectives on Accounting, vol. 14, no. 8, November 2003, pp. 813–53.

Bernard Sellin
University of Nantes

Exile and Expatriates in Robin Jenkins' Novels

Scotland has a long history of migration, not only to England, but also to the rest of the world. There is a "migrant tradition" which has been well documented by historians or sociologists. Studies devoted to Scotland's involvement in the Empire or to the Scottish diaspora show that emigration has become a leitmotiv which is difficult to ignore.[1]

Writers themselves have often either been directly affected by this migration or have felt the need to address Scotland's relations with the outside world.[2] One example is Robin Jenkins (1912–2005), presented by Isobel Murray as Scotland's finest contemporary novelist.[3] In a lecture entitled "The Novelist's Quest for a Suitable Theme" Jenkins himself made this unexpected comment on the subject:

> It is a curious fact that Scots novelists have never regarded it as their duty to write about Scotland. I mentioned Sir Compton (Mackenzie), who presides over the literary scene in Edinburgh; but his reputation was established by books that had nothing to do with Scotland. Mr Eric Linklater is another as likely to write about the Fidji Islanders as about his countrymen.[4]

Taken out of context, the statement may seem surprising. The sarcastic tone and exaggeration should not blur the point which Jenkins wanted to make: the necessity of considering Scottish society as a valid subject of fiction as long as it was rendered truthfully. In another essay he added: "In the past Smollett, Scott and even Stevenson, drew a large proportion of their material from outside their native country with, I believe, a

---

1. Tom Devine (ed.), *Scottish Emigration and Scottish Society*, Edinburgh, 1992.
Marjory Harper, *Adventurers and Exiles: The Great Scottish Exodus*, Profile Books, 2004.
Billy Kay, *The Scottish World*, Edinburgh and London, Mainstream Publishing, 2006.
2. For general criticism on the subject see Nigel Leask, "Scotland's Literature of Empire and Emigration, 1707–1918", in *The Edinburgh History of Scottish Literature*, vol. 2, pp. 153–62.
Douglas S. Mack, *Scottish Fiction and the British Empire*, Edinburgh, Edinburgh University Press, 2006.
3. Isobel Murray, "Robin Jenkins obituary", *The Scostman*, 1 March 2005.
4. Robin Jenkins, "The Novelist's Quest for a Suitable Theme", *Proceedings of the Annual Conference*, Coatbridge, Scottish Library Association, 1956, p. 21.

weakening effect on their work, and on Scottish literature."[5] Here again his intention was to invite authors to write primarily about Scotland. The novelist should write about what he knows best, he added, quoting Milton: "In my own country, where I most desire."[6]

These judgements were expressed in the mid-fifties, when Jenkins was still at the beginning of his career, despite having already published some of his best books, among them *The Thistle and the Grail* (1954), *The Cone-Gatherers* (1955) and *Guests of War* (1956), all of which offer a perceptive, though disenchanted, portrait of the Scottish scene.

And yet, shortly after the aforementioned declarations, Robin Jenkins himself was to break links with his home country, thus giving his life and work an unexpected turn. Though we do not know the actual reasons for his departure, Jenkins often expressed disillusion with Scotland. On several occasions he had vented his frustrations about the limitations of the Scottish scene and its imaginative possibilities, even though, ultimately, he recommended novelists "to stay at home".[7]

An abrupt change in his teaching career took him to several foreign countries. In 1957 he was appointed to a position in Kabul, Afghanistan. He was then offered the post of Cultural Officer with the British Council in Barcelona. This was, in his own words, a "plum job", which he nevertheless gave up after two years, to everybody's astonishment. The decision was apparently motivated by the fact that most of his time was taken up with administrative work and representation, leaving him little opportunity to write. He returned to live in Scotland for another two years but was restless and longed to discover the Far East. From 1963 to 1968, Robin Jenkins then lived in Borneo, the longest and most enjoyable of his stays abroad.

Throughout those years Jenkins never stopped writing and the result was eight novels and one collection of short stories, all dealing with foreign themes. These appeared between 1960 and 1974, and were all set in the countries which the author had visited.[8] They gave his work a new form and inspiration which contrasted with the Scottish novels though the Scottish identity remains present in the background and the general philosophy remains the same.

On the whole, this second period has received little critical attention, presumably because it does not affect readers as intimately as the

---

5. Robin Jenkins, "Novelist in Scotland", *Saltire Review*, vol. 2, no. 5, 1955, p. 7.

6. *Ibid.*, p. 7.

7. Robin Jenkins, "The Novelist's Quest for a suitable Theme", *Proceedings of the Annual Conference*, Coatbridge, Scottish Library Association, 1956, p. 25.

8. One novel belonging to that background was published late in 1995, *Leila*.

Scottish books, although one at least (*Dust on the Paw*, 1961, which deals with Afghanistan) has been highly praised and even compared with E.M. Forster's *Passage to India*.[9] It is also true that for some years many of the books were out of print. Unexpectedly, today's political tensions in Afghanistan are lending new interest to some of them. It is noticeable that only one novel is available in French, the recently translated *Some Kind of Grace* (1960), also set in Afghanistan.[10] One is set in Catalonia (*The Sardana Dancers*, 1964), while the rest are all concerned with the Far East, and particularly Malaysia (Borneo).

Bearing in mind the circumstances of Jenkins' travels, we should not expect to come across a problematic of exile as defined by Edward Said: "the unhealable rift forced between a human being and a native place, between the self and its true home".[11] In the same essay, Said mentions "the crippling sorrow of estrangement" associated with exile. Jenkins, on the contrary, speaks freely about his love of travelling, and about the pleasure of being in a strange city where you don't understand the language.[12]

Consequently, Jenkins' novels are seldom about "exile", a word he does not often use, except ironically. Dealing with expatriates and the experience of living abroad, they therefore require a new relationship to be defined, both with the country of origin, which can even be obliterated (although this is rare), and with the country of adoption and its inhabitants, traditions, language, climate, etc.[13]

The subject can be examined from two opposite angles. On the one hand we have the novelist writing about his own experience at one given moment, living in a foreign country which he has, if not selected, at least accepted, experiencing a situation which he endorses and which has therefore little to do with Said's sense of loss. The separation is known to be temporary. The expatriate can put an end to it whenever he chooses and decide to return home. On the other hand we have the literary expression

---

9. That part of Jenkins' work has been examined by Douglas Gifford in his *Scottish Literature, in English and Scots*, Edinburgh University Press, 2002, pp. 850–4, and by Ingibjörg Agústsdóttir in "Full Circle: The Function of Place in the Fiction of Robin Jenkins", *Terranglian Territories: Proceedings of the Seventh International conference on the Literature of Region and Nation*, Frankfurt am Main, Peter Lang, 2000, pp. 179–86.

10. *La colère et la grâce*, Paris, Albin Michel, 2008.

11. Edward Said, *Reflections on Exile and other Literary and Cultural Essays*, London, Granta Books, 2001, p. 173.

12. Isobel Murray (ed.), *Scottish Writers Talking, 3*, Edinburgh, John Donald, 2006, p. 124.

13. On the difference between expatriate and exile, see Peter Costello: "an expatriate is someone who sloughs off his country like an old skin; an exile, on the other hand, however far he may go, has his country always on his mind." (Peter Costello quoted by Patrick Ward, *op. cit.*, p. 11.)

of that estrangement which presents characters who experience a similar situation to, but who are distinct from, the novelist: engineers, clerks, embassy staff, administrators, teachers. The period is usually the 1960s, a post-imperial context in which, though Britain is still in a position of authority overseas, independence has either already achieved by former colonial territories or is imminent, with the result that members of the British delegations no longer hold effective power. Only once do we come across a writer adjusting to his new life, in the person of Jonathan Broxmead in *The Sardana Dancers* (1964), an Englishman with whom Jenkins can hardly be suspected of sharing affinities. More interesting is the other artist of the book, the Scottish painter John Lynedoch who, better than any other character, expresses the tensions and frustrations of Scottish connections, including both the rejection of home and the emotional richness which these tensions produce. As mentioned above, Lynedoch shares some features with the author, in particular his working class background, his frustrations and uncertainties, and his absence of involvement.

Thus Jenkins' foreign novels describe the experiences of Scottish or English expatriates viewed critically by a writer who seldom considers himself as one of them, a writer who, as usual, seems to be testing his characters and particularly their abilities to adapt to a foreign world. Themes which are treated include the vulgarity of British expatriates and, in contrast, the dignity of native peoples, race and racism, prejudice, interracial relationships and especially mixed marriage, political and administrative power, corruption, and occasionally nationalism.

Obviously, there is no single model. On the contrary, Jenkins is always careful to change perspectives. For example, some novels focus on the native peoples (*Dust on the Paw, The Holy Tree, Bonny Chung*), while others devote their attention to the expatriates (*A Far Cry From Bowmore, A Figure of Fun, The Sardana Dancers*). Interracial relationships are common and are explored in many different forms ("Imelda and the Miserly Scot", *The Expatriates, Dust on the Paw,* "A Far Cry from Bowmore"). These works are not so much about homesickness, a necessary component of the experience of exile, as about the difficulty of breaking links with the country of adoption (*The Sardana Dancers, The Expatriates*).

Although the books offer many parallels between home and abroad in terms of landscape, behaviour or religion, these never appear to be the priority for the narrator. In one story (*The Expatriates*, p. 115) the hero is, as it were, carrying a part of Scotland with him: a Celtic cross tattooed on his arm representing St Martin's Cross in Iona. But this is an exception and, in an ironic way so characteristic of Jenkins' rejection of sentimentality, the reader learns that the tattoo was the result of an impulsive, though highly symbolic decision taken during a drinking spree, which, surely, reduces the commitment.

Readers seldom come across scenes of nostalgic recollection or a sense of kinship with other expatriates. One exception is to be found in the short story "A Far Cry from Bowmore", which gives its title to the whole collection, when Macpherson visits McArthur on his death bed.[14] The dying man wants Macpherson to talk about his birthplace and their conversation evokes the Western Isles, Macpherson's plan of retiring on Islay, Gaelic songs, etc. A second instance is the meeting between McCleod and Kemp in *Some Kind of Grace* (1960). Once again, death is impending and the meeting is mediated through Gaelic, which appears here as the language of emotion and of roots. It's noticeable that many of Jenkins' expatriates are Highlanders or, at least, have Highland origins, perhaps in recollection of the part that Highlanders played in the formation of the British Empire, through their role in the military, for example, or as the result of evictions. In a review of *Some Kind of Grace*, James Meek makes an interesting suggestion when he parallels the Highlands with the foreign sub-culture in terms of poverty, dispossession and political exploitation. "Being an atheist among believers and a wealthy foreigner among the poor, McLeod, in the glens of Afghanistan, is a Highlander among highlanders, seeing the squalor and the dignity both as an outsider and, through history, from within".[15] After all, you do not have to go a long time back to find Highlanders being treated like savages, as Meek reminds us. In the two examples mentioned here, attachment to the home country is expressed more through reference to the Highlands than to Scotland at large. This is even more restricted if we bear in mind that Bowmore is a village on Islay.

Such scenes of nostalgia are, however, scarce in Jenkins' work for the simple reason that they do not stand up to comparison with oriental values and settings. Consequently, we do not find a romantic scene of homecoming in the tradition of exilic nostalgia as exemplified in Waugh's *Put out more Flags* (1942).[16] In this book the reader encounters the typical situation of a character who has spent most of his life overseas as a dutiful servant of the Empire and been dreaming of returning to the house he bought, "meaning to retire there when the time came". The homecoming scene is imbued with a sense of pleasant return to the past as if the stay abroad had been a mere parenthesis during which time

---

14. *A Far Cry from Bowmore*, London, Victor Gollancz, 1973, pp. 162–6.

15. James Meek, "A Scot in the Afghan glens", *The Guardian*, 18 September 2004.

16. Evelyn Waugh, *Put out more Flags* [1942], Penguin Books, 1943, pp. 90–1. Evelyn Waugh was one of Jenkins' favourite authors.

had been suspended. The colours of home are rich and mellow and "the scent of the gillyflowers are sweet and fresh on the breeze" (pp. 90–1), we read. The place is unchanged after so many years spent abroad, still untouched by modernity. Needless to say that this description is closer to a dream than to reality but it is characteristic of exilic imagination, however ironic the passage may be.

Turning from Waugh to Jenkins' *The Expatriates*, the contrast can hardly be more abrupt. Not only is home nearly absent from the book but it is actually known as "Martyrs' Brae", a name which suggests not rebirth and fulfilment but death and sacrifice, in recollection of an historical episode in which two covenanters were killed long ago. The past may still be alive but it has taken a threatening form: just as someone will one day have to pay for this past murder, there is the suggestion that going home will be a form of punishment for the expatriate's betrayal of his Asian mistress.

For another family in this book, homecoming, even when temporary, becomes an ordeal when they realise that, after so many years spent abroad, they do not belong any more. The girls look like mere visitors cut off from their roots, while the father, the aptly named Bill Livingstone, realises:

> with all his expatriate advantages left behind in far-off Kalimantan, he was here in Scotland purposeless and disconsolate. Living crampedly in his parents' small council house, with his wife grumbling at him most of the time, he had the sense to know that boasting of his distant Mercedes Benz would be more pathetic than impressive.[17]

Most of his foreign books give a harsh, sardonic view of the expatriate community where gin and lechery lead to sordid adventures and where gossip, jealousy and stupidity are the norms. Even those who mean well often find themselves trapped in their own contradictions or carried away by decisions which they can no longer control, such as Harold Moffatt in *Dust on the Paw* or Alistair Campbell in *A Figure of Fun*. For those men who have left their wives behind in Europe, there are female compensations abroad which few of them have the strength to resist.[18] This critical view, however, is probably the least interesting aspect of this fiction as satirical excess tends to stifle the message.

More fundamental is the relationship which is established with the local community, although, in many cases, characters may in fact live in a

---

17. *The Expatriates*, London, Victor Gollancz, 1971, p. 78.

18. John Melrose in *The Holy Tree*, p. 105: "Melrose had a wife at home in Scotland to whom every month he made a generous allotment of money, out of duty, however, not love."

ghetto of white expatriates. The point is made particularly in the only novel set in Catalonia, *The Sardana Dancers*. It is a complex narrative set on the Costa Brava which involves several young characters, among them two English twins, Jonathan and Madeleine Broxmead, who have been in Catalonia for some three years. They have been enjoying the sun and their new carefree life, but they also realise its emptiness. The novel touches on many themes (social class, political commitment, art, spiritual values) but one which recurs throughout is the necessity of understanding and engaging closely with other people. This is what Jonathan, a writer whose novels have been repeatedly rejected, learns at the end of the book; indeed, this realisation may be what stirs his creative genius again. The Sardana, the Catalan dance whose symbolic motif runs through the book, expresses this sense of a human communion which everybody is invited to join.

The Broxmead twins are in keeping with stereotypes of English upper middle class snobbery: wealthy, refined in speech and manners, aloof. For that reason the reader is on the lookout for any breach in their superiority complex. This happens in a double confrontation with the local Catalan community and with a Scottish painter from Glasgow, John Lynedoch.

Lynedoch, one of Jenkins' most interesting figures, fulfils the role of the powerful working class artist whose undeniable genius feeds on his own tensions and doubts. He also highlights the complex, even problematic, relationships with the native country since he carries with him a shame of his background, reasserted in the painful meeting with three Glasgow girls. "Though only four or five years his juniors, they had brought with them all the stultifying confusion, dreary bigotry, and petty arrogance of their country and class" (p. 75). In that sense, the foreign setting serves to remind characters that they cannot escape from their identity and roots. One single meeting is enough to abolish distance: "You are what you were brought up to be […]; it's in your blood, and in the remotest crannies of your brain; you cannot get rid of it" (p. 76). Running away to Spain or the Far East will not hide this fact.

However, what one can—one must—do is open oneself to others, in a gesture that will be all the more valuable if the Other belongs to a different culture. Thus most of Jenkins' novels raise the issue of interracial or international understanding on the assumption that exile involves a double aspect of dispossession and encounter with a new culture. It is, in the words of one critic, "a cross-cultural, cross territorial and cross-linguistic experience".[19] In the end, Jenkins is really more interested in

---

19. Kinga Olszewska, *Wanderers across Language. Exile in Irish and Polish Literature of the Twentieth Century*, London, Legenda, Modern Humanities Research Association and Maney Publishing, 2007, p. 1.

this cultural confrontation than in the arrogant behaviour of his Scottish or English characters. For many of them the situation is hopeless, a mere transplantation of Western communities abroad, with many vices and few virtues. Among the former is, in the words of one character, "the characteristic British failing" of obtuseness, or "the centuries-old irremovable unawareness that other people in other countries ordered some things better".[20]

Jenkins has confessed that he personally found a great lesson of humility in his successive stays overseas. His books also show what poverty, disease and despair mean while pointing out the responsibilities of the local elites in terms of corruption and backwardness.

Not only does his fiction take pains to depict the arrogance, vulgarity and emptiness of expatriates, but it also attempts to draw attention to what is positive about the foreign setting. This is achieved particularly through plots involving interracial marriages or relationships, such as in *Dust on the Paw*, *The Expatriates*, *The Sardana Dancers* and "Imelda and the Miserly Scot", among others. Of course, having a native mistress is part of the conventional image of the expatriate but beyond that cliché we also come across situations of expatriates who genuinely fall in love with native women, an experience which often ends tragically for lack of courage and honesty ("Imelda and the Miserly Scot", *The Expatriates*), but which also occasionally opens prospects of redemption and human greatness. It follows that the most interesting of Jenkins' characters are those who learn something from their experiences abroad in terms of generosity, dignity, understanding and relativity. Exile then is not limited to a separation from home. It also represents, if not a union with, at least the discovery of an unknown world. For Jenkins, those who keep longing to return home (and few actually do) are relatively shallow characters. The interesting ones are those who are so radically transformed by their experience that they can no longer go back home. "To emigrate is to change, to become 'Other', different, plural", writes Patrick Ward in the context of Irish literature.[21] This is also relevant for Jenkins' fiction, and we can easily draw a line between the characters who accept change and question their own identity, and, those who are unable to face this because of prejudice, rigidity or a feeling of superiority. Few of them accept the Other as he/she is, but for those that do so the consequence is an experience that thoroughly affects them, in a way reminiscent of a Joycean epiphany. Like Macpherson in "A Far Cry from Bowmore", they may return home, but utterly transformed. This transformation, though

---

20. *Dust on the Paw*, London, MacDonald, 1961, p. 51.
21. Patrick Ward, *op. cit.*, p. 245.

positive, is also the prelude to more dissatisfaction and frustration, the result of the intimate breach which exile has opened in the self.

Jenkins' foreign novels and stories open interesting perspectives for anybody interested in the production of this major Scottish author. They offer a view which is less grim perhaps, and one which is less obsessed with national identity and the limitations of the Scottish scene. They also offer a release and, for that reason, seem to contradict the problematic of exile with its insistence on notions of nostalgia and return, and on the pain of separation.

Leaving Scotland in the late 1950s was never regarded as a form of exile by the author, though the temptation of exile is forever present in his fiction. Like Mungo Niven at the end of *A Very Scotch Affair* as well as several others of his heroes, Jenkins himself never excluded the option of departing from Scotland at times of failure and despondency. From Mungo Niven's dubious attraction to a "beautiful place of banishment" to other characters' deep commitment to the foreign world, many differences can be found. What they have in common, though, is a sense of dissatisfaction with the Scottish scene which finds an outlet in its confrontation with another setting, rendered in more positive, though not at all idealistic, terms. In various forms, Jenkins' stories of expatriates tell the same message of tolerance and opening towards the rest of the world. Scots have much to learn from others and, in that sense, his fiction breaks with the stereotypes of the sentimental, nationalistic superiority of home to offer a disquieting questioning of commonly accepted values. No wonder Jenkins has been described as an "ambivalent patriot"[22] as his foreign books often depict Scottish (or English) heroes who discover more affinities with the Other than with their own people.[23]

Bibliography

Fiction by Robin Jenkins

Some Kind of Grace, London, Macdonald, 1960.
Dust on the Paw, London, Macdonald, 1961.
Tiger of Gold, London, Macdonald, 1962.

---

22. Paul Binding, "Ambivalent Patriot. The Fiction of Robin Jenkins", *New Edinburgh Review*, Spring 1981, pp. 20–2.
23. Though English characters are few, they are not totally absent from Robin Jenkins' fiction. Three examples of such heroes falling in love with a foreigner are Laura Johnstone in *Dust on the Paw*, Jonathan Broxmead in *The Sardana Dancers* and Andrew Sandilands in *Leila*.

The Sardana Dancers, London, Jonathan Cape, 1964.
The Holy Tree, London, Gollancz, 1968.
The Expatriates, London, Gollancz, 1971.
A Far Cry from Bowmore, London, Gollancz, 1973.
A Figure of Fun, London, Gollancz, 1974.
Leila, Edinburgh, Birlinn, 1995.
La colère et la grâce, Paris, Albin Michel, 2008, trad. Françoise du Sorbier.

General bibliography

AGÚSTSDÓTTIR Ingibjörg, "Full Circle: The Function of Place in the Fiction of Robin Jenkins", *Terranglian Territories: Proceedings of the Seventh International conference on the Literature of region and Nation*, Susanne Hagemann (ed.), Frankfurt am Main, Peter Lang, 2000, pp. 179–86.

BINDING Paul, "Ambivalent Patriot. The Fiction of Robin Jenkins", *New Edinburgh Review*, Spring 1981, pp. 20–2.

DEVINE Tom (ed.), *Scottish Emigration and Scottish Society*, Edinburgh, 1992.

GIFFORD Douglas, DUNNIGAN Sarah, and MACGILLIVRAY Alan, *Scottish Literature*, Edinburgh, Edinburgh University Press, 2002.

HARPER Marjory, *Adventurers and Exiles: The Great Scottish Exodus*, Profile Books, 2004.

JENKINS Robin, "Novelist in Scotland", *Saltire Review*, vol. 2, no. 5, 1955, pp. 7–10.

—, "The Novelist's Quest for a Suitable Theme", *Proceedings of the Annual Conference*, Coatbridge, Scottish Library Association, 1956, pp. 21–7.

KAY Billy, *The Scottish World*, Edinburgh and London, Mainstream, [2006], 2008.

LEASK Nigel, "Scotland's Literature of Empire and Emigration, 1707–1918", in *The Edinburgh History of Scottish Literature*, vol. 2, pp. 153–62.

MACK Douglas S., *Scottish Fiction and the British Empire*, Edinburgh, Edinburgh University Press, 2006.

MEEK James, "A Scot in the Afghan glens", *The Guardian*, 18 Sept. 2004.

MURRAY Isobel (ed.), *Scottish Writers Talking, 3*, Edinburgh, John Donald, 2006, pp. 101–46.

—, "Robin Jenkins obituary", *The Scotsman*, 1 March 2005.

OLSZEWSKA Kinga, *Wanderers across Language. Exile in Irish and Polish Literature of the Twentieth Century*, London, Legenda, Modern Humanities Research Association and Maney Publishing, 2007.

SAID Edward, *Reflections on Exile and other Literary and Cultural Essays*, London, Granta Books, 2001.

WARD Patrick, *Exile, emigration and Irish Writing*, Dublin, Irish Academic Press, 2002.

WAUGH Evelyn, *Put out more Flags* [1942], Penguin Books, 1943.

Jean Berton
CIEREC, Université Jean Monnet, Saint-Étienne

Le retour d'exil dans l'œuvre de Iain Crichton Smith

L'aventure est un événement positif dans la vie d'un homme. L'exil est associé à la séparation, à l'abandon, à la perte[1]. Le retour est lié à la restitution, la revendication, la reprise, même partielle. Chez Crichton Smith[2], cependant, le retour ne peut être combiné qu'avec la perte, la déchéance et la mort. C'est pour cela que certains personnages exilés refusent le retour. Pour le fils prodigue, il n'y a pas de veau gras pour atténuer le formidable sentiment de culpabilité. La nouvelle fantastique «Les frères[3]» est l'histoire de la culpabilité qui rend fou : le héros ne pourra retrouver la paix de l'esprit qu'au moment où il acceptera de rentrer chez les siens pour prendre la défense de la langue maternelle à l'agonie.

Iain Crichton Smith ne partage pas la croyance chrétienne qui fait du pécheur une brebis égarée qui peut retrouver le troupeau, un exilé de Dieu qui se rachète, obtient le pardon et se retrouve purifié. Dans son œuvre, le retour d'exil heureux ne l'est jamais entièrement, car l'exilé qui ne revient pas au bercail pour se coucher dans sa tombe se trouve dans un monde qui lui paraît mort, ou plus précisément dans un monde auquel il ne peut pas s'adapter parce qu'en son absence ce dernier a changé à un rythme différent du monde qu'il vient de quitter. Dans le monde smithien il n'est nulle joie, encore moins d'exultation; les personnages restent terre à terre, aucune cosmogonie ne s'offre en échappatoire.

---

1. Voir Jean Berton, *La Hantise de l'exil dans l'œuvre de Iain Crichton Smith*, Villeneuve-d'Ascq, Septentrion, 1998.

2. Iain CRICHTON SMITH, un seul prénom et un double patronyme sans tiret, (mais on le trouve indexé à Smith, comme dans *Scottish Literature* de D. Gifford) est né en 1928 et mort en 1998. Il a grandi sur l'île de Lewis, il a commencé à écrire durant ses années à l'université d'Aberdeen. Ses vingt premières années d'écrivains sont celles d'un jeune auteur en colère. Dès les années 1970 son œuvre révèle une véritable culture du sens de l'humour, notamment avec la création de son personnage clownesque «Murdo». Il est remarquable de voir qu'il a conclu son œuvre avant de mourir dans la sérénité.

3. Dans *Le télégramme et autres nouvelles d'exil*, Paris, Éditions Praelego, 2009, p. 91. Traduction française d'un choix de vingt-cinq nouvelles en anglais ou en gaélique de Crichton Smith. Les références suivantes à ce recueil de nouvelles choisies seront : («… *autres nouvelles d'exil*, p. … »).

Les romans et nouvelles, les poèmes et œuvres dramatiques de Crichton Smith sont pour la majeure partie ancrés dans le territoire de l'Écosse — phénomène que Dominique Maingueneau identifie comme l'effectuation bio/graphique[4] — mais chaque lieu de retour est assimilable à l'île natale symbolique. L'histoire de l'Écosse offre des exemples d'exil et de retour d'exil à foison : se pouvait-il que Crichton Smith échappe à la référence à l'archétype de « Bonnie Prince Charlie », dont le grand-père avait subi l'exil ? Les fiascos des retours des Stuarts bannis n'ont pu que causer davantage d'exil. Le roman *Consider the Lilies*[5] se défend d'être un roman historique bien que la toile de fond en donne l'impression puisqu'il s'agit de la période des Évictions. Dans ce récit, il n'y a pas de cas de retour d'exil : le mari de l'héroïne fuit le domicile conjugal et meurt six mois plus tard sur un champ de bataille ; son fils s'en va au Canada pour toujours. Et cette Mrs Scott, au nom symbolique, est impuissante à les retenir ou les ramener à la maison. *Consider the Lilies* se lit comme une accusation faite à l'Écosse pour les choix qu'elle fait qui engendrent l'exil : « [...] Mrs Scott is both the suffering soul of Scotland and the Highlands, Lewis and Strathnaver, in the past[6]. » Cette Mrs Scott est tout à la fois la cause et la conséquence d'exil : « Tu détestes tout le monde[7] » ; Crichton Smith ne cherche pas de coupable à l'extérieur du topos écossais tant pour l'exil que pour le retour d'exil.

L'issue heureuse ou malheureuse du retour d'exil est fortement dépendante des conditions de l'exil et de la réussite de cet exil. L'évaluation, dans l'œuvre de Crichton Smith, est faite par le narrateur qui garde le village, métaphorique ou non, comme repère paradoxalement fixe et mouvant pour l'exilé en partance ou de retour ; et au cœur de la communauté, l'image de la mère demeure l'élément le plus implacable, bien que victime, aux yeux du narrateur. Cette étude s'organise autour d'un jeu d'oppositions d'abord sur les natures de l'exil et le caractère fatal du retour, puis sur les causes de l'exil et celles du retour, avant de mener à l'évidence de l'impossible retour au *statu quo ante*.

Le retour d'exil est un autre exil

Les natures et les formes de l'exil sont multiples et complexes, le retour est tantôt incertain, tantôt létal, tantôt impossible, comme dans « Les

---

4. D. Maingueneau, *Le contexte de l'œuvre littéraire*, Paris, Dunod, 1993, p. 53-54.

5. *Consider the Lilies*, Londres, Gollancz, 1968.

6. D. Gifford (dir.), *Scottish Literature*, Edinburgh University Press, 2002, p. 892.

7. Le roman a été traduit en français par François Happe : *Murdina Scott*, Nantes, Le Passeur, 2004, p. 41.

exilés» (… *autres nouvelles d'exil*, p. 35). Le récit relate la rencontre de deux exilés, un étudiant pakistanais qui finance ses études en faisant de la vente à domicile et une vieille femme venue des Hautes Terres avec son fils qui a vendu la maison familiale. L'étudiant est sûr de rentrer au pays bientôt, la vieille femme sait que son exil est sans retour possible. De surcroît, son fils s'est marié et l'a abandonnée dans la banlieue glaswégienne. Pour ce personnage, l'exil géographique se charge d'une valeur affective pour être équivalent à la déportation dont la seule perspective est la mort dans la solitude. Cependant, l'issue prévisible de la nouvelle, «La mer et les mouettes» (… *autres nouvelles d'exil*, p. 31), qui met en scène Napoléon en exil à Sainte-Hélène, n'occulte pas la question première qui n'est ni l'éloignement ni le souvenir obsédant du passé mais la perte d'identité : c'est ainsi que Napoléon, esseulé sur la plage, s'adresse aux mouettes pour leur demander de manière insistante «Qui suis-je?». Son nom est «personne», car l'exilé de retour est tantôt un absent, tantôt un être sans valeur. Crichton Smith a intitulé plusieurs nouvelles du même titre, le retour, mais le traitement est différent. Dans «Le retour de Nouvelle-Zélande» (… *autres nouvelles d'exil*, p. 131) le jeune homme que l'on n'attend pas trouve porte close. Tandis que dans «L'étranger» (… *autres nouvelles d'exil*, p. 151), le jeune homme trouve sa mère devenue aveugle mais en se comportant comme un idiot, il ne parvient pas à la tromper. La nouvelle se termine sur le portrait du retour d'un exilé piteux.

La majorité des cas de retour d'exil concerne des jeunes hommes. Cela confère un caractère réaliste au traitement du thème, puisque les jeunes filles qui partent des Hautes Terres ou des Hébrides se marient à des autochtones des Basses Terres et ne reviennent pas dans leur village natal après avoir fondé une famille. Crichton Smith transforme l'exil en exportation dans «Le mariage» (… *autres nouvelles d'exil*, p. 49) : la mariée, devenue urbaine, blêmit de honte lors du discours maladroit que fait son père, sa robe blanche devient linceul. Mais c'est plus tard, lorsque l'on se met à chanter des chansons traditionnelles que le père intervient pour léguer en cadeau de mariage la culture des Hautes Terres dont personne ne veut mais dont, paradoxalement, tous ont besoin. Il ne sera pas nécessaire que la mariée retourne au village natal car elle est désormais passeur de la culture de la Haute Écosse.

Crichton Smith rejette tout sentiment de nostalgie dans le traitement du retour d'exil, gardant en point de mire le personnage totémique de la Mrs Scott de *Consider the Lilies*. C'est là un sujet majeur qui transparaît dans la plupart des textes traitant ce thème : que trouve celui qui revient? La réponse est pessimiste et fait débat. Crichton Smith a recours au fantastique dans «The Ghost[8]» pour noircir le tableau : quelques mois après son mariage avec un artiste d'Édimbourg, Sheila emmène son mari pour quelques jours de vacances chez ses parents sur l'île de Lewis. Le séjour est catastrophique car Sheila prend conscience de la réalité de la jeune femme qu'elle était avant son mariage : «[she's] frightened by the sight of her own true nature.» Sur la route du retour, le couple s'arrête dans un hôtel isolé. La nuit, Sheila perçoit dans le miroir de l'hôtel le fantôme d'une vieille femme enveloppée d'un châle, qui n'est autre qu'elle-même sous les traits prémonitoires de «an old woman struggling against that eternal wind of death in her black clothes». Le lecteur est poussé à conclure que le retour d'exil à Lewis est mortifère : «It was as if she had returned to an aboriginal guilt.» Dans cette nouvelle, les villageois inflexibles font resurgir ce que l'exilé revenant a de pire en lui. Ce cas est atypique dans l'œuvre de Crichton Smith puisque dans la plupart de ses textes, l'exception confirmant la règle, c'est le village qui a changé, rendant ainsi impossible le retour de l'exilé nostalgique de son enfance : «[…] to be an exile is to be a double man, living in a new world while still enchanted by the fantasies of the old[9].» La projection d'un rêve est irréalisable puisque, dans cet essai, l'écrivain répète que l'île natale appartient au domaine du réel.

Pour dépeindre la solitude de l'exilé social, Crichton Smith utilise son propre reflet dans le miroir — Carole Gow mentionne un double miroir : «The self is perceived in two mirrors; a Gaelic, Calvinistic culture and an English culture of learning and books[10].» Il n'a pas deux ans quand son père meurt de la tuberculose. Sa mère décide de rentrer au village natal de son mari défunt avec ses trois fils[11]. Ce retour d'exil dans une communauté qui n'est pas vraiment la sienne puisqu'elle n'y est pas née est un échec car elle subit l'hostilité de la communauté puisqu'elle était native d'un autre village. Quelques années plus tard, le jeune Iain doit supporter l'agressivité du groupe qui lui reproche d'être différent : en effet, Iain souffre, pour faire court, de la maladresse des intellectuels. Ce handicap est décrit dans «La tache» où le jeune élève est violemment pris à partie par la maîtresse pour avoir taché son cahier. Sa survie n'est alors possible que dans la fuite de la rêverie, une forme d'exil temporaire

8. Dans *The Black Halo*, Édimbourg, Birlinn, 2001, p. 425.

9. *Towards the Human*, «Real people in a real place», Édimbourg, Macdonalds Publishers, 1986, p. 22.

10. C. Gow, *Mirror and Marble, the poetry of Iain Crichton Smith*, Édimbourg, Saltire, 1992, p. 19. Carole Gow est enseignante à l'université de Dundee.

11. Peut-être par souci de brièveté, la majorité des notices biographiques indiquent que Iain Crichton Smith est né à Lewis… C'est ce que l'on peut lire à la première ligne introduisant Crichton Smith dans *Scottish Literature*, ouvr. cité, p. 766.

dans un milieu où l'adresse du manuel est un gage de qualité. Le retour nécessaire à la réalité est cause de mal-être persistant.

Embrasser une carrière militaire pour Crichton Smith est une forme d'exil, tant est particulier ce mode de vie qui devient métaphore de la vie en communauté. L'inadaptabilité de la jeune recrue est tout aussi cruelle que celle du jeune élève maladroit. Dans *Survival without Error*[12], le héros, Lecky, est aliéné par son incapacité à marcher au pas ; et harcelé par ses camarades de chambrées souvent punis par sa faute, il finit par se suicider. Ce jeune homme, exilé dans un mode de vie auquel il n'a pu s'adapter, a préféré refuser de vivre dans l'absurde. Dans le roman *An Honourable Death*[13], Crichton Smith présente une biographie fictionnelle du général de division Hector A. Macdonald, d'origine écossaise. La bravoure de ce militaire et les distinctions obtenues dans les conquêtes de l'Empire ne l'ont pas protégé du déshonneur d'une conduite sexuelle déviante étalée dans la presse. Rentré à Londres pour affronter ses juges, il passe sa dernière journée en tenue de ville, ce qui symbolise son retour à la vie civile. Mais ce retour est un échec puisque le militaire déclaré indigne avant d'être jugé se suicide.

Toutes ces formes d'exil social mettent en avant le sentiment de solitude qu'éprouvent tous les exilés. Crichton Smith analyse avec acuité une forme d'exil et de retour vécue quotidiennement : celle du lycéen quittant son village tous les matins et rentrant le soir encore plus différent des gens qui forment son milieu social, dont son frère cadet. Cet exil suivi du retour est décrit dans la nouvelle « Le premier jour » (… *autres nouvelles d'exil*, p. 65) qui indique le modèle de journée d'un lycéen qui va se répéter pendant des années. Ce premier jour, l'élève rencontre son professeur de latin qui leur fait apprendre la déclinaison de « *insula, insulam, insulae, insulae, insula* » : le choix du mot *insula*, une île, est comme une invitation tacite au lecteur à associer les prépositions au mot décliné, telle que *ex insula*, en dehors de l'île, une forme concrète de l'exil (ou ex-île / ex-isle). Ce détail narratif est une manière appuyée de souligner la conscience de l'insularité. L'exil du village vers le lycée permet de mesurer l'écart sans cesse grandissant que subit l'élève qui rentre tous les soirs chez lui. Il sait que sa réussite scolaire l'aliène du groupe de camarades qui sont passés de l'école primaire à la vie active. Cet exil culturel devient définitif le jour où il quitte l'île pour aller à l'université. L'émancipation devient exil pour l'étudiant lorsqu'il doit rompre avec la pratique religieuse. Cet exil progressif est décrit dans une nouvelle

---

12. « Survival without Error », dans *The Red Door*, Édimbourg, Birlinn, 2001, p. 29.
13. *An Honourable Death*, Londres, Macmillan, 1992.

épistolaire, «The Black and the Red[14]», dont la tension progressive entre l'étudiant et sa mère, alimentée par la culpabilité, mène à un point de rupture : il est parti adolescent, il est devenu un jeune homme désormais inadapté à la vie sur l'île natale, mais qui devra gérer pendant des lustres ce sentiment de culpabilité.

L'exil linguistique

Toute l'œuvre de Crichton Smith est imprégnée de la question linguistique concernant les probabilités de survie du gaélique écossais depuis la deuxième guerre mondiale jusqu'au référendum de 1997 sur la réouverture du Parlement d'Écosse, qui en avril 2005, allait voter la parité linguistique entre l'anglais et le gaélique. Les correspondances linguistiques entre l'anglais, qui s'est imposé en Haute Écosse à partir du XVIIIe siècle, et le gaélique, qui s'est implanté à compter des IIIe et IVe siècles, sont toujours sujettes à caution. Le terme Hébrides traduit l'anglais «Hebrides», qui aujourd'hui a cédé devant l'appellation factuelle géographique «Western Isles», qui est l'égal sémantiquement de «Na h-Eileanan an Iar». Mais cette aire géographique qui correspondait à la Seigneurie des Îles pendant les siècles où elle a dépendu du royaume viking norvégien est aussi connue sous l'appellation «Innse Gall», signifiant littéralement, les îles des étrangers. La plus norroise des îles gaélophones des Hébrides est Lewis, bien que le norrois en soit disparu depuis des siècles! Ainsi, Lewis a été sous la domination des Vikings qui ont progressivement adopté la langue vernaculaire. Le gaélique, qui n'avait pas reculé devant l'écossais, issu du nord-anglien, allait-il s'effacer devant l'anglais par l'effet conjugué de l'exil des gaélophones et l'implantation d'anglophones? Crichton Smith, tout en œuvrant activement pour la rénovation de sa langue maternelle, était très inquiet de sa survie et de l'effacement de la Gaélie, terme qui traduit littéralement Gàidhealtachd (et Gaeldom), l'aire linguistique du gaélique d'Écosse.

Crichton Smith décrit de façon humoristique l'apprentissage forcé de l'anglais dans le premier texte de *Thoughts of Murdo*[15], «Murdo and the language» : le jeune héros, en apprenant cette langue étrangère, risque la schizophrénie, maladie métaphorique de l'exil linguistique. Crichton Smith aborde sérieusement la question linguistique dans son essai, «Real people in a real place[16]» : «For we are born inside a language and see

---

14. «The Black and the Red», dans *The Red Door*, ouvr. cité, p. 253.
15. «Murdo and the language», dans *Thoughts of Murdo*, Nairn, Balnain, 1993, p. 11.
16. Dans *Towards the Human*, ouvr. cité, p. 20.

everything from within its parameters: it not we who make the language, it is the language that makes us.» Interdire la pratique d'une langue maternelle, c'est désorienter le sujet et l'exiler de sa réalité. Exiler un gaélophone, pour Crichton Smith, c'est aliéner un locuteur, acte criminel, s'il en est.

En dehors de toute considération pour les déclarations internationales visant à protéger les langues menacées, Crichton Smith a souvent intégré la question de la survie du gaélique dans ses écrits, dont le recueil de poèmes *An t-Eilean agus an Canan*[17] (L'île et la langue). Le poème N° 6, qui débute par ce vers : «Tha am Frangach seo ag ionnsachadh na Gàidhlig…», décrit un certain étudiant français qui s'entraîne à traduire des textes gaéliques en français. Loin d'encourager ce linguiste, le poète reproche la perte de milliers de jeunes locuteurs gaélophones morts dans les tranchées de la Première Guerre mondiale… L'acte d'apprentissage du jeune traducteur est dénoncé comme une saignée supplémentaire de la langue, comme si une fois traduits, les textes cessaient d'être en gaélique ; comme si cet exil linguistique ne pouvait qu'être sans retour. On pointera ici la contradiction chez Crichton Smith qui a publié quelques traductions en gaélique de textes en langue étrangère.

Les universitaires qui font parfois l'objet de romans et nouvelles sont généralement impliqués dans l'enseignement de la langue et la culture gaéliques. Ainsi, dans *The Dream*[18], Martin prépare sa retraite de l'enseignement et envisage de revenir dans son île natale. Sa femme, Jean, s'oppose violemment à cette décision car elle ne souhaite pas revenir sur les lieux de son enfance malheureuse : enfant illégitime abandonnée, elle a été élevée par une tante intolérante. Le couple est partagé entre le désir du retour chez Martin et le rejet de l'injustice d'une culpabilité imposée chez Jean. L'idée même du retour d'un exil dans les métropoles écossaises est cause de souffrance et de rupture mortifère.

L'impossible communication dont souffrent les personnes ayant une déficience mentale est une forme d'exil social et affectif pour lequel nul retour vers la pleine communication sociale n'est envisageable. C'est le thème de la nouvelle «Timochenko» (… *autres nouvelles d'exil*, p. 75). Le personnage tenant le rôle-titre est une femme adulte simplette tyrannisée par son frère handicapé aigri. Elle poignarde ce frère d'un geste impulsif avec le couteau à pain. Le drame est découvert par le narrateur qui parvient à calmer Timochenko et à lui faire expliquer son geste : le frère s'était ingénié à la faire passer pour vraiment folle, notamment auprès d'un fiancé bienveillant qui avait fini par l'abandonner. En évacuant le

---

17. *An t-Eilean agus an Canan*, Glasgow University Press, 1987.
18. *The Dream*, Londres, Macmillan, 1990.

pathétique, on découvre l'impossibilité du retour à la vie mentale saine de celui qui en a été exclu malgré lui. Puis, *mutatis mutandis*, le schéma d'exclusion de la minorité poussée à l'exil se précise, où les notions de justice et d'humanité peuvent surgir en contrepoint.

La métaphorisation de l'exclusion atteint un paroxysme dans le poème «Deer on the High Hills[19]» où le cerf, animal qui partage la niche écologique du poète, appartient pourtant à un autre monde. L'écart est irréductible, avant tout pour une raison linguistique :

> And you, the deer, who walk upon the peaks,
> Are you a world away, a language distant?
> Such symbols freeze upon my lips.

La métaphore étant toujours une fuite du réel, «an evasion» selon Colin Nicholson[20], Crichton Smith prône le retour au réel («There is no metaphor. The stone is stony.») pour connecter l'isolement des hommes avec celui du cerf qui brame sur la colline.

La posture du poète est conforme à celle de l'homme : Crichton Smith a eu dans la première moitié de sa vie d'écrivain une attitude de violent rejet de la religion presbytérienne. Les pasteurs inflexibles, les anciens bornés, les femmes bigotes ont été les cibles favorites de sa colère. Une des raisons majeures est que, selon Crichton Smith, ils poussaient les fidèles à fuir la réalité quotidienne pour se réfugier dans une lecture de la Bible délétère. L'exemple de la nouvelle au titre ironique «Le dialogue» (… *autres nouvelles d'exil*, p. 111) en est caractéristique : le jeune homme qui se meurt de la tuberculose est accompagné par le pasteur. Mais le lecteur est amené à penser que le pasteur aliène le jeune homme de la tendresse de sa mère en le persuadant de se tourner exclusivement vers la lecture de la Bible. En précisant qu'il «lui fallait penser à Dieu et au feu de l'enfer», le narrateur indique que le jeune homme s'exile de l'amour des siens autant que de l'amour de Dieu. Sous la tonalité pathétique de la cruauté, le lecteur entend la possibilité de la croyance au déterminisme le plus extrême : le jeune Norman qui vient de mourir était-il un élu de Dieu? Si la réponse est négative, Dieu ne l'accueillera pas au paradis. Pour l'auteur, qui se déclarait athée, le pire est que le jeune homme a été détourné du dialogue naturel avec sa mère dans sa langue maternelle («Il était plus silencieux qu'avant») au profit d'une lecture muette et sans échange possible de la Bible («[…] il a commencé à lire la Bible comme s'il avait pris peur»). Norman meurt symboliquement de l'interdiction

---

19. *Deer on the High Hills*, Édimbourg, Giles Gordon, 1962.

20. C. Nicholson, «Deer on the High Hills, a meditation on meaning», dans *Iain Crichton Smith, Critical Essays*, C. Nicholson (dir.), Edinburgh University Press, 1992, p. 102.

qui lui est faite de dialoguer avec les siens par le pasteur armé de sa Bible et de ses certitudes.

Les causes de l'exil, les causes du retour

Toutes les familles d'Écosse ont été touchées par l'exil d'un membre, et celle de Crichton Smith offre des exemples banals propres à alimenter fables et récits. Deux de ses oncles ont émigré au Canada, l'un a réussi et l'autre non. Dans un long poème narratif, « My Canadian Uncle[21] », Crichton Smith fait le récit, de manière réaliste, de la vie de cet oncle auquel il a rendu visite. Mais cet oncle-ci sert de repoussoir à cet autre oncle, Danny, qui a dû rentrer d'exil : il est érigé en archétype de l'exilé qui a failli, qui a sombré dans l'alcool, et qui rentre pour se perdre dans une pratique calviniste extrême. Danny a fait l'objet d'un poème sarcastique, « Returning Exile[22] » :

> Home he came after Canada
> where for many years he drank
> his failure into the ground.
> Westward lay Lewis. He never wrote.
> The snow needs a gay pen.
> However at the age of fifty-five
> he put on his hat, his painted tie,
> and packed his trunk (being just alive).
> Quietly he sailed over waters
> which made him cry secretly by rails
> through which he saw his home all green
> and salmon leaping between deer's horns.
> Arrived home he attended church
> (the watch chain snaking his waistcoat).
> None was as black or stiff as he.
> He cast his bottles into outer darkness
> where someone gnashed his teeth
> each evening by the quay
> watching the great ship sail out
> with the girls laughing
> the crew in white
> and the bar mazy with mirrors.
> Some called her SS. Remorse
> others the bad ship Envy.

---

21. *My Canadian Uncle*, Édimbourg, Cencrastus (n° 30), 1988.
22. *Collected Poems*, Manchester, Carcanet, 1992, p. 62.

L'attitude pharisaïque de l'émigré déchu interdit la compassion mais permet à Crichton Smith de comparer ce retour d'exil à la mort de l'homme qui se présente alors devant le Dieu inflexible des Calvinistes qu'il a vénéré : « [...] to return home is not simply to return home, it is to return to a community, for one's gains or losses to be assessed[23]. »

Crichton Smith avait deux frères, mais contrairement au dénouement des paraboles, il n'y a pas eu de retour. Le frère cadet a vécu son échec en Australie[24], le frère aîné s'est installé durablement en Afrique australe où il a connu une vie assez prospère. C'est ce frère-là qui a servi de modèle pour la nouvelle «Chez soi» (... *autres nouvelles d'exil*, p. 19). Fier de sa réussite, l'émigré revisite l'immeuble de sa jeunesse mais il doit vite remonter dans sa voiture pour échapper à la vindicte des jeunes délinquants. Le retour aux sources se termine dans un hôtel à la clientèle internationale : il n'y a pas de retour pour l'exilé car il est forcément apatride.

La guerre, pour un Hébridien du vingtième siècle, est synonyme d'exil puisque le soldat volontaire doit se battre sur un sol ou sur une mer qui est loin de son île. Crichton Smith a privilégié le point de vue de l'îlien qui attend le retour du fils aimé. La nouvelle «Le télégramme» (... *autres nouvelles d'exil*, p. 9) met en scène deux exilés : la mère parce qu'elle n'est pas native du village, et le fils qui navigue sur quelque mer inconnue. La mère est mise en contraste avec une autre mère qui vit la même angoisse lorsque sur la route apparaît l'ancien, préposé aux télégrammes fatidiques qui sont autant de métaphores de non-retours.

C'est dans un poème, «Iolaire» (*Collected Poems*, p. 237), que Crichton Smith évoque le retour de la grande guerre des soldats lewisiens le 1er janvier 1919. Le ferry a fait naufrage en pleine nuit, et Crichton Smith prend le point de vue d'un ancien dont la foi vacille alors qu'il cherche le corps de son fils parmi tous les noyés qui flottent dans la baie :

In sloppy waves,
in the fat of water, they came floating home
bruising against their island. It is true,
a minor error can inflict this death.

Le retour est ici synonyme de mort. Et les survivants ne pourront pas s'adapter à la vie de leur île natale.

---

23. *Towards the Human*, ouvr. cité, p. 24.
24. Crichton Smith a raconté sa rencontre avec ce frère dans un roman, *The Search* (Londres, Gollancz, 1983).

Les causes du retour d'exil peuvent être aussi paradoxales que la mort physique inopinée ou prévisible du personnage. Crichton Smith illustre de cette façon une réalité historique propre aux îles : tout au long des dix-neuvième et vingtième siècles, les Hébrides ont vu le retour d'exilés souffrant de tuberculose contractée, pour la plupart, dans les villes métropoles de Grande-Bretagne. Les malades contaminaient très souvent les membres de leur famille vivant dans les chaumières souffrant d'un déficit d'hygiène patent. La fiction permet de mettre à profit ce phénomène réaliste afin de souligner le rôle néfaste de l'exil et du retour tant pour l'émigré que pour la communauté. Ainsi voit-on dans le roman, *The Last Summer*[25], Dicky renvoyé de la Royal Navy pour mourir chez lui. Dans le recueil de nouvelles, *On the Island*[26], Jim rentre d'Amérique et meurt soudainement au chapitre 12 sans explications. Enfin, dans la nouvelle « Le Rhodésien » (... *autres nouvelles d'exil*, p. 117), le protagoniste rentre à Glasgow à la suite de la mort de sa femme : tout en se vantant d'avoir écrit l'hymne national rhodésien, il tousse beaucoup, ce qui laisse entendre qu'il n'aura pas le loisir de repartir en Afrique et de partager la tombe de sa femme.

Dans la nouvelle qui illustre la philosophie existentialiste de Crichton Smith, « La lettre » (... *autres nouvelles d'exil*, p. 167), c'est un maître d'école, installé dans le village depuis un quart de siècle, qui tient le rôle de l'émigré : en effet, il n'est pas natif de la localité. Il annonce son suicide dans cette lettre : sa mission d'éducation a échoué, explique-t-il. Et il estime qu'il doit repartir en choisissant de se donner la mort. Le suicide est, pour l'exilé qui estime être dans l'échec, un acte de retour impossible au stade du choix : ce maître d'école ne peut pas revenir au jour où il a décidé de devenir enseignant et faire un autre choix de vie.

Crichton Smith a donné plusieurs versions en anglais et en gaélique de la longue nouvelle, « The Hermit[27] », dont un des aspects est de montrer que l'île de Lewis est aussi une terre d'exil : le héros anonyme est un homme jeune qui vient vivre en ermite dans un ancien abri préfabriqué abandonné par la RAF à quelque distance du village. L'ermite ne fait scandale que par sa présence discrète : il est comme un menhir isolé qui attire le regard et fait naître des réactions malsaines. La pression des habitants est telle que l'ermite doit fuir : cette nouvelle est un miroir dans lequel les autochtones peuvent observer leurs comportements injustifiables envers ceux qui choisissent de venir vivre parmi eux.

---

25. *The Last Summer*, Londres, Gollancz, 1969.
26. *On the Island*, Glasgow, Drew Publishing, 1979.
27. *The Hermit and Other Stories*, Londres, Gollancz, 1977.

De l'appel du large au chant de l'île

Dans la nouvelle «Le retour» (... *autres nouvelles d'exil*, p. 105), l'émigré devenu homme analyse les raisons qui l'ont poussé à partir à l'âge de seize ans en laissant Peggy : il n'y avait pas de raison autre que celle de partir à l'aventure. L'homme rentré après avoir gagné de l'argent retrouve sa famille, mais Peggy est partie récemment se marier en Angleterre. Le héros est rentré parce qu'il a entendu le chant de la sirène, mais la morale de la fable est que la vie est une voie à sens unique où se succèdent les actes d'exil : chaque choix implique un abandon.

Les multiples raisons de retour d'exil, explicables et injustifiables, sont rassemblées dans le poème en prose, «You're at the bottom of my mind» (*Collected Poems*, p. 175), dont le titre en est un résumé.

> Without my knowing it you are at the bottom of my mind, like one who visits the bottom of the sea with his helmet and his two great eyes: and I do not know properly your expression or your manner after five years of the showers of time pouring between you and me.
>
> Nameless mountains of water pouring between me, hauling you on board, and your expression and manners in my weak hands. You went astray among the mysterious foliage of the sea-bottom in the green half-light without love.
>
> And you will never rise to the surface of the sea, even though my hands should be ceaselessly hauling, and I do not know your way at all, you in the half-light of your sleep, haunting the bottom of the sea without ceasing, and I hauling and hauling on the surface of the ocean.

Dans «Going Home» (*Collected Poems*, p. 176), Crichton Smith entrevoit le retour comme une fuite du monde réel, une forme d'exil vers le monde de l'enfance.

> Tomorrow I will go home to my island, trying to put a world into forgetfulness. I will lift a fistful of its earth in my hands or I will sit on a hillock of the mind, watching "the shepherd with his sheep".
>
> There will ascend (I presume) a thrush. A dawn or two will rise. A boat will be lying in the glitter of the western sun: and water will be running through the world of the similes of my intelligence.

Enfin, dans «Returning Exile» (*Collected Poems*, p. 226), le poète faisant fi de toutes les raisons du retour, exprime la nécessité d'abandonner orgueil et préjugés pour accepter l'enfant prodigue :

> You who come home do not tell me
> anything about yourself, where you have come from,

why your coat is wet, why there is grass in your hair,
[…]
Do not tell me where you have come from, beloved stranger.
It is enough that there is light still in your eyes,
that the dog rising on his pillar of black knows you.

Carol Gow, dans *Mirror and Marble*[28], fait une lecture différente («The silence is prescribed by the community») et plus intime du poème : «[…] but "home" is also poetry itself, and a poet who finds a space in which to write, who accepts the silence of those seven years and yet who finds a new and rich productivity : "it is enough", […].» Il s'agit, pour Gow, du retour à l'écriture du poète qui se remet d'une dépression.

Après avoir décrit la souffrance physique et morale de l'exilé qui s'en revient, et la joie, même agressive, de celui ou celle qui l'accueille; après avoir énoncé l'inutilité de la culpabilisation, Crichton Smith expose une observation paradoxale qui fait valoir l'impossible retour au *statu quo ante*. En effet, le renversement de situation dans le poème «The Departing Island» (*Collected Poems*, p. 60), est une aporie.

Strange to see it—how as we lean over
his vague rail, the island goes away
into its loved light grown suddenly foreign:
how the ship slides outward like a cold ray
from a sun turned cloudy, and rough land draws down
into an abstract sea its arranged star.
[…]
It's the island that goes away, not we who leave it.
Like an unbearable thought it sinks beyond
assiduous reasoning light and wringing hands,
or, as a flower roots deep into the ground,
it works its darkness into the gay winds
that blow about us in a later spirit.

Cette inversion permet d'évacuer la tragédie hébridienne historique des Évictions consécutives à la défaite des Jacobites en 1746 à Culloden, et d'accéder à l'universel; elle contourne l'aliénation de la culpabilité de l'exilé, fût-il de retour; elle facilite l'exploration des multiples aspects de l'exil tels qu'ils ont été énoncés plus haut. En s'échappant du réel tangible et matériel, le poète pose les prémisses de sa démonstration : l'espace entre l'île et moi s'agrandit; je ne bouge pas sur mon bateau poussé par le vent, le courant ou la puissance du moteur. La conséquence semble aller

---

28. C. Gow, *Mirror and Marble*, ouvr. cité, p. 125.

de soi : c'est l'île qui s'éloigne. Il s'ensuit qu'en retournant sur cette île, je ne la retrouverai pas à la même place.

L'exilé de retour doit reconnaître les changements en lui-même et ceux de son île natale et les accepter. Crichton Smith a très tôt eu conscience de sa difficulté d'adaptation à son milieu social, ce qui lui a permis d'analyser l'écart toujours grandissant entre lui et son île. C'est après qu'il est rentré de l'hôpital où il avait été admis pour cause de dépression en 1985 et qu'il a publié le récit de son expérience dans ce roman d'autofiction, *In the Middle of the Wood*[29], qu'il a donné libre cours à ce personnage clownesque, Murdo[30] — un archétype d'endo-exilé propre à endosser les paradoxes des humains. Le recueil de textes de genres les plus divers, *Thoughts of Murdo*, expose de manière humoristique les travers de la société dans le prisme de cet esprit libre. Ce personnage loufoque non seulement permet à Crichton Smith de se tenir en dehors de la société pour en faire une critique plus libre, mais encore lui sert de support pour une nouvelle autobiographique décalée, « Life of Murdo[31] ». Enfin, la forme la plus aboutie de ce personnage-clone apparaît dans la pièce *Lazybed*[32] : Murdo œuvre à la réconciliation de son auteur avec la communauté hébridienne. Lorsque le rideau tombe, le spectateur peut penser que le héros n'est pas plus fou que la nation tout entière engluée dans les excès aliénants du libéralisme économique importé par les Sassenachs.

Crichton Smith a fixé son masque sur le personnage de Murdo, alias Meurdoc, pour mieux se libérer du rôle de l'exilé vindicatif. Demeurant sur la côte d'Argyll, en plein cœur de la Gaélie, Crichton Smith a pu, tout à loisir, envoyer son clone hanter les « îles occidentales » voisines.

L'exil-retour *ad patres*

Le dernier voyage de Crichton Smith est une réponse à l'aporie de l'image de l'île en partance. Il est remarquable que son recueil de poèmes dont le titre est oxymorique, *The Leaf and the Marble*[33], soit sorti de presse quelques jours avant la mort de son auteur. Le poète s'en revient à Rome, tout en s'adressant à la bien-aimée, pour y retrouver les personnages

---

29. *In the Middle of the Wood*, Londres, Victor Gollancz, 1897.

30. La première apparition du personnage de Murdo date de la publication du recueil de nouvelles : *Murdo, and other stories* (Londres, Victor Gollancz, 1981). Le Murdo de Crichton Smith paraît être une forme amplifiée du personnage principal, Murdo Anderson, de *The Albannach*…

31. « Life of Murdo », dans *Murdo, the Life and Works*, S. Conn (dir.), Édimbourg, Birlinn, 2001.

32. *Lazybed* a été traduite (par J. Berton) et publiée sous le titre *Le lectorium, ou le souffroir du Picte existentialiste*, aux Presses de l'université de Saint-Étienne en 2008.

33. *The Leaf and the Marble*, Manchester, Carcanet, 1998.

et les maîtres qu'il a côtoyés toute sa vie. Les images se superposant, le couple archétypal de Didon et Énée épouse les contours du couple Crichton Smith et le dernier poème, avant l'épilogue, reprend l'aporie annoncée plus haut :

> You
> among others I weep for
> in my guilt
> that my sail took you from me
> [...]

La dernière étape du retour *ad patres* est celle de l'Égypte des pharaons : l'épilogue est un ensemble de cinq poèmes (ou un poème en cinq actes) inspirés par un tableau représentant Toutankhamon et sa femme Ankhésenamon. Le poète rentre dans le tableau pour partager l'immortalité du pharaon et nous lègue un condensé de sa vie sous forme d'oxymore modulé conclu par une épanalepse :

> An
> almost questioning wonderment
> elegantly so.

La fiction requiert un enchaînement logique d'actions et ne peut montrer un exilé que face à ses dilemmes et à sa culpabilité et à l'échec de son éventuel retour. Seule la poésie parvient à poser des paradoxes et à résoudre les apories hiéroglyphiques, dont celle de l'île en partance. Après avoir décliné *insula* toute sa vie, et médité sur tous les aspects de la relation entre le narrateur et son objet, le poète retourne vers son île intérieure.

Bibliographie

Traduction de textes de Iain CRICHTON SMITH, par Jean Berton :
Le lectorium, ou le souffroir du Picte existentialiste, Saint-Étienne, PUSE, 2008.
Le télégramme et autres nouvelles d'exil, Paris, Éditions Praelego, 2009. Sélection de vingt-cinq nouvelles en anglais ou en gaélique.

De Iain CRICHTON SMITH

Murdo, the Life and Works, S. Conn (dir.), Édimbourg, Birlinn, 2001.
The Black Halo, K. MacNeil (dir.), Édimbourg, Birlinn, 2001.
The Red Door, K. MacNeil (dir.), Édimbourg, Birlinn, 2001.
The Leaf and the Marble, Manchester, Carcanet, 1998.

Thoughts of Murdo, Nairn, Balnain, 1993.
An Honourable Death, Londres, Macmillan, 1992.
Collected Poems, Manchester, Carcanet, 1992.
The Dream, Londres, Macmillan, 1990.
My Canadian Uncle, Édimbourg, Cencrastus (n° 30), 1988.
An t-Eilean agus an Canan, Glasgow University Press, 1987.
A Life, Manchester, Carcanet, 1986.
Towards the Human, Édimbourg, Macdonalds Publishers, 1986.
The Exiles, Manchester, Carcanet, 1984.
The Search, Londres, Gollancz, 1983.
Murdo, and other stories, Londres, Victor gollancz, 1981.
Selected Poems, 1955–1980, Loanhead, Macdonald, 1981.
On the Island, Glasgow, Drew Publishing, 1979.
The Hermit and Other Stories, Londres, Gollancz, 1977.
The Last Summer, Londres, Gollancz, 1969.
Consider the Lilies, Londres, Gollancz, 1968.
Deer on the High Hills, Édimbourg, Giles Gordon, 1962.
In the Middle of the Wood, Londres, Victor Gollancz, 1897.

Autres

GIFFORD Douglas (dir.), *Scottish Literature*, Edinburgh University Press, 2002.
GOW Carole, *Mirror and Marble, the Poetry of Iain Crichton Smith*, Édimbourg, Saltire, 1992.
MAINGUENEAU Dominique, *Le contexte de l'œuvre littéraire*, Paris, Dunod, 1993.
NICHOLSON Colin (dir.), *Iain Crichton Smith Critical Essays*, Edinburgh University Press, 1992.
WATSON Moray, «Iain Crichton Smith: exile, sparseness and the Clearances», *Studies in Scottish Literature*, vol. 33, 2004.
—, «Iain Crichton Smith» [en ligne], *The Literary Encyclopedia*, 2009, disponible sur <http://www.litencyc.com/php/speople.php?rec=true&UID=4117>.

Jane Gray

Sciences Po Bordeaux

The Woman with the Ibo Nose and the Scottish Tongue: Expressions of Belonging and Return in Jackie Kay's Writing

My grandmother is like a Scottish pine,
tall, straight-backed, proud and plentiful,
a fine head of hair, greying now
tied up in a loose bun.
Her face is a ploughed land.
Her eyes shine rough as amethysts.
She wears a plaid shawl
of our clan with the zeal of an Amazon.
She is one of those women
burnt in her croft rather than moved off the land.
She comes from them, her snake's skin.
She speaks Gaelic mostly, English only
when she has to, then it's blasphemy.

My grandmother sits by the fire and swears
There'll be no darkie baby in this house

My grandmother is a Scottish pine,
tall, straight-backed proud and plentiful,
her hair tied with pins in a ball of steel wool.
Her face is tight as ice
and her eyes are amethysts.[1]

Originally published in 1991, in the now out-of-print collection entitled *That Distance Apart*, "My Grandmother" was reprinted in Kay's collection of new and selected poems entitled *Darling* (2007). By way of introduction, this poem will serve to outline some of the themes I wish to develop in relation to the expressions of belonging and return in Jackie Kay's writing.

---

1. J. Kay, *Darling: New and Selected Poems*, Northumberland, Bloodaxe, 2007, p. 12.

First of all, since Kay is an adopted child of Scottish/Nigerian descent, brought up by a white Glaswegian couple, the poem hints at the autobiographical nature of much of Kay's work. But although personal experience informs her writing, Kay is interested in exploring the threshold between fact and fiction, between reality and imagination, creating, rather, out of her own experience. The poem "My Grandmother" illustrates this point, since the grandmother being described can only be a product of the imagination, the reader having been led to understand that the poetic persona is the "*darkie baby*" in question, verbally banished from the family home before it was even born. Leading on from this idea is the question of identity, of the need to know one's origins, the importance of affiliation, of belonging to a particular place, of knowing where one's home is. This resolutely Scottish grandmother is inextricably linked to her land, to her home, to her language and to her origins. However, following her blatant racist declaration—pronounced almost as a statement of high moral principle—the protagonist proceeds to distort these images, the ballad-type refrain thus hinting at a somewhat ambivalent vision of Scotland and its people.

It also alludes to another of Kay's thematic preoccupations: the notion of "Blackness" in contemporary Britain, exploring issues of divided identity, hybridity, home and exile, loss and longing. Placed as it is at the opening of the *Darling* collection, the poem appears almost as a prologue to *The Adoption Papers*, which immediately follows it, and could be seen, therefore, as the starting point of an imaginary poetic journey undertaken by Kay to retrace her origins, and find her home(s). The aim of this paper is therefore to analyse—by focussing on a selection of Kay's poetry and prose—how the writer comes to terms with these questions of identity, home and belonging, and more significantly, how the theme of *return* to her African origins is expressed in her work.

Many of the interviews that Kay has given over the years highlight the way in which she draws on her personal experience of being Black and Scottish as creative inspiration for her poetry. Kay describes this position as having been unusual when growing up; a contradictory state of being in which she felt isolated. She refers to having been subjected to racist abuse as a teenager, which led her to begin writing "revenge poems".[2] In other words, the powerful tool of the imagination—which was perhaps initially considered to be "therapeutic"—developed into a means for Kay to create images for herself, to define a space she could be at home with,

---

2. Jackie Kay expressed these feelings during a radio interview with Eleanor Wachtel aired on 7 October 2007 on the Canadian programme *Writers and Company*, <www.cbc.ca/wordsatlarge/blog/2008/08/eleanor_wachtel_talks_with_poe.html>.

to which she could belong. Of course, even if the "revenge poems" of her youth are no longer part of her poetic agenda, she has continued to express a double relationship to her country of birth as well as an ambivalent sense of belonging. This is illustrated in several of her poems and short stories: "So You Think I'm A Mule" (*A Dangerous Knowing*, 1988), "In My Country" (*Other Lovers*, 1993), "The Broons' Bairn's Black" (*Off Colour*, 1998), or "The Oldest Woman in Scotland" (*Why Don't You Stop Talking*, 2002), to name but a few examples. An incident Jackie Kay actually experienced is poetically expressed in "So You Think I'm A Mule".[3] Kay describes in an interview with Rebecca Wilson how a woman approached her and questioned her Scottish identity, insisting: "You're not pure, are you? You're a mulatto."[4] The opening lines read:

"Where do you come from?"
"I'm from Glasgow."
"Glasgow?"
"Uh huh, Glasgow."
The white face hesitates
The eyebrows raise
The mouth opens
Then snaps shut
Incredulous
Yet too polite to say outright
Liar

The woman insists on obtaining a more satisfactory answer to comfort her suspicions, until she utters the fatal word "mulatto", resulting in a fierce poetic diatribe, the use of alliteration insisting on the "dialectics of mixtures" that the speaker finds so insulting:

Listen. My original father was Nigerian
to help with your confusion
but hold on right there
If you dare mutter mulatto
Hover around hybrid
Hobble on half-caste
And intellectualize on the
"mixed race problem",
I have to tell you:

3. Jackie Kay, "So You Think I'm a Mule?", in *A Dangerous Knowing: Four Black Women Poets*, London, Sheba Feminist Publishers, 1988.
4. R. Wilson and G. Somerville-Arjat (eds), *Sleeping With Monsters: Conversations with Scottish and Irish Women Poets*, Edinburgh, Polygon, 1990, p. 121.

Take your beady eyes offa my skin;
Don't concern yourself with
The "dialectics of mixtures";
Don't pull that strange blood crap
On me Great White Mother

The concluding lines allude to the question of "belonging", and the speaker proceeds to take on a feminist stance and identify herself politically with other women of the Black diaspora:

So take your questions, your interest,
Your patronage. Run along.
Just leave me.
I'm going to my Black sisters
To women who nourish each other
On belonging
There's a lot of us
Black women trying to define
Just who we are
Where we belong
And if we know no home
We know one thing:
We are Black
We're at home with that.

These lines become problematic, however, when they are considered in relation to the place—Glasgow—the speaker initially identifies herself with, since it suggests that a sense of belonging can only be found elsewhere. The statement: "I'm going to my Black sisters" thus implies a form of exile—be it geographical or imaginary, forced or voluntary—from Scotland.

The purpose of this paper is by no means to question racism in Scottish society, and indeed, I would tend to agree with Gavin Miller's assertion—borrowing from Walter Benn Michaels—that "even when *we* are racist, the society to which we are committed is not".[5] However, this feeling of being a "contradiction", or an "anomaly" (*SWM*, p. 121)—to quote some of the words used by the poet herself—is echoed in other examples of how Black or Asian Scots negotiate with the idea of Scottishness. In 2002, Tom Devine and Paddy Logue brought together the reflec-

---

5. W. B. Michaels, *The Trouble with Diversity: How We Learned to Love Identity and Ignore Equality*, New York, Metropolitan, 2006, pp. 82–3, in G. Miller, "Scotland's Authentic Plurality: The New Essentialism in Scottish Studies", *Scottish Literary Review*, vol. 1, no. 1, Spring/Summer 2009, p. 168.

THE WOMAN WITH THE IBO NOSE AND THE SCOTTISH TONGUE

tions of what they described as a "balanced cross-section of Scots"[6] into a book entitled *Being Scottish: Personal Reflections on Being Scottish Today*. The accounts given by Robina Qureshi (born and brought up in Glasgow to Pakistani immigrants) and Mukami McCrum (born in Kenya and Chief Executive of Central Scotland Racial Equality Council), reiterate—to varying degrees—Kay's preoccupations with belonging within a Scottish context. Mukami McCrum's contribution is particularly interesting in that she notes parallels between the Scots and the people of Unjiru where she grew up. However, brought up in the Church of Scotland tradition in Kenya, she writes:

> For me, being Scottish is about a sense of belonging, identity and how others see me. While Kenyans often remind me that I am Scottish, not all Scots have come to terms with my colour and ethnic background. When I say that I come from Linlithgow, political correctness makes some people accept it, while others ask me, where do you really come from [...] My Scottish teachers in Kenya never told us about the inherent fear and dislike that some Scots have for people like me. [...] Clearly my colour and being Scottish were mutually exclusive and a challenge for many people. (*BS*, pp. 156–7.)

Robina Qureshi's contribution is conveyed with much more anger. Both personal experience and her active involvement in Scotland in challenging institutionalised racism and government policy towards refugees lead her to describe Scottish society as "deeply racist" (*BS*, p. 219) and one in which the refrains: "'Go back home, Paki', 'Go back to where you belong'" (*BS*, p. 218) that she heard in her childhood perhaps too many times for comfort, make it difficult for her to "feel Scottish". She writes:

> I don't really feel Scottish unless I go abroad, but then I say "I am from Scotland", not "I'm Scottish". No way, not unless it is to annoy the hell out of someone who is determined that I don't come from here. Scotland is not my home in that sense of the word... (*BS*, p. 218.)

Even though we must bear in mind—as do the editors of the book in which these accounts were published—that these examples are but "one snapshot of Scottish identity" (*BS*, p. XIII), they do tend to highlight a common sense of alienation and a difficulty in finding a "home". In Jackie Kay's case, though, and in the case of writers such as the late Maud Sulter, or "New Scots" such as Leila Aboulela or Imtiaz Dharker, this particular position has been a continuing source of creative tension.

---

6. T. Devine and P. Logue (eds), *Being Scottish: Personal Reflections on Scottish Identity Today*, Edinburgh, Polygon, 2002, p. XII.

Kay's White Scottish upbringing adds a further dimension to her writing. Having been "steeped in Scottish culture" (*SWM*, p. 122), she claims that:

> If you're brought up in a place, you get that identity very, very fixedly. And you don't necessarily get a sense of your being Black, because there's nothing else around you affirming that you are. (*SWM*, p. 122.)

The poem "Watching People Sing" (*Other Lovers*, 1993), illustrates this point particularly well. It evokes a family gathering, during which the persona's relatives take turns to demonstrate their singing talents. The titles and lyrics from traditional Scottish ballads, which punctuate this poem, serve, as Alison Lumsden suggests, to:

> [...] provide the singers with a link to "The mouths of the people of the past", who offer the speaker both a context in which she may belong, and the possibility of a future grounded in that context.[7]

Furthermore, Alison Lumsden suggests that such "an overtly Scottish poem" (*CSWW*, p. 84) as this one immediately following her sequence of "Bessie Smith" poems (*Other Lovers*)—which engage in expressions of Black identity—serves to "de-stabilise" any implication that "blackness may be a more important aspect of identity for the poet" (*CSWW*, p. 84). The different sequences in Kay's poetry do tend to juxtapose these themes and can be interpreted as a means of further highlighting the poet's artistic negotiation with being *both* Black *and* Scottish, of belonging to two cultures, as it is expressed elsewhere in her work. Music is another device the poet uses to convey this state of being. Both ballad and jazz music thematically, stylistically and rhythmically punctuate Kay's writing and serve as a way, she says, "of being Black and being Scottish at the same time in words".[8]

Hence, the juxtaposition of themes in Kay's collections may serve rather to define a space in which one's identity can be both one and the other, both "Kail" *and* "Callaloo" as Kay's poem of the same name suggests, a place where it is possible to be an "Afro-Scot" or a "Celtic-Afro-Caribbean", where you can "dance a reel *and* a salsa / remember Fannie Lou Hamer *and* Robert Burns" (my italics).[9]

---

7. A. Lumsden, in A. Christianson and A. Lumsden (eds), *Contemporary Scottish Women Writers*, Edinburgh, Edinburgh University Press, 2000, p. 84.

8. Jackie Kay interviewed for *The Poetry Archive*, <www.poetryarchive.org>.

9. J. Kay, "Kail and Callaloo", in S. Grewal, J. Kay, L. Landor, G. Lewis, and P. Parmar (eds), *Charting the Journey: Writings by Black and Third World Women*, London, Sheba Feminist Publishers, 1988, p. 195.

We may also suggest that, as a writer who has now been living in England since the 1980s, her "overtly Scottish" poems may be seen as a way to reconnect with her Scottish origins, in the same way as poets or writers such as John Burnside or Carol Ann Duffy have done. Distance, according to Kay, has given her "an outside way of looking back in".[10] She has stated in interviews that moving to England has given her more confidence and courage as a lesbian writer (*SWM*, pp. 126–7). She also explains that the more "multi-cultural" nature of Manchester (where she now lives) was important for her because she did not want her son to be "quizzed permanently about his identity".[11] Although these remarks hint at the complex "double" relationship Kay has with Scotland, some of her work echoes the recurring themes of loss and (be)longing, of displacement and of return in relation to Scotland that can be found in Burnside's "Exile's Return" (*Dream State*, p. 9)[12] and "Out of Exile" *(ibid.)*, or in Carol Ann Duffy's poems "Originally", "Plainsong" and "The Way My Mother Speaks" for example. In Duffy's poem "Originally"[13], the protagonist's expression of exile is reminiscent of Edward Said's description of "estrangement", as that "unhealable rift forced between a human being and a native place, between the self and its true home".[14] The opening lines read:

> We came from our own country in a red room
> which fell through the fields, our mother singing
> our father's name to the turn of the wheels.
> My brothers cried, one of them bawling *Home*,
> *Home*, as the miles rushed back to the city,
> the street, the house, the vacant rooms
> where we didn't live any more.

To the physical, geographical displacement is added linguistic alienation, reminding the speaker that she does not belong, because her accent is "wrong". Then follows the expression of sadness and longing as the speaker cries: "*I want our own country.*" The concluding lines evoke the role of memory, as "you forget, or don't recall, or change":

> I remember my tongue
> shedding its skin like a snake, my voice

---

10. In L. Brooks, "Don't tell me who I am", *The Guardian*, 12-01-2002, [online edition].
11. Interview with Eleanor Wachtel, *op. cit.*
12. D. O'Rourke (ed.), *Dream State: The New Scottish Poets*, Edinburgh, Polygon, 1994, 231 p.
13. C. A. Duffy, "Originally" (1990), in *Selected Poems: Carol Ann Duffy*, London, Penguin Books, 1994, p. 65.
14. E. Said, "Reflections on Exile", in *Reflections on Exile and Other Essays*, Harvard University Press, 2000, p. 173.

in the classroom sounding just like the rest. Do I only
think
I lost a river, culture, speech, sense of first space
and the right place? Now, *Where do you come from?*
strangers ask. *Originally?* And I hesitate.

As memory fades through time, there is an inherent sense of something irretrievably lost which is much more than just an accent or a place:
it is—as Margery Palmer McCulloch has suggested in reference to this
poem—a progressive loss of the *self* [15], made all the more painful by the
protagonist's *awareness* of it. These sentiments of loss of Scottish accent
through exile as synonymous with the loss of the "self" are reiterated in
Kay's poem, "Old Tongue" [16]:

When I was eight, I was forced south.
Not long after, when I opened
my mouth, a strange thing happened.
I lost my Scottish accent.
Words fell off my tongue:
eedyit, dreich, wabbit, crabbit
stummer, teuchter, heidbanger,
so you are, so am ur, see you, see ma ma,
shut yer geggie or I'll gie you the malkie!

My own vowels started to stretch like my bones
and I turned my back on Scotland.
Words disappeared in the dead of night,
new words marched in: ghastly, awful,
quite dreadful, *scones* said like *stones*.
Pokey hats into ice cream cones.
Oh where did all my words go—
my old words, my lost words?
Did you ever feel sad when you lost a word,
did you ever try and call it back
like calling in the sea?
If I could have found my words wandering,
I swear I would have taken them in,
swallowed them whole, knocked them back.

Out in the English soil, my old words
buried themselves. It made my mother's blood boil.

---

15. M. P. McCulloch, "Scottish Women's Poetry 1972–1999: Transforming Traditions", in
A. Christianson and A. Lumsden, *Contemporary Scottish Women Writers*, p. 21.
16. J. Kay, "Old Tongue", in *Life Mask*, Northumberland, Bloodaxe, 2005, p. 50.

I wanted them back; I wanted my old accent back,
my old tongue. My dour soor Scottish tongue.
Sing-songy. I wanted to *gie it laldie*.

Again we have the use of the metonymical, melopoeic Scottish "tongue" as bearer of the "self", as well as the emotions of sadness and longing induced by the experience of loss. It is interesting to note the reference to the mother in this context, who serves to remind the protagonist of his/her origins; of the "mother tongue". The same idea is conveyed in Carol Ann Duffy's poem entitled "The Way My Mother Speaks".[17] The persona takes the train back down to England after a visit "home", repeating throughout the duration of the journey her mother's characteristically Scottish syntax in the expression: "*What like is it*", and concluding: "I am homesick, free, in love / with the way my mother speaks."

For Jackie Kay, therefore, themes characteristic of displacement permeate her work in a similar way. But as we have seen, there are constant reminders that "home" is also to be found *elsewhere*, either through the refusal of others to acknowledge her Scottish identity due to the colour of her skin, or through her own awareness of her being an adopted child of African descent. Brought up by White Scottish parents, Kay has said that as a child, she "never had any sense of Black culture at all, until (she) went about finding and creating it for (her)self" (*SWM*, p. 122). In one interview she relates with humour to having created an "imaginary Black family" in the jazz and blues singers Bessie Smith, Duke Ellington, Count Basie or Sarah Vaughan, "in the absence of having Black neighbours or Black friends".[18] This "extended family"—as it were—implies the possibility of being "someone else", and is creatively expressed in her poetry and prose alike. In the poem "The Red Graveyard"[19] the speaker recalls visual memories of her childhood home, and of her father dancing to Bessie Smith, and wonders: "Why do I remember her voice […]. Why do I remember the blues?" In her sequence "The Adoption Papers", which tells the story of adoption through the voices of the biological mother, the adoptive mother and the daughter, the daughter finds self-recognition in the African-American jazz artists Pearl Bailey and Bessie Smith and in human rights activist Angela Davis. Kissing the poster of Angela Davis she has on her bedroom wall, the girl reflects upon their skin colour:

17. C. A. Duffy, *Selected Poems*, p. 88.
18. Interview with Eleanor Wachtel, *op. cit.*
19. J. Kay, "The Red Graveyard" (*Other Lovers*, 1993), in *Darling: New & Selected Poems*, p. 73.

I can see my skin is that colour
but most of the time I forget,
so sometimes when I look in the mirror
I give myself a bit of a shock
and say to myself *Do you really look like this?*
as if I'm somebody else. I wonder if she does that. [20]

In the same way, the poetic persona in "Somebody Else" laments: "It's no laughing matter going about the place / all the time being somebody else: / people mistake you; you mistake yourself." [21] This theme is also at work in the novel *Trumpet*, the story of a famous Black Scottish trumpet player, Joss Moody, who after his death is revealed to have been a woman. His adopted son, Colman, is deeply upset at this revelation, and begins questioning his own identity, and the possibility of being someone completely different, had he not been adopted. Reflecting on his original name, he claims:

If I'd stayed William Dunsmore all my life I'd have been a completely different man. Definitely. I mean a William Dunsmore smile would be different from a Colman Moody's smile. All my facial expressions would have been different. I bet even my walk would have been heavier if I'd have been William Dunsmore. Heavy-footed. Maybe a bit lopsided. [22]

Finally, and perhaps even more significantly, the poem "Pride" [23]— which tells of a chance encounter between a Black woman and a Black man on a train—evokes an imaginary *return* to the woman's African origins when the man recognizes the features of the Ibo people on her face. As the man excitedly claims: "That nose is an Ibo nose. / Those teeth are Ibo teeth", the speaker says: "There was a moment when / my whole face changed into a map, / and the stranger on the train / located even the name / of my village in Nigeria / in the lower part of my jaw." As their conversation develops, the woman imagines her return to this other "home":

I saw myself arriving
the hot dust, the red road,
the trees heavy with other fruits,
the bright things, the flowers.
I saw myself watching

---

20. J. Kay, *The Adoption Papers*, Northumberland, Bloodaxe, 1991, p. 27.

21. J. Kay, "Somebody Else", in *Off Colour*, Northumberland, Bloodaxe, 1998, p. 27.

22. J. Kay, *Trumpet*, London, Picador, 1998, p. 56.

23. J. Kay, "Pride", in *Off Colour*, p. 62.

the old people dance towards me
dressed up for me in happy prints.
And I found my feet.
I started to dance.
I danced a dance I never knew I knew.
Words and sounds fell out of my mouth like seeds.
I astonished myself.
My grandmother was like me exactly, only darker.

When I looked up, the black man had gone.
Only my own face startled me in the dark train window.

What is significant at this point is the *vagueness* of the African imagery the woman conjures up. She evokes "*other* fruit", "bright *things*", "*happy* prints", "*a* dance", "*words*" and "*sounds*", alluding to the oneiric quality of her return to Africa but at the same time reflecting Koye Oyedeji's claim that "for many of a Black generation born in Britain, a knowledge of Africa remains no more than facing The Unexamined River. A rippling river across which you can see Africans on the other side".[24] Colman Moody in *Trumpet* alludes to this notion of a "fantasy" Africa as opposed to a "real" Africa:

> We never actually got to go to Africa. Joss had built up such a strong imaginary landscape within himself that he said it would affect his music to go to the real Africa. Every Black person has a fantasy Africa, he'd say. Black British people, Black Americans, Black Caribbeans, they all have a fantasy Africa. It's all in the head. (*T*, p. 34.)

Nigerian academic Afam Akeh—who considers Jackie Kay as a writer of the "African" diaspora—asserts that such writers' "representations of home" (i.e. Africa):

> remain poignantly estranged, as they focus, like tourists, on what is strange, what is different, what might elicit laughter, disgust or some other strong interest or response from outsiders about that distant location or memory they interpret as home.[25]

---

24. K. Oyedeji, "Prelude to a Brand New Purchase on Black Political Identity: A Reading of Bernadine Evaristo's *Lara* and Diran Adebayo's *Some Kind of Black*", in K. Sesay (ed.), *Write Black Write British: From Post Colonial to Black British Literature*, Hertford, Hansib Publications, 2005, p. 355.
25. A. Akeh, "'Poor' African Writers Travelling: Home and Exile in Younger Nigerian Diasporic Writing", in *Sentinel Poetry*, no. 48, November 2006 [online journal], <www.sentinelpoetry.org.uk/1106/Afam_Akeh.html>.

He insists on "the diasporic personal experiences of these 'African' writers as being influential in 'how they write, (and) what they write'".[26] For Jackie Kay, in "the absence of an intimate knowledge of the material realities of Africa",[27] the sequence of African poems published in the collection *Life Mask* comprises a fusing and juxtaposition of reality and the imagination pertaining to magic realism, intertwining her personal experience of travelling to Nigeria to meet her birth father with African myths, stories, rituals and masks, landscapes, and animal and food imagery. This imagery provides the backdrop for dream-like journeys along the "hot dust, red road(s)"[28]—a recurring image in Kay's work—as the protagonist negotiates with finding a sense of belonging in her father's country in poems such as "Things Fall Apart", "A White African Dress" or "Kano", for example. Brenda Cooper, in her analysis of the works of diasporic women writers of African background, sees this "excavating" of African stories and beliefs as a way of "stak[ing] a claim [...] to Africa".[29] However, she sees their use of magic realism as "stretched taut, given that they have had neither first hand experience of the supernatural world of the African oral tradition, nor of the material cultural background of their [...] African parents".[30] This is not to undermine the legitimacy of their African-inflected writing, but rather to insist on the way that such writers—including Jackie Kay—use it to represent their personal experience of being between two cultures. Gina Wisher refers to Jackie Kay along with Monica Ali *(Brick Lane)* and Zadie Smith *(White Teeth)* as being among UK Asian and Black writers who:

> negotiate potential and real difficulties of working within the diaspora, developing and articulating a hybrid existence and identity, charting passages between cultures and between their perceptions of those within and without their own communities.[31]

Jackie Kay's creative "return" to her African roots has also led to poetic expressions of Britain's colonial past, lending a voice to those who suffered enslavement or racial intolerance. This can be seen in poems from the collection *Off Colour* such as "Hottentot Venus" or "Gambia",

---

26. *Ibidem.*
27. B. Cooper, "'Birthed in the Third Space': Myth and Language in Diasporic Women Writers of African Background" [online], University of Pittsburgh, August 2006, p. 13, <www.english.pitt.edu/.../Cooper%20--%20African%20Novels%20paper.pdf>.
28. J. Kay, "Kano" *(Life Mask)*, in *Darling*, p. 180.
29. B. Cooper, *op. cit.*, p. 1.
30. *Ibid.*, p. 13.
31. G. Wisher, "Negotiating passages: Asian and Black Women's Writing in Britain", 2004-05-01, Hecate publication [online article], p. 16.

for example, or from a specifically Scottish perspective in "Christian Sanderson", the story of a Black Scotswoman deported to Australia after poverty and hunger drove her to steal "sixteen shillings".[32]

In 2007 Kay published the dramatised epic poem *The Lamplighter*, the multi-vocal story of slavery focussing on the lives of four women. Based on original accounts and testimonies, it bears witness to the horrific pain and suffering felt by those people forced from their lands onto ships and taken to the Caribbean plantations or to Britain to build the industrial cities of Glasgow, Liverpool or Bristol. The women's autodiegetic narratives overlap one another, individual accounts thus fusing together to recount the experience of an entire people. The expression of loss pervades the poem: "I lost my family. I lost my name. / I lost my country. I lost my freedom. I lost my weight. / I lost my sense of smell. [...] I lost my bearings. I lost faith / (for a while.) / I lost my words. / I lost my tongue. / I lost my sense of fun."[33] Memory, home and belonging are leitmotifs in the opening pages as the women recall images, smells and tastes from their "own country" (*L*, p. 24). But as the poem progresses, these images are replaced by the terrible reality of slavery. The will to return home, however, remains constant, and is symbolically rendered by the Negro spirituals that punctuate the monologues or by the accounts of relentless—albeit vain—attempts to escape. They are given new names: "Constance", thus named so that she "would forever be constant" (*L*, p. 33); "Black Harriot": "So that white Harriot / Never needed to be called / *White Harriot* / And could just be Harriot" (*L*, p. 34). As for "Mary MacDonald", we read: "Original meaning uncertain" (*L*, p. 33). The "uncertain" origin of this final name appears of course highly ironic, alluding possibly to the poet's criticism of Scotland's problematic lack of acknowledgement of its forebears' role in the slave trade. In an article published in *The Guardian*, Kay writes:

> Being African and Scottish, I'd taken comfort in the notion that Scotland was not nearly as implicated in the horrors of the slave trade as England. [...] Scotland is a canny nation when it comes to remembering and forgetting. The plantation owner is never wearing a kilt.[34]

The Lamplighter was a commissioned work written to mark the 200th anniversary of abolition. Although no city is spared, there is an insistence on how Scotland profited from the triangular slave trade in the slaves' singing in unison of the words "*I belong to Glasgow*" and "Glasgow belongs

---

32. J. Kay, *Off Colour*, p. 29.
33. J. Kay, *The Lamplighter*, Northumberland, Bloodaxe, 2008, p. 18.
34. J. Kay, "Missing Faces", *The Guardian*, 2007-03-24 [online article].

to me" (*L*, p. 74), claiming the rightful acknowledgement of their part in building this city, in putting Glasgow "on the map" (*L*, p. 72). Glasgow streets named after Caribbean islands and tobacco lords are evoked as are the "one hundred Black people / Called MacDonald" on the "slave island of Jamaica" (*L*, p. 81). Having been repeatedly raped by a Scottish slave owner, Black Harriot claims: "My daughters have Scottish blood. Scotland has my blood" (*L*, p. 81).

Kay has written about her personal experience of writing this piece of work. Reluctant at first to embark on such a project, which she feared would "pigeonhole" her as a Black writer, she finally accepted, having become aware of her ignorance on the subject through "the shocking original testimonies" [35] she discovered during her research. The actual writing process, she explains, "felt as if I was writing a love letter to my ancestors". [36]

Once again, therefore, we witness in Kay's writing a conscious effort to negotiate "passages between cultures and histories", [37] creatively bringing forth—through this highly symbolic return to Africa's tragic past and Scotland's shameful role in slavery—connections between the two countries. Thus, through her poetry and prose, through the poetic expression of her belonging both to Scotland and Africa, and above all through the juxtaposition of imagery and experiences related to both cultures, I have tried to illustrate how Kay manages to come to terms with what she has described as the "multiplicity" [38] of her own identity. Like other Black British writers, one might argue that she has sought to define a new space: a 'third space' [39]—to borrow Homi Bhabha's terms—one in which she might feel at home.

---

35. *Ibidem.*
36. *Ibid.*
37. G. Wisher, *op. cit.*, p. 4.
38. In C. Whyte (ed.), *Gendering the Nation*, Edinburgh, Edinburgh University Press, 1995, p. 10.
39. Homi Bhabha refers to the notion of cultural "hybridity" as the "third space", which "gives rise to something different, something new and unrecognisable, a new area of negotiation of meaning and representation". It is defined as a space "which enables other positions to emerge". See J. Rutherford, "The Third Space. Interview with Homi Bhabha" [online], in Ders. (Hg), *Identity: Community, Culture, Difference*, London, Lawrence and Wishart, 1990, p. 211, <ccfi.educ.ubc.ca/Courses_Reading_Materials/ccfi502/Bhabha.pdf>.

Camille Manfredi

University of Brest, HCTI/CEIMA (EA 4249)

Internal, imaginary and ontological exile in Peter Urpeth's *Far Inland* (2006)

In 2006 Peter Urpeth published his first, and so far only, novel entitled *Far Inland*. The novel tells the story of Sorley MacRath, a native of Lewis, who left the island to make a living as a bookseller in "the Big City" (p. 79) of Glasgow. After he is brutally assaulted and falls into a coma, Sorley discovers that he has a "gift", the power to let his spirit travel out of his body. During his skyward travels back through time and to the place of his ancestors, Sorley becomes increasingly aware of his uniqueness and vocation as a modern-day shaman. The realisation, while bearing much resemblance to a posttraumatic stress symptom, triggers Sorley's compulsion to move back to his native island and find out about the origin of his vocation. *Far Inland* is thus set partly in Glasgow and partly in Lewis. But there is also a third setting, one that allows another form of travel writing: in his trances, Sorley travels to an allegorical, imaginary homeland hidden somewhere up North, caught in the ice of the Arctic. This "wild country of the mind" (to quote Wallace Stevens) overlaps the traditional dichotomy between island and city blurred by the tripartite structure, while offering Sorley a magical alternative to his native island.

The novel repeats the general pattern of the *Bildungsroman* and is organised along two parallel narrative threads: Sorley's redemptive physical homecoming to the wilderness of north-east Scotland and his ritual and spiritual journey back to the origins of his gift, the elusive "far inland" of the title. The analysis of the two embedded return narratives soon reveals that Sorley suffers from three forms of alienation or exile that are not exactly new to the Scottish hero: one from his native island, another one due to his "shamanic election", and a third one that arises out of his suspected mental disorder. Sorley appears exiled all at once from his birthplace, from his community and, last but not least, from himself. What is more, the modern sense of loss makes Urpeth's protagonist acutely sensitive to his own experience of renewal and atavism, estrangement and normality, issues that are intrinsically connected with the problematics of exile as they are identified by Edward Said in his *Reflections on Exile* of 2000.

| 169

The dispossessed hero's struggles to make sense of the world will draw interesting parallels with the narrative genre of fantasy theorised by Jean Le Guennec's *États de l'inconscient dans le récit fantastique* (2003), while illustrating Said's views on the necessary debunking of romantic ideas about exile. By analysing the structural and thematic interactions between the two return narratives, this paper will attempt to highlight the competing claims of a return to reality and a particular form of both willing and unwilling exile into the imaginary. Peter Urpeth's attempts at re-enchanting Scotland will also raise the issues of representation and identity that are central to our reflection. The point will be to explain how Urpeth uses Sorley's extravagant daydreams to formulate an original proposal for an alternative cultural identity, a proposal that may, however, remain enduringly romantic and thus exemplify the difficult journey from essentialist immaturity to progressive identity.

We can consider that there are two return narratives in *Far Inland*, the first being the story line of the novel which tells of the linear, contemporary and realistic return of Sorley to Lewis—a journey through space. Embedded within the first one, however, we also find Sorley's fantastic, onirical journey to the mythological North—a journey through time. The main "Glasgow-Lewis" narrative relies on the opposition between island and city, a *topos* that has had a long tradition in Scottish literature and is exemplified in the works of major Scottish writers such as Edwin Muir, Iain Crichton Smith, Sorley MacLean, Alasdair Gray and A. L. Kennedy among many others. The contrastive pattern has of course featured in postcolonial discourse studies as a parable of the denunciation of the evils of colonisation. The juxtaposition of small rural communities enjoying a largely unspoilt nature with life in the evil, corrupt city—the classical opposition of virtue and vice—has often turned into a structuring principle. *Far Inland* is no exception to the rule, with its suggestion that life in the city tends to equal persecution and gratuitous violence. Meanwhile, Urpeth hints at the issues of island depopulation and cultural dispossession. He does so obliquely, through a rather low-key reference to emigration to Canada (p. 131) or the metaphor of the lost swarm of bees that epitomises the many young islanders who "never came back" (p. 132).

We learn that Sorley left Lewis as a young adult, lured like so many others by the promise of a better life on the "Big", English-speaking mainland. The assumption that all that is English is "big and modern" (p. 79) and that all that is related to the old ways (including the vernacular) is therefore small and obsolete is quickly undermined. The city brings but linguistic deprivation: significantly enough, the depiction of the world when seen from Glasgow is characterised by its impoverished language as shown through the systematic use of situational articles. "The city", "the island", "the loch" or "the village" have all lost their names as if the world had shrunk to almost nothing but a limited stock of words, for a limited stock of landscapes. This is perhaps why Young Sorley had guessed, and rightly so, that the island boys, belonging as they did to a place where words still had meaning, "would always be strangers in the city" (p. 79). The feeling of estrangement sharpens after Sorley is brutally assailed and left for dead in the gutter:

> He went towards [the pub] and pushed on its sprung doors expecting to be greeted by the familiar faces behind the bar but all he saw was a face he had not seen before, a young woman behind the bar who did not know him. He looked about the public bar, one or two were sitting that he half-recognised but who showed no obvious sign of knowing him. (p. 91)

Sorley's sudden loss of bearings is of course the perfect harbinger of fantasy. The physical abuse he went through and his subsequent discovery of his "gift" add another experience of alterity to the one caused by his internal migration. It is finally the inclusion of fantastic elements in Sorley's urban environment that prompts his return to the island and to an original situation of unity with the land of his ancestors:

> The gift of sight, the flight, the cave, the saving of Calum, all of it was true, all of it was his and all of it related to another world, an archaic place and time where and when such things mattered. These were not gifts for the city, but gifts for the open wilderness. (p. 98)

When compared to Glasgow, Lewis appears to Sorley as a sanctuary on "an ocean of peace, a place where life could begin again and where there was escape from the insanity of the city". "Maybe", Sorley continues, "it was a place where he would be wanted and he would be taking the gift home" (p. 113). Sorley's homecoming to Lewis is therefore not so much a mere journey through space as the deluded pursuit of some alternative sense of belonging. Going back to the island leads Urpeth's protagonist to explore notions such as culture, ancestry, origin and time, as well as to question the reasons why he left in the first place. Sorley's original departure, and this becomes more and more explicit, occurring out of necessity as much as out of cowardice: "He was the one that left, that went, that turned his back. He was the one who ran away as a child and as an adult" (p. 134).

Sorley's return is then bound to make him face up to the sense of betrayal, and therefore of guilt, that his flight to Glasgow had only served to magnify:

> I suppose I've carried that with me all my life since then, since leaving the island, a deferred guilt. The pain put off until another, better time when it would be all the more terrible, and I think that time has come. (p. 80)

Returning to Lewis is then inevitable. Sorley's search for redemption and atonement with the parents he admits to having "turned his back on" (p. 67) marks the beginning of his self-mythologising journey and the transfiguration of the native space into a gateway to some other magical world. The first step he takes through this gateway is once again linguistic:

> When Sorley heard Alex's voice he knew at once that he was making the right decision, almost as if the sound of a voice, the inflection of the Gaelic in the English, the shaping of the vowels somehow changed the constitution of his blood. More of a transfusion than a journey, Sorley knew, or at least hoped he knew that going home would bring sense to the happenings of the last few weeks and months. (p. 116)

Sorley's unconscious need to transform his return to Lewis into a reintegration ritual is already perceptible. The Gaelic speakers even come to form a secret society that Sorley calls "the community of knowing" (p. 144), keeping the secret of the poetic and elemental song of the vernacular. A simple list of place names becomes a sacred litany comparable to "the sound of the Gaelic Salm" (p. 144), somewhat magically lifting the mist, opening the gates to the long-forgotten beauty of the natural world. The sea passage to the island functions as an "ecstatic" (p. 127) introductive miracle that would have been enough to reterritorialise Sorley's identity, had the novel been less elaborate:

> Sorley said the names again and again in his head. As their sounds resonated so the sun broke over the exposed, ice-scoured rock of a sea cliff, its reflection a brilliant orange in the deep blue waters of the loch. (p. 123)

But the traditional structure of the *Bildungsroman* is disrupted by the strand of fantasy introduced in the thirteen embedded visions of Book Two. These spill over into the main narrative, as Sorley proves unable to renounce the great myth of origins he had caught a glimpse of in his coma-induced visions. He fails to retransfer his spiritual centre of gravity from the unknown zone of the Arctic back to reality: Sorley keeps mistaking himself for an Inuit shaman exactly as he mistakes the Highlands for—oddly enough—Mount Fuji (p. 85) or his personal return trip for an epic, mythological journey. Sorley's hallucinatory perceptions of the native space triggered by his near-death experience are thus grafted onto the island, turning the whole novel into a composite work of fiction that bears most of the characteristics of Joseph Campbell's "monomyth" as it is exposed in *The Hero with a Thousand Faces* (1949). The very structure of the novel mirrors the standard pattern of adventure and the sequence of ordeals or initiation stages identified by Campbell in the hero's passing from ignorance to self-knowledge: the "departure" section is narrated in books one and two, the "initiation" stage in book three and the first half of book four, the hero's "return" in the second part of book four and book five. Parallel to that of a conventional return narrative, a second reading of *Far Inland* is then made possible: Sorley receives a "call" (a keyword in the novel) to adventure that is first dismissed by others as "voodoo" (p. 108), "dreams of the coma" (p. 61) or even "bloody witch-craft" (p. 114). Once he has committed to the quest for his vocation, Sorley is mysteriously provided with artefacts (the Rasmussen volume, Sorley's "memento", p. 117) and protective figures (Morag, as well as animal totems such as the Arctic fox, p. 17) that help him all along his road of trials and across the threshholds leading to the supernatural world. There, Sorley undergoes a number of transformations ("His skin was now white fur, and he ran on his feet and hands", p. 13), is magically gifted with "some other tongue" (p. 14) passed onto him by the *angakok*. Finally, he dies a symbolical death that triggers his return journey to the ordinary world where he is to bestow his healing gift onto his fellow men.

The transcription of Sorley's visions is highly metaphorical and loaded with Jungian archetypes. These visions suggest that Sorley's alleged vocation as a shaman (as the ultimate exile or, as Urpeth writes, "an isolated wanderer of the remote places", p. 144) might turn him into a stranger in his own land, forever displaced and forever alienated. As the timeless landscapes of the Arctic invade the novel, Lewis falls back into the mists of oblivion.

The solipsistic forces that work upon Sorley, and perhaps also on Urpeth, are not entirely devoid of a social historical perspective. The stories of the Arctic brought back by 19th and 20th century Scottish whalers allow Urpeth to introduce a poetic dialogue between Inuit and Gaelic cultures. The very genealogy of his protagonist (it is said that Sorley's great-grandfather took an Inuit wife and brought her back to Lewis [p. 65]) provides him with an alternative, yet not so unlikely narrative of national identity, as history has attested to marriages between Lewismen who worked for the Hudson's Bay Company and native American women. Pre-modern northern Hinterland offers Sorley everything he could expect from an idealised home: virginity, remoteness, wilderness, a syncratic history and the heroic aesthetic potential that poor, rural, depopulated Lewis does not provide:

> He was flying again and in the song he heard, as though coming from the
> distance, the slow beat of the shaman's drum. Its skin was from the north,

its voice from the north and in the ancient voice was the voice of the Norse, the Inuit, the Sami and the Gael, all as one in one moment, all following the same drum. In its ancient skin of the drum was the spirit of the animal, the spirit of the person, the shaman dancing with them both on the skin of the drum. The rhythm a path to ecstasy, they danced on and on. (p. 127)

There, and there only, can he be "a dead man, a feral man" and, by freeing himself from the burden of reality, "walk out of the place he really belonged" (p. 69). But Sorley, in his own deluded mind, does not return to Lewis. He exiles himself to an existential territory in which he hopes to recreate an atopic and atemporal identity, one in which thresholds between realms and cultures are easily crossed, where he would belong everywhere and nowhere at the same time. At this point, we could perhaps suggest that Urpeth's idealised North owes as much to his own experience as an incomer as to his interest in Kenneth White's concept of geopoetics. The "infertile, acidic, moonless wilderness of the upper globe" (p. 69) then offers two opportunities: one, to tie the Borromean knot (used by Jacques Lacan to theorise the interrelation between the real, the imaginary and the symbolic) where Urpeth's literary ideal lies, and two, to offer his protagonist an abstract territory where his identity would escape political and historical circumstances. We could of course argue that this is, too, a betrayal of some sort.

Added to the inclusion of a fantastic sub-narrative (or imaginary self exile) within the story of Sorley's return to Lewis, is Urpeth's attempt to import apparently allogeneous literary material within an otherwise very "Scottish" novel. On the one hand, Urpeth resorts to standard (e.g. Western) narrative devices and motifs easily recognizeable in the field of Scottish studies such as issues of guilt and election, linguistic schizophrenia, alcohol abuse, attempted suicide by drowning …

On the other hand, Urpeth uses literary structures to implicitly reflect the spiritual beliefs of the Inuit culture: extended or open-ended dream sequences, an overall holistic view of reality, or a magical-psychological interpretation of phenomena such as paramnesia, hypermnesia and xenoglossia. The elements of Inuit symbolism present in the novel are perfectly consistent with the issues of exile and return explored in the main storyline: the shaman's power to resuscitate the dead from their naked bones, together with the running metaphor of whale, salmon or seabird migration (pp. 65, 123) all serve to echo Sorley's irrational wish to travel back through time. It is then no wonder that his visions often draw on the notion of time reversal:

> The small boy took a fistful of the sand from where she lay and held it until it was again a boulder of wind-cut granite falling to the sea from the northern cliffs. And then another fist of sand he held until it was a stone journeying in a river far inland, flowing among frost-split boulders. The small boy held that river in his hands until it was again a mountain glacier burdened with a moraine as it clove the island glens. (p. 42)

We could, however, argue that the archetypal figure of the Inuit shaman is but a northernized version of that of the witch, and the Arctic North another, colder version of Brigadoon. Both ways, Urpeth's northernization of literary materials and the Inuit concepts he resorts to enable him to deal with his protagonist's homecoming from literal and symbolical perspectives simultaneously. Urpeth then dwells on the problems inherent in writing a modern western narrative about a non-western culture to compel his protagonist (and reader) to examine how his (their) urge to escape into the imaginary may eventually derail the return journey's completion. Sorley's conclusive failure to bring his gift back to the world of common day suggests that he is neither permitted nor able to "dream [his] dreams and have them too". There comes the limit of the myth: Sorley will only be able to return to Lewis when he renounces reframing his journey as metaphor. His return home (or incorporation) is only completed when he re-enacts the symbolical death of the incipit and finds himself "back at the beginning" (p. 158), that is, when he regains consciousness in hospital after a failed suicide attempt. He is then able to come to terms with the fact that his life is devoid of any metaphysical dimension and that he has no grasp on either space or time.

> He was calm then, his mind had emptied as he walked that path and listened to the river, and he realised that for the first time since he returned to the island he saw and felt nothing in that empty landscape, no yearning, no struggle, no sorrow. He wanted to be nothing but a part of its movement, its emptiness and its presence. [...] He did not want the wings for flight, or the cave or the bay or the boat; as he looked at the night sky he knew that his being was enough and the great flight would come by watching, listening, remaining, and they would be the gifts he kept. (p. 161)

Sorley's homeostasis is finally achieved through a non-teleological interpretation of life. The "great flight" mentioned in the last lines of the novel clearly refers to the end of the misplaced nostalgia that had prompted Sorley's negative exile into the realm of the magical, together with his beliefs in the "taghairm" and his own unalterable self-definition as shaman.

The story of an individual's journey from an essentialist to an existentialist notion of self and from a negative to a positive form of exile,

Far Inland celebrates as much as it questions its protagonist's desperate desire for identity. The necessity to give up on the dream of a homeland that would have been miraculously left unscathed by time underlies the predicament of all exiles—and is explored by a number of Scottish writers (among whom Iain Crichton Smith, Robin Jenkins and Sorley MacLean), whether the latter write from or about Scotland.

Through Sorley's allegorical exile into a fantasised version of Northern Pangaea and his final, redemptive re-inscription in "real" Scotland, Urpeth then suggests that there are many things that one has to unlearn in order to *become* what one is. The transmutation of a regressive journey into a progressive one thus implies entering a state of positive, ontological exile reminiscent of Said's necessary acknowledgement of loss, a form of exile that would finally be rid of determination or necessity, whether these are personal or collective.

Bibliography

BOUCHARD Joë, CHARTIER Daniel, and NADEAU Amélie, *Problématiques de l'imaginaire du Nord en littérature, cinéma et arts visuels*, PUQ, 2004.

CAMPBELL Joseph, *The Hero with a Thousand Faces*, New World Library, [1949] 2008.

ÉLIADE Mircea, *Le chamanisme et les techniques archaïques de l'extase*, Paris, Fayot, [1951] 1983.

LE GUENNEC Jean, *États de l'inconscient dans le récit fantastique 1800-1900*, Paris, L'Harmattan, 2003.

ONFRAY Michel, *Esthétique du pôle Nord*, Paris, Grasset, 2002.

SAID Edward, *Reflections on Exile and Other Essays*, Harvard University Press, 2000.

SALADIN D'ANGLURE Bernard, *Être et renaître Inuit*, Paris, Gallimard, 2006.

URPETH Peter, *Far Inland*, Edinburgh, Polygon, 2006.

WHITE Kenneth, *On the Atlantic Edge: a Geopoetics Project*, Sandstone Press, 2006.

Résumés

[p. 19]   **Exile and Return from the Far North of Scotland from the Reformation to the Revolution**
Thomas Brochard

The exile and return of individuals from the far north of Scotland from 1560 to 1640 can be viewed within the perspective of a "civilizing process" and its dual core of social discipline from above and social regulation from below. Indeed, the Government promoted "exile" as a way to channel clan militarism. It intended to relocate the potential offered by private armies into the public sphere—i.e. as an official, governmental institution—and regulate it. The rationale behind this exile policy points towards its own "civilizing" agenda. In that sense, the clan military force and network survived by its transposition into an official body, equally military in its nature. The experiences of returning soldiers proved just as multifarious as their reasons for joining the army and as a result remoulded both individuals and communities in a process of social regulation. The military co-optation allowed the elite, this middling sort (at the State level), both in exile and on their return to Britain to position itself for the promotion of their own interests and that of the clan. A parallel phenomenon was at work in the exile and return of primarily, but not solely, members of the clan elite not only to other Scottish towns outside their native environment but also to Europe for educational motives. It (re)shaped, *mutatis mutandis* and in a more pronounced way, their native culture into a pre-existent hybrid society in their integration into a Lowland and British genteel model. The response of the northern High-landers, as *homo peregrinator*, to the push and pull factors of exile and return was to adapt and utilize the opportunities forced onto or presented to them by the State or which arose from *Rinascimento* culture. They used their various kinship ties and other networks to the full for a constant re-alignment according to their respective interests. Social transformations came from below too perhaps most visibly and profoundly at the cultural level. To some extent, what the Crown tried with difficulties to impose in the so-called "civilizing" of the far north was somewhat accomplished almost imperceptibly by cultural influences. It helped redefine and re-assess the perception of an immovable and immutable society immersed in clan warfare. The result is a picture less of a retrograde, stultified, and monolithic society, though with some elements of this remaining, but more of a slowly moving and diverse one engaged in and selectively responding to a pre-existing but amplified early-modern bicultural process. *In fine*, this remained an ongoing process best studied over the *longue durée* and with significant variations both in terms of geography and, within communities, within clans and families themselves.

Exil et retour : le cas du Nord de l'Écosse, de la réformation à la révolution

On peut considérer l'exil et le retour des habitants de la partie la plus septentrionale de l'Écosse de 1560 à 1640 du point de vue d'un «processus de civilisation». En effet, le gouvernement voyait dans l'exil une façon de canaliser le militarisme des clans. Son but était de transférer le potentiel des armées privées vers la sphère publique. Les forces militaires et les réseaux des clans perduraient grâce à leur transposition dans un organisme officiel, tout aussi militarisé. Les expériences des soldats qui rentraient dans le pays étaient aussi diverses que les raisons motivant leur départ; il en résultait que les individus et les communautés se voyaient transformés dans un processus de régulation sociale. Cette cooptation militaire permettait à l'élite de promouvoir leurs propres intérêts ainsi que ceux de leur clan, à la fois lors de leur exil et après leur retour. Un phénomène parallèle s'opérait lorsque des membres de l'élite des clans partaient loin de leur environnement natif pour faire des études, que ce soit dans d'autres villes écossaises ou en Europe. Leur adoption d'un modèle social britannique ou des Basses Terres (re)transformait la culture au sein d'une société hybride préexistante. La réponse des Highlanders face à l'exil et au retour était de saisir les opportunités qui leur étaient présentées (ou imposées) par l'État ou qui émergeaient de la culture de la Renaissance. Ils se servaient pleinement de leurs réseaux et de leurs liens familiaux afin de mieux servir leurs propres intérêts. Des transformations sociales se sont également opérées par le bas, surtout au niveau culturel. D'une certaine manière, c'étaient les influences culturelles qui, de manière imperceptible, faisaient avancer le projet de «civilisation» du nord de l'Écosse que la couronne tentait avec difficulté d'imposer. Il en résultait une réévaluation d'une société clanique martiale, souvent considérée comme immobile et immuable. Cette nouvelle image était moins celle d'une société monolithique et rétrograde que celle d'une société qui avançait lentement vers la diversité à travers son engagement dans un processus biculturel typique de l'époque moderne. Ce processus était de longue durée et connaissait des variations significatives selon des facteurs géographiques et également selon les particularités des clans, des communautés et des familles eux-mêmes.

[p. 41]   English and Scottish Exiles in Northwest Germany c. 1683–1709

Kathrin Zickermann

The politically and culturally diverse north western territories of the Holy Roman Empires so far lack an analysis of Scottish exile communities which could hold up to the work published on seventeenth century exiles communities in the United Provinces or Poland-Lithuania. This is unfortunate as some German territories and cities received intensive attention from English and Scottish religious and political exiles who had left or were in the process of leaving the British Isles during the Restoration period seeking refuge on the continent. Although a majority of these exiles found support within expatriate communities established in Dutch cities, some Scots and Englishmen aimed to relocate to other Northern European locations due to safety issues or economic opportunities. In November 1683 the Englishman Sir William Waller, accompanied by the Scots Adam Freer and Sir George Melville, led negotiations with the senate of the Calvinist and Imperial city of Bremen for the settlement of Scottish and English exiles. When these failed due to pressure exerted by Charles II, talks continued with the Lutheran duke Georg Wilhelm of Braunschweig-Lüneburg. On 9 August 1684, the latter issued religious and economic privileges to families and individuals of reformed faith belonging to any nation who were willing to settle in the city of Lüneburg. These freedoms led not only to English and Scottish but also to French and Dutch migration of religious and political exiles as well as of economic opportunists. This article analyses the aims of the exiles and their negotiations with the local authorities in North West Germany. It also examines the success and failure of the communities in Bremen and Lüneburg and their long-term impact on individuals such as the Scottish entrepreneur Robert Hog. Furthermore, the articles analyses if the diverse migration of individuals of several nationalities resulted in the formation of a single British or multi-ethnic religious community or if the migrants organised themselves in several groups, divided by nationality or other criteria.

Les exilés anglais et écossais dans le nord-ouest de l'Allemagne c. 1683-1709

Le rôle des communautés d'exilés écossais dans les territoires politiquement et culturellement diversifiés du Saint-Empire romain germanique n'a pas fait l'objet d'études, à l'opposé de celles qui existent sur les communautés d'exilés aux Provinces-Unies ou en Pologne-Lituanie au XVIIᵉ siècle. Cela est regrettable car certains territoires et villes allemands suscitaient un très vif intérêt chez les exilés religieux et politiques de l'Écosse et de l'Angleterre qui quittaient les Îles Britanniques pendant la Restauration afin de trouver refuge sur le continent. Bien que la majorité de ces exilés fussent accueillis au sein des communautés d'expatriés des villes néerlandaises, certains Écossais et Anglais espéraient s'installer dans d'autres villes du nord de l'Europe pour des raisons de sécurité ou des motifs économiques. En novembre 1683, un Anglais, Sir William Waller, accompagné par deux Écossais, Adam Freer et Sir George Melville, mena des négociations avec le Sénat de Brême, ville impériale et calviniste, au sujet de l'installation d'exilés écossais et anglais. Suite à l'échec de ces pourparlers, dû à la pression exercée par Charles II, des négociations se poursuivirent avec le duc luthérien Georg Willhelm de Braunschweig-Lüneburg. Le 9 août 1684, ce dernier accorda des privilèges religieux et économiques aux familles et aux particuliers adhérant à la foi protestante qui souhaitaient s'installer à Lüneburg, sans considération de leur pays d'origine. Ces libertés ont attiré nombre d'exilés religieux et politiques d'origine anglaise et écossaise, mais aussi française et néerlandaise, venant s'ajouter à ceux qui s'exilaient pour des raisons économiques. Cet article cherche à analyser les objectifs des exilés ainsi que leurs négociations avec les autorités locales dans le nord-ouest de l'Allemagne. Nous étudions également la réussite et l'échec des communautés de Brême et de Lüneburg ainsi que leur impact durable sur des individus comme l'entrepreneur écossais Robert Hog. En dernier lieu, cet article cherche à savoir si la migration de ressortissants de nationalités différentes résultait en la création d'une seule communauté religieuse britannique ou multiethnique, ou si les migrants s'organisaient en différents groupes selon des critères nationaux ou autres.

[p. 59]   The Scottish painters' exile in Italy in the eighteenth century
Marion Amblard

In the eighteenth century, a prolonged stay in Rome was essential in the career of a painter. In this city, which was then the main artistic centre of Western Europe, they studied the works of the Renaissance masters and they tried to find patrons among the aristocrats on the Grand Tour. For Scottish painters a stay in Rome was of prime importance as this was the means to complete the basic artistic training acquired in their native country. Indeed, in Scotland there was no fine art academy providing thorough training before 1798; most painters left Scotland to study in Italy for several years. In Rome, they enrolled in the studio of a fashionable painter and they attended the classes of the *Accademia di San Luca* and of the *Académie de France*.

The aim of this article is to come back to the question of Scottish painters' training in Italy and to underline the contribution of Italian art to eighteenth-century Scottish painting. First of all we will present the places traditionally visited by Scottish painters in Italy: they did not only visit Rome, they also went to Venice, Bologna, Florence and Naples. Then we will talk about the life of the artistic community in Rome and about the painters' activities in the *Académie de France* and the *Accademia di San Luca*. Thanks to a study of several drawings and paintings made by Scottish painters when they returned to Britain, we will notice that Scottish artists were deeply influenced by Italian art.

L'exil des peintres écossais en Italie au dix-huitième siècle
Au dix-huitième siècle, un séjour prolongé à Rome était une étape obligatoire dans la carrière des peintres. Dans cette ville, qui était alors le principal centre artistique de l'Europe occidentale, ils étudiaient les œuvres des maîtres de la Renaissance italienne et tentaient de trouver de nouveaux mécènes parmi les aristocrates engagés dans le Grand Tour. Pour les peintres écossais un séjour

à Rome était d'autant plus indispensable qu'il leur permettait de compléter la formation artistique rudimentaire qu'ils avaient reçue dans leur pays natal. En Écosse, il n'y eut effectivement pas d'académie des beaux-arts dispensant un enseignement complet avant 1798; la plupart des artistes écossais quittèrent donc leur terre natale plusieurs années afin de venir étudier en Italie. À Rome, ils s'enrôlaient dans l'atelier d'un peintre reconnu et fréquentaient les cours de l'Académie de Saint-Luc et de l'Académie de France.

Cet article propose de revenir sur la formation des peintres écossais en Italie et sur l'apport de l'art italien à la peinture écossaise du dix-huitième siècle. Nous retracerons tout d'abord l'itinéraire traditionnellement effectué par les peintres écossais en Italie; leur visite ne se limitait pas à Rome, ils se rendaient aussi à Venise, Bologne, Florence et à Naples. Nous nous intéresserons ensuite à la vie de la communauté artistique écossaise établie à Rome et aux activités des peintres au sein de l'Académie de France et de l'Académie de Saint-Luc. Enfin, une étude de quelques dessins et tableaux réalisés à leur retour en Grande-Bretagne, nous permettra de constater que les peintres écossais ont été profondément marqués par l'art italien.

[p. 79] The transportation of the "Scottish Martyrs" in 1793: a particular form of exile?

Christian Auer

This article will focus on some of the essential traits of the concept of exile through the study of the transportation of the Scottish Martyrs, the supporters of the radical cause who marked the political history of the eighteenth century, and more particularly of their emblematic figure Thomas Muir, a lawyer from Glasgow and a passionate defender of the French revolution. Fearing the spread of radical ideas, the authorities decided to arrest the leaders of the movement and sentenced them to transportation to Australia.

Drawing on the case of Thomas Muir, this article will try to determine whether the time of political exile differentiates itself from the time of other forms of exile, whether political exile is characterized by a state of "fundamental discontinuity", to use the words of Edward Said, and whether the political, intellectual or ideological dimension of political exiles enables them to overcome, maybe more than other exiles, the essential sadness of exile.

La déportation des "martyrs écossais" de 1793 : une forme particulière d'exil?

Cet article a pour objet d'étudier certains des contours du concept d'exil en prenant pour appui la déportation des «martyrs écossais», ces partisans de la cause radicale qui marquèrent l'histoire politique de la fin du dix-huitième siècle, et notamment leur figure emblématique, Thomas Muir, avocat originaire de Glasgow, ardent défenseur de la révolution française. Les autorités, craignant de voir le radicalisme se répandre dans la population, arrêtèrent les principaux dirigeants du mouvement et les condamnèrent à des peines de déportation en Australie.

Cet article tentera de déterminer, en prenant comme point d'ancrage le cas de Thomas Muir, si l'exil politique se différencie des autres formes d'exil. La temporalité de l'exil politique présente-t-elle des traits différents des autres formes d'exil ? L'exil politique se caractérise-t-il lui-aussi par un état de « discontinuité fondamentale », pour reprendre une formule d'Edward Said ? Enfin la dimension politique, intellectuelle ou idéologique de l'exilé politique ne lui permet-elle pas de surmonter peut être mieux que d'autres l'essentielle tristesse de l'exil ?

Si l'on se réfère à ce commentaire d'Emmanuel Levinas, qui estime que l'exil s'apparente à une violence qui « ne consiste pas tant à blesser et à anéantir, qu'à interrompre, à faire jouer des rôles où [les individus] ne se retrouvent plus, à leur faire trahir, non seulement des engagements mais leur propre substance », il apparaît que les autorités judiciaires qui condamnèrent Thomas Muir à l'exil ne parvinrent pas à atteindre leur objectif car Muir ne trahit aucun de ses engagements en faveur des valeurs de réforme, de liberté, de justice et de démocratie.

[p. 91]   Radical Returns in an Age of Revolutions
Gordon Pentland

The exile and especially the transportation of political radicals in the late eighteenth and early nineteenth centuries forms a key theme in both an academic historiography and a popular mythology of radicalism in Scotland. In particular, the exiles of the "Scottish Martyrs" of the 1790s and the men transported in 1820 for their role in the "Radical War" loom large and have received some scholarly treatment. This essay focuses on the theme of radical "return". The more obvious rhetorical power provided by transported "martyrs" has tended to obscure the ways in which those radicals who did return from exile could continue to play important roles in popular politics. It explores three types of radical return through a number of case studies. First, it looks at an unrepentant radical, who could return from long exile and become involved, once again, in those very activities for which he had been exiled. Secondly, it explores radicals who returned and whose experience of exile proved "politically usable" within subsequent movements. Finally, it explores less tangible ideas of return, such as the sending of letters or "relics" to Scotland from exile.

Le retour des radicaux à l'époque des révolutions

L'exil, et surtout la déportation, de radicaux politiques à la fin du XVIIIᵉ siècle et au début du XIXᵉ siècle constitue une thématique centrale de l'historiographie universitaire du radicalisme écossais mais aussi de sa mythologie populaire. En particulier, l'exil des « martyrs écossais » des années 1790 et celui des hommes déportés en 1820 à cause de leur rôle dans « l'Insurrection écossaise » ont fait l'objet de certaines études. Cet article prend comme sujet le thème du retour du radical. Le pouvoir rhétorique plus évident du «martyr» déporté a tendance à nous faire oublier la façon dont les radicaux qui rentraient suite à une période d'exil pouvaient continuer à jouer un rôle politique important. Nous analysons trois types de retour chez les radicaux à travers plusieurs études de cas. D'abord, nous examinons le radical non repenti qui rentrait de son exil puis s'engageait encore dans les activités pour lesquelles il avait été exilé. Ensuite, nous étudions le retour des radicaux dont l'expérience d'exil s'avérait, par la suite, «exploitable» sur le plan politique pour certaines mouvances. Enfin, nous nous tournons vers les manifestations moins tangibles du «retour d'exil», comme l'envoi vers l'Écosse de lettres ou autres «reliques».

[p. 103] Homecoming and Liminality in Walter Scott's *Guy Mannering*
Céline Sabiron

In 2009 Scotland celebrated its first Homecoming year which aimed to encourage the international Scottish Diaspora to return home. During this event emblematic Scottish writers have been commemorated, like Robert Burns or Walter Scott who made the question of exile and return the central topic of his writings, with the long narrative poem *The Lay of the Last Minstrel* (1805), or the novels *Redgauntlet* (1824), *St Ronan's Well* (1824), and above all *Guy Mannering* (1815) which focuses on the movement homeward. The fiction stages three different types of homecoming, from the simplest and the most straightforward, the return of a Scottish heir after his early abduction away to Holland, to the most problematic, the return of foreigners, i.e. a homeless English tourist Guy Mannering ("a stranger in the [Scottish] land" [II, 9: 162]), and his nomadic and traditionally homeless counterpart, the wandering gypsy Meg Merrilies. On their return home the exiles are constantly out of place and out of time, as they live in a liminal space (in-between space) at the periphery of a country and at the margin of society, and in a liminal time (in-between time) between chronological linearity and cyclical circularity.

And yet, returning home does not necessarily lead to homecoming. These three parallel returns are questioned for they threaten the centripetal movement triggered off by the motion homeward; the home of their choice is indeed located on the Borders, at the edge of Scotland. They are also mutually exclusive as these homecomers all try and return to the same home, the Ellangowan property. Homecoming can only take place within the literary home created by the author.

Retour et liminalité dans *Guy Mannering* de Walter Scott

En 2009 l'Écosse a célébré, pour la première fois, l'année du Retour *(Homecoming)* dont le but était d'encourager la Diaspora écossaise internationale à revenir au pays et à ainsi revisiter la terre de leurs ancêtres. Des écrivains écossais emblématiques de l'Écosse ont été commémorés, comme Robert Burns ou Walter Scott qui a fait de cette question de l'exil et du retour le thème phare de ses écrits, avec le poème narratif *Le Lai du dernier ménestrel* (1805), ou les romans *Redgauntlet* (1824), *Les Eaux de Saint-Ronan* (1824) et surtout *Guy Mannering* (1815) qui insiste sur le mouvement du retour au foyer. Cette fiction met en scène trois différents types de retour, du plus simple, le retour d'un héritier écossais après son enlèvement en Hollande, au plus problématique, le retour d'étrangers sans foyer comme le touriste anglais Guy Mannering («a stranger in the [Scottish] land» [II, 9 : 162]) et son double itinérant, la bohémienne Meg Merrilies. Déplacés et déphasés, ils vivent dans un espace liminaire, un entre-lieu, à la périphérie d'un pays et en marge de la société, et dans un entre-temps, à mi-chemin entre des temporalités chronologique et cyclique.

Et pourtant, le retour au pays n'implique pas nécessairement une restauration ou une installation définitive. Ces trois retours parallèles sont remis en cause car ils menacent le mouvement centripète du retour au foyer; la maison de leur choix est en effet située en périphérie, à la frontière anglo-écossaise. De plus, ils s'excluent mutuellement puisque les exilés migrent tous vers la même maison, la propriété d'Ellangowan. Le foyer ne peut donc prendre qu'une forme littéraire et émerger de la plume de l'auteur.

[p. 119] The Displaced Naturalist: W. F. Campbell's life of exile in Normandy

Lesley Graham

This article examines the dynamics of rootedness and displacement; bourgeois authority and peasant ways of life; signified and signifier, that are at work in Walter Frederick Campbell's *Life in Normandy* (1863).

Walter Frederick Campbell (1798–1855) spent the last years of his life in Avranches, Normandy as an economic refugee. He had been Laird of Islay for thirty-two years and his financial ruin was in large part due to the agricultural and economic reforms he had implemented on the island. He was in many ways a benevolent proprietor and was described as "a man of kind heart and generous nature". The reforms he introduced were farsighted, visible in the landscape still today, while he resisted the temptation to clear the overpopulated island.

Life in Normandy is a fictionalized account of Campbell's experience in and around Avranches. His son, John Francis Campbell edited the two volumes and declared them to be primarily a philanthropic effort to teach Scottish peasants how to improve their practices: "It was suggested that a good cheap dinner would tempt a poor man from bad dear drink abroad, and that a poor Scotchman's wife might be taught to do that which poor wives do elsewhere" (p. v). Hope and Cross, the protagonists of the narrative are clearly Campbell's alter egos and are both passionately interested in nature, fishing and shooting. The action in

Normandy takes place against the background of rumblings from the 1848 Revolution in Paris.

The account can be read as a long reflection on the dislocation of identity and the precarious meaning of home for the economic exile as well as for the Scottish and French peasant.

Le naturaliste déplacé : W. F. Campbell et sa vie d'exil en Normandie

Cet article traite de la dynamique d'enracinement et de déplacement, de l'autorité bourgeoise et de la vie paysanne ainsi que du signifié et du signifiant en jeu dans l'ouvrage *Life in Normandy* de Walter Frederick Campbell (1863).

Exilé pour des raisons économiques et financières, Walter Frederick Campbell (1798-1855) passa les dernières années de sa vie à Avranches en Normandie. Auparavant, il avait été propriétaire de l'île d'Islay pendant trente-deux ans et sa ruine financière fut en partie due aux réformes agraires et économiques introduites sur cette île par ses soins. Il était, à bien des égards, un propriétaire bienveillant, décrit comme un homme de cœur et de nature généreuse. Il sut résister à la tentation d'expulser la population de l'île par des *clearances*. Ses réformes visionnaires sont encore perceptibles de nos jours sur la terre d'Islay.

Life in Normandy est l'histoire romancée de la vie de Campbell à Avranches et ses alentours. Son fils, John Francis Campbell édita les deux volumes, les décrivant comme avant tout un effort philanthropique pour inciter la paysannerie écossaise à améliorer ses pratiques : «On suggéra qu'un bon dîner à peu de frais inciterait un Écossais pauvre à rester chez lui plutôt que de dépenser son argent sur des beuveries à l'extérieur, et qu'on pourrait enseigner à sa femme à faire ce que font les femmes ailleurs» (p. v). Hope et Cross, les protagonistes du récit sont très clairement les alter ego de Campbell, tous deux passionnés de nature, de pêche et de chasse. L'action se déroule en Normandie sur fond révolutionnaire parisien en 1848.

On peut considérer que le récit constitue une longue réflexion sur la dislocation, le délitement du sentiment identitaire de l'auteur et sur la signification instable et mouvante de la notion du «chez moi» pour l'exilé économique et pour le paysan, français aussi bien qu'écossais.

[p. 129]   Exile and expatriates in Robin Jenkins' Novels
   Bernard Sellin

Robin Jenkins (1912-2005) is one of the most distinguished novelists of post war Britain. In a career which lasted some fifty years, he became a perceptive, though disenchanted, observer of Scottish society.

However, we are less familiar with a second aspect of his work, nine novels and collections of short-stories which are set abroad and find inspiration in the author's own experience as a teacher in Afghanistan, Catalonia and Malaysia in the 1960s.

For Jenkins this withdrawal from the Scottish scene offered a much needed distance at a time when he was increasingly dissatisfied with Scottish society and the lack of vitality of the literary scene. It also gave the opportunity for a discovery of new cultures and territories.

What the books have in common is the experience of a majority of Scottish expatriates abroad, their mixed feelings, ambiguities and cowardice in front of the Other. Titles like *The Expatriates*, *A Far Cry from Bowmore*, *Dust on the Paw*, *The Sardana Dancers*, among others, offer a complex literary discussion of themes of exile and possible return, the pain of separation, the tensions between home and abroad, the vulgarity of the Scottish and English communities overseas. Inevitably, expatriation or exile is integrated into Jenkins' spiritual quest for values until it merges with a possible experience of rebirth and self-discovery.

Exil et expatriés dans les romans de Robin Jenkins

Robin Jenkins (1912-2005) est l'un des écrivains les plus remarquables de la Grande-Bretagne de la seconde moitié du XXᵉ siècle. Au fil d'une carrière qui s'étendit sur quelque 50 années, il jeta sur la société écossaise un regard aigu bien que désenchanté.

Mais c'est ignorer un autre aspect de son œuvre, neuf romans et recueils de nouvelles, tous situés à l'étranger, dans des pays que fréquenta l'auteur comme enseignant en Afghanistan, Catalogne et Malaisie dans les années 1960.

Pour Jenkins, ce retrait de la scène écossaise signifia une prise de distance salutaire à un moment où l'écrivain se montrait de plus en plus critique à l'égard de la société et du manque de vitalité de la scène littéraire. Ce fut aussi l'occasion de découvrir de nouvelles cultures. Ces livres partagent tous l'expérience d'expatriés, en majorité écossais, leurs ambiguïtés, hésitations et lâcheté face à l'Autre. *The Expatriates*, *A Far Cry from Bowmore*, *Dust on the Paw*, *The Sardana Dancers* sont quelques-uns des récits dans lesquels Jenkins se livre à un complexe examen des thèmes de l'exil et d'un possible retour, les tensions entre l'éloignement et la découverte de nouveaux horizons, la vulgarité quasi générale des expatriés, qu'ils soient anglais ou écossais. Inévitablement, expatriation et exil finissent par être intégrés à la quête spirituelle qui sous-tend tous ses livres jusqu'à suggérer renaissance et découverte de soi.

[p. 139] Return from exile in Iain Crichton Smith's fiction and poetry
Jean Berton

This paper is concentrating on the varied aspects of returning from exile which Iain Crichton Smith investigated, from migrants coming back from Canada to soldiers returning from wars, or from workers retiring from the Lowlands to their Gaelic-speaking native islands and glens to young men and women who, after being educated out of their villages, realise, before or when returning, they can no longer adapt because times have changed—to them all, returning from exile is yet another exile.

By means of the aporia of "The Departing Island" Iain Crichton Smith relishes on reversing common perceptions of reality. His study on exile and return from exile first of all sets the major issue of the loss of the native language. If all reasons for exile can be summed up in the call of the sea, those for the return from exile are best epitomised in the title of the prose poem, "You are at the bottom of my mind". Finally, Crichton Smith's answer to the aporia of the departing island is his own return *ad patres*, as developed in his last collection of poems, *The Leaf and the Marble*.

Le retour d'exil dans l'œuvre de Iain Crichton Smith

Cette étude traite surtout des divers aspects du retour d'exil que Iain Crichton Smith a explorés : des émigrés rentrant du Canada aux soldats revenant de guerre, des employés quittant les Basses Terres pour vivre leur retraite dans les îles ou les vallées gaélophones de leur enfance aux jeunes gens partis après leurs études et qui s'aperçoivent, à leur retour, de la difficulté à s'adapter parce que ces lieux, aussi, ont changé pendant leurs années d'absence. Pour eux tous, le retour d'exil est un autre exil.

C'est à l'aide de l'aporie de « The Departing Island» que Crichton Smith ose retourner la perception habituelle de la réalité. Son analyse de l'exil et du retour d'exil développe d'abord la question de la langue maternelle que l'on abandonne. Si toutes les raisons d'émigrer peuvent se résumer à l'appel de la mer, celles du retour se concentrent dans le titre du poème en prose : «You are at the bottom of my mind». En fin de compte, la réponse que fait Crichton Smith à l'aporie de l'île en partance se trouve dans son dernier recueil de poèmes, *The Leaf and the Marble*, où il décrit son retour progressif *ad patres*.

[p. 155] The Woman with the Ibo Nose and the Scottish Tongue: Expressions of Belonging and Return in Jackie Kay's Writing
Jane Gray

Questions of identity—or more appropriately of identities—are at the core of much of Jackie Kay's writing, and are often intimately linked to the writer's personal experience of being Scottish, Black and adopted. The expression of this multiplicity necessarily implies the question of belonging, and also in the particular case of Jackie Kay, of a painful recognition of *not* belonging, of the refusal of others to acknowledge her Scottish identity due to the colour of her skin.

The aim of this paper is to analyse how this writer comes to terms with such questions, and more significantly, how the theme of *return*—be it real or imaginary—to her African origins is expressed in her work. In order to achieve this aim, it focuses on a selection of Kay's poetry and prose which is representative of preoccupations with themes of belonging and estrangement within the context of both Scotland and Africa, for example, *The Adoption Papers* (1991), *Off Colour* (1998), or *Life Mask* (2005). Kay's epic poem *The Lamplighter* (2007), a portrayal of Britain's involvement in the slave trade through the experience of four women, is also dealt with in this context.

La femme au nez ibo dont la langue est écossaise : expressions d'appartenance et de retour dans l'écriture de Jackie Kay

La question de l'identité — ou plus précisément des identités — est un thème récurrent dans l'œuvre de Jackie Kay qui est intimement liée à son expérience personnelle en tant qu'Écossaise d'origine africaine, adoptée par des parents blancs. L'expression de la multiplicité de son identité implique nécessairement la question de l'appartenance, et dans le cas particulier de Jackie Kay, de la reconnaissance parfois douloureuse de ne pas appartenir, du refus des autres d'admettre son identité écossaise en raison de la couleur de sa peau.

Dans cette optique, cet article analysera la manière dont l'écrivaine aborde de telles questions, et plus précisément, comment le thème du *retour* — qu'il soit réel ou imaginaire — à ses racines africaines est exprimé dans son œuvre. Afin d'y parvenir, une sélection de poésies et de prose représentative de ses préoccupations avec les thèmes de l'appartenance et de l'éloignement, voire même de l'exil, sera analysée, extraite d'ouvrages tels que, *The Adoption Papers* (1991), *Off Colour* (1998) et *Life Mask* (2005), qui abordent tous ces thèmes dans un contexte à la fois écossais et africain. Une attention particulière sera accordée à son poème épique intitulé *The Lamplighter* (2007), qui dépeint de manière poignante le rôle de la Grande-Bretagne dans la traite des Noirs à travers l'expérience de quatre femmes arrachées de leur pays et réduites en esclavage afin de construire les grandes villes industrielles de Glasgow, Liverpool ou Bristol.

[p. 169] Internal, imaginary and ontological exile in Peter Urpeth's *Far Inland* (2006)
Camille Manfredi

The paper proposes to examine how Peter Urpeth, in his first published novel *Far Inland* (2006), attempted to re-write the traditional dichotomies between island and city, magic and reality, origin and exile.

Central to the issues of exile and return, the notions of change, solitude (whether it is voluntary or not) and solipsism will be explored through the analysis of a novel set in Lewis that focuses on the figure of the wanderer. The latter's home-coming is the occasion for Urpeth to explore the place of origin through space, time and spirituality. By resorting to an imposing array of symbols inspired from Inuit shamanism, Urpeth suggests the possibility of a return to an original, pre-Christian and re-enchanted Scotland. While considering how this new (?) proposal for an alternative collective identity is grounded in the paradoxical notion of ontological exile, the paper offers to inscribe the novel within the desire, shown by many contemporary Scottish artists, to "re-imagine" Scotland and provide it with new surfaces of inscription and existential territories.

Figures de l'exil interne, imaginaire et ontologique dans *Far Inland* (2006) de Peter Urpeth

À travers l'étude du roman *Far Inland* (2006) de Peter Urpeth, cet article se propose d'examiner les modalités de réécriture de l'éternelle polarité entre île et ville, magie et réel, origine et exil.

L'étude du roman permettra d'aborder les questions de rupture, d'errance, de solitude (subie et choisie) et de solipsisme soulevées lors du colloque. Ainsi *Far Inland*, roman insulaire, vient déterritorialiser les notions d'exil et de retour, faisant de la rencontre entre l'être et l'espace clos de l'origine le lieu d'une exploration non seulement géographique et temporelle, mais aussi et surtout spirituelle. L'auteur renonce aux modèles pour amorcer en rêve le retour vers une autre Écosse, pré-chrétienne et ré-enchantée. Cette dernière peut constituer une nouvelle proposition identitaire fondée sur le chamanisme inuit et une certaine forme, complexe, de nomadisme ontologique. Cette proposition, dont on tentera d'évaluer la validité, sera mise en perspective avec le processus de réinvention de l'Écosse largement initié en littérature écossaise contemporaine à travers la recherche de nouvelles surfaces d'inscription et de nouveaux territoires existentiels.

COMPOSITION ET MISE EN PAGE
Ellug / Revues

Ce volume est composé en Baskerville
et Myriad Pro sous Adobe InDesign

IMPRESSION ET FAÇONNAGE

Atelier de reprographie
Université Stendhal - Grenoble 3

Achevé d'imprimer, septembre 2010